LIONS OF KANDAHAR

MAJOR RUSTY BRADLEY
and KEVIN MAURER

LIONS OF KANDAHAR

The Story of a Fight Against All Odds

Bantam Books   *New York*

Published in the United States by Bantam Books,
an imprint of The Random House Publishing Group,
a division of Random House, Inc., New York.

BANTAM BOOKS and the rooster colophon are registered
trademarks of Random House, Inc.

LIBRARY OF CONGRESS CATALOGING-IN-PUBLICATION DATA

Bradley, Rusty.
Lions of Kandahar : the story of a fight against all odds / Rusty Bradley
and Kevin Maurer.
p.   cm.
ISBN 978-0-553-80757-8
eBook ISBN 978-0-440-42345-4
1. Afghan War, 2001–   —Campaigns—Afghanistan—Panjwa'i
(District).   2. Afghan War, 2001–   —Commando operations.   3. Afghan
War, 2001–   —Personal narratives, American.   4. Taliban.   5. Bradley,
Rusty.   I. Maurer, Kevin.   II. Title.
DS371.4123.P38B73 2011
958.104'742—dc22   2010053026

Printed in the United States of America on acid-free paper

www.bantamdell.com

9 8 7 6 5 4 3

Book design by Virginia Norey

Dedicated to those few who live every day
like September 12, 2001

Contents

——

Glossary

Operation Medusa
September 2–September 17, 2006

AAF	Anti-Afghanistan Forces; also used to designate the Afghan Air Force
AC-130	gunship
ANA	Afghan National Army
ANP	Afghan National Police
API	armor-piercing incendiary rounds
AT4	disposable light anti-tank round
CAS	close air support
CCP	casualty collection point
CSM	command sergeant major
EOD	explosive ordnance detachment
ETT	embedded trainer with the Afghan Army
FBCB2	Force XXI Battle Command, Brigade and Below—navigation system and force tracker
FOB	forward operating base
GFC	ground force commander
GMV	truck
Goose	90-mm recoilless rifle

GSR	gunshot residue and explosives test
IED	improvised explosive device
IR	infrared
ISAF	International Security Assistance Force
JTAC	joint tactical aircraft controller
KAF	Kandahar Airfield
LAWS	Light Anti-Armor Weapons System
LZ	landing zone
MREs	Meals, Ready to Eat
NODS	night-vision device
PKM	*Pulemyot Kalashnikova,* or Kalashnikov's Machine Gun
PUC	personnel under confinement (prisoners)
QRF	quick reaction force
RPG	rocket-propelled grenade
TOC	tactical operations center
WIA	wounded in action

Key Afghan words

Amerkaianu Mushakas Kawatuna   American Special Forces

badal   blood feud, revenge

hamla   attack

mesher   a senior, elderly person

turan   captain

wa sahib   yes, sir

za   go

Author's Note

———

The most important challenge I faced in writing this book was trying to capture the significance of this event on paper and to articulate its magnitude for the reader. This book is not just about a series of intense firefights that stretched over days. It was the most strategically significant battle in Afghanistan that you never heard of, and its effects would have a direct impact in the War on Terror (WOT). What originated as a preplanned military operation designed by the International Security Assistance Force (ISAF) to clear a known enemy sanctuary soon developed into a ferocious, pivotal engagement that would push untested NATO troops to the limit and cause the Taliban and its foreign fighters to completely change the way they confronted coalition forces. It was an all-out fight to hold the line against a resurgent enemy and a catalyst to a new understanding of what would be required as the United States and its allies continued to prosecute the war.

The initial phase of Operation Medusa raged for nearly two weeks in the late summer of 2006. This operation and its subsequent phases would eventually extend combat operations over the course of several months. My team was one of five that directly participated in all phases of the entire operation and was the primary element chosen to stay in the volatile Panjwayi district following the conclusion of

Operation Medusa. Designated as Operational Detachment Alpha (ODA) 331, my team was tasked to "clean out" the Taliban and foreign fighters, mitigate their influence, reinstate local, legitimate governance, and assist in the reconstruction and security of an underdeveloped urban area the size of Rhode Island. This Herculean task was given to ten men. Such are the fortunes of war, and that truth comes with a price.

This story is my recollection, to the best of my ability, of what my Special Forces team endured from August to September 2006. It is intended to be an honest portrayal of the trials Special Forces soldiers face in Afghanistan. The language and humor are genuine, if not necessarily for the weak, fainthearted, or politically correct. This project has no ulterior motives or hidden agenda and is in no way intended to cause controversy or to point fingers. It is simply a story of ordinary men who did extraordinary things in the face of overwhelming adversity.

Every legal and operational consideration has been exercised in writing this book. I have only used first names and nicknames to protect those persons discussed, unless individuals' names have been previously released. Some call signs have been changed because of operational security. In writing this, I have made every attempt to abide by the security requirements of the U.S. Army Special Operations Command and old-fashioned common sense.

My intent in writing this story was not to gratify any particular rank or ego, or to make any political statements. In portraying events, I adhere strictly to facts, not opinions. It either did or did not happen. There will be those who choose to armchair-quarterback my decision to write this book and the depiction of the events in it. I will simply add that the validity of this account comes not just from myself, but from nearly three dozen Special Forces operators and commanders, ISAF members, and Afghan National Army soldiers who served there with me and who were subsequently interviewed for this project, to ensure its accuracy. Conversations and dialogue have been reconstructed from these interviews, action reports, and my own notes and recollections.

These men were my compass, my guide, and ground truth for this project. The Afghans have a saying in Pashto, *Dagga tse dagga da*—It is what it is.

Such is this story. This is our story. *De opresso liber.* March or die.

Rusty Bradley
April 2009
Kandahar, Afghanistan

Disclaimer: The views presented are those of the author and do not necessarily represent the views of the Department of Defense (DOD), its components, or its personnel.

LIONS OF KANDAHAR

Chapter 1

———

FIRST CONTACT

*The only thing necessary for the triumph of evil
is for good men to do nothing.*

—ATTRIBUTED TO EDMUND BURKE

September 2006

The first rounds slammed into the windshield like a jackhammer. I winced, expecting the worst. Luckily, the bullet-resistant glass did its job, otherwise my brains would have been blown all over the truck. Rocket-propelled grenades (RPGs) shot by just feet away, so close I could see the spring-loaded stabilizer fins that can easily shear off men's heads, arms, legs, and destroy a small vehicle with appalling quickness. Their vapor trails hung in the air. The roar of machine guns was deafening, overwhelming. We had just arrived at the battlefield.

Operation Medusa, the largest NATO-led offensive in history, was turning into an absolute disaster. Nearby, the main Canadian advance had stalled, and then stopped altogether, ambushed by anti-armor assaults and then enveloped in urban firefights. My Special Forces team and our Afghan allies were five minutes into a savage firefight at the base of Sperwan Ghar, a remote hill in the Panjwayi district

in western Kandahar Province. Two other SF teams were also leading Afghan soldiers up the hill under heavy fire. If we could seize the
hill, we could call in air strikes to help our NATO allies.

The first two minutes of a fight are the most precious. You know
who you are up against in the first thirty seconds, if you live that
long. The machine guns that raked our Ground Mobility Vehicles
(GMVs) and the volleys of RPGs told me that we were up against
enemies who knew exactly what they were doing. Already, the Taliban fighters had dealt the nearby Canadian mechanized units a severe blow, killing nearly a dozen and destroying several vehicles. I
could hear the Canadians on the radio. They were fighting for their
lives. We all were.

This was my third tour in Afghanistan, and when I'd departed
seven months earlier we'd nearly chased the Taliban out of Kandahar. They were supposed to be broken and defeated. But since then,
NATO forces had assumed control of southern Afghanistan, replacing American units with a collection of troops from around the
world. The NATO commanders focused heavily on setting up reconstruction teams and less on combat and maintaining security, critical
to the reconstruction efforts. Five years into the war, the change in
strategy would result in the bloodiest period since the fall of the
Taliban regime in 2001.

We'd been warned that the Taliban had returned in force. They
had massed thousands of fighters in Panjwayi, their heartland, and
had their sights set on overrunning Kandahar city, the capital of the
province and of southern Afghanistan. These guys weren't bush-
league Taliban villagers. This wasn't the Taliban of old that "sprayed
and prayed," hoping Allah willed them to kill the infidel and live another day. These Taliban were using well-coordinated and synchronized movements. After a volley of airburst rocket-propelled-grenade
rounds, the enemy followed up with well-placed RPG rounds aimed
directly at our heavy machine gunners, hoping to disable the guns or
kill their operators. This was our first glimpse of a resurgent Taliban

movement wholly focused on pushing the coalition forces out of southern Afghanistan. Now, hunkered down in our trucks, we faced firepower rarely seen since the first months of the war.

Hard thumping cracks of gunfire from the right rear of my truck startled me. I sat sidesaddle, facing out, and turned my head just in time to see the intense red glow of another RPG slam into the ground. The red tracers that immediately followed from the Taliban machine guns struck our vehicles and the earth around us, ricocheting in all directions. I swung my M240 machine gun in that direction as fast as I could. The matrix of irrigation ditches, which ran six feet deep in some places, thick vegetation, and grape-drying huts exploded with enemy fire.

"Contact right, contact right!" I screamed over the roar of the guns. Every machine gun and grenade launcher on my team's trucks erupted toward the Taliban positions. The race was on to pour as much firepower into the enemy as possible.

Just as we were beginning to gain an edge, a mud fortress and its surrounding buildings directly in front of my truck suddenly opened up. We were in the open and exposed. Rounds skipped all around inside and outside the vehicle, then the flash. An RPG exploded on the truck's front bumper. My teeth hurt and I had the strong metallic taste of explosives in my mouth. The confusion and pain assured me I was alive. We had enemy fighters to our right, front, and left. Their ambush almost cut our column in half, preventing any reinforcements from getting into the fight. This was their goal from the start. Divide the unit, cause confusion, and destroy each of us individually. We needed air support NOW!

Dutch Apache helicopter gunships circled above us. The thumping sound of the Apaches' 30-mm cannon fire was sweet music. The gunships made runs on the heavily defended buildings to drive out the occupants. The first two of four 2.75-inch rockets from the Apaches slammed high into the grape house less than a football field away. The sharp cracks of the explosions marked a good hit. As the dust cleared from the rocket blasts, our Afghan Army soldiers opened fire and cut down the four or five Taliban fighters who came stumbling out of the building, dazed and confused. Good kills usually drop like rag dolls, as these did.

I figured we were facing about fifty to eighty fighters in and around the hill. We had about sixty Afghans and thirty Special Forces soldiers in three A-teams and one command and control B-team. This B-team was supposed to be composed of twelve additional men, but this was just four in one truck. Our target, Sperwan Ghar, jutted out of the valley of farms separated by deep irrigation ditches. It was prime real estate because whoever owned it could see up and down the valley and across the river, where the Canadians were getting mauled.

As we desperately tried to push up the hill, we radioed back to the tactical operations center (TOC) for more information. They were watching a live feed from a Predator drone flying over the battlefield that revealed a drastically different scenario than we had been briefed on.

"Talon 30, this is Eagle 10. Here is your situation: The enemy count is not dozens, but hundreds, maybe even a thousand. They are everywhere! Do you copy, over?"

We'd already shot half of our ammo. Now we knew we were horrifically outnumbered and outgunned. We faced hundreds of Taliban fighters, with more pouring in from all directions.

We were in very serious trouble.

Chapter 2

———

THAT SEWER SMELL

Intuition is often crucial in combat,
and survivors learn not to ignore it.

—COLONEL F. F. PARRY, USMC (Ret.)

August 2006

The wheels of the massive gray C-17 cargo plane screeched as they hit the pavement of Kandahar Airfield (KAF). The plane shook violently, its powerful engines screaming, until it finally rolled to a stop at the end of the runway.

Ten minutes before, we had been told to strap in for landing. We all gave up our somewhat comfortable nooks within the belly of the aircraft and took seats along the sides of the cargo bay. Guys crawled off large pallets of supplies or rolled off the hoods of the trucks. No one talked. We all just sleepwalked to our seats. The jolt of the wheels hitting the tarmac helped wake us up. Wiping the sleep from my eyes, I stretched and scanned the cargo hold. The rest of my team seemed groggy, but awake. The roaring engines pushed the huge plane and its cargo forward to the twenty-foot white W painted on the runway and then we taxied over to the terminal.

The flight for me was always the major turning point. It was when reality set in that there was a war going on and we would again be put into the middle of it. Seventeen hours earlier, as the plane climbed into the sky, I tried to shed all my concerns about the life I was leaving at Fort Bragg. It was a mental separation as much as a physical one. For the next eight months, I'd have to be a diplomat, peacemaker, teacher, and hunter. On bad days, I'd be the hunted.

Leaving my family was always the hardest part. It was worse than the combat, worse than the crappy living conditions, and worse than being injured. What made it hard was the unknown. I never knew if I was saying my last good-bye. When I was young and thinking about getting married, I prayed for a strong, independent wife who could take care of my family should anything ever happen to me. That is exactly what God gave me. But the good-byes took a toll. My wife had a weary look. Leaving my child was excruciatingly painful. You can't explain why you're going, and that's all they want to know. But the why, for me, is really simple. My family is why I fight, but it's hard for them to understand the reason I had to travel thousands of miles away to do it. We didn't have any special rituals. I just tried to spend as much time as I could with them before they dropped me off at Fort Bragg. After the final hug, I went numb and pushed home deep inside, to a safe place no one could get to.

When I'd joined, the Army was drawing down after Desert Storm. I had a college degree, but there were no slots available in Officer Candidate School (OCS). It didn't matter to me. I was just out to pay off my debts and see the world. It wasn't long before I found my niche in the Noncommissioned Officer Corps. I loved the camaraderie and was eager for any and all training my senior sergeants could give me. I just tried to be a sponge and absorb everything I could learn. I got my Ranger tab, graduated from airborne and air assault schools, and even went to Malaysian tracking school. It wasn't until years later that I finally got my shot to attend Officer Candidate School and eventually survived selection to Special Forces. I have always felt that being an NCO first, understanding how they function, operate, motivate, and lead men as part of the backbone of the Army, made me a better officer. The skills and the attention to detail I was taught would serve me well in the future.

When I graduated from the Special Forces Qualification Course, I inherited a Super Bowl–caliber team. After my first SF rotation, a few of my senior guys were forced under standing policy to rotate off the team and assume other assignments. I thought removing guys with so much combat experience from a team that was so clearly cohesive was a ridiculous requirement. But I did not have a vote in this; we were, after all, in the Army. Thankfully, the remaining members of my team were great mentors. When new guys arrived, they were immediately molded into the team structure and we moved on.

Very soon after joining my unit I realized that Special Forces soldiers and our organization in general have a particular mystique. It's something you can't put your finger on and definitely does not derive from a Hollywood movie. We lived, trained, and operated within a unique paradigm. On one hand, every day was like September 12, 2001. We were truly the tip of the spear, out there in the enemies' backyard with little or no support, living wholly within the indigenous culture. Our country wanted blood, brains, and balls on the wall in Afghanistan, and we would deliver. On the other hand, we were simultaneously trying to build a country and free its people from the tyrannical ideology of the Taliban—the more difficult challenge. In order to fulfill this key aspect of our mission, it was necessary to separate ourselves from Western thinking and adopt the mind-set of an Afghan, immersing ourselves in their society, tribes, languages, culture, religion, and fundamental philosophy. It was imperative to establish and meet the needs of the Afghan people as they undertook the huge transition from a warring society to a peaceful one. They needed security, education, organization, honest political representation, and civil infrastructure. We understood that this transition would take several generations and a whole lot of money. We understood, strategically, that Afghanistan as a nation had to prevail. If it followed its historical track record, and we could not secure a country for these people, all our sacrifices would be for naught. The Afghans do not see their country as a graveyard for another empire. We were not there to conquer but to rebuild and help, and they knew it.

As the C-17 glided through the night sky, I concentrated on my last rotation as a Special Forces team commander, reviewing our premission training and preparation for the upcoming deployment. There is not another unit in the U.S. military as versatile as a Special Forces team. Born after World War II, Special Forces fields some of the most highly trained units in the U.S. military. The standard SF team, called an Operational Detachment Alpha, or ODA, is designed to operate independently and consists of twelve men led by a captain and a warrant officer. The rest of the team is made up of NCOs—sergeants. Two senior sergeants serve as the team sergeant and intelligence sergeant. Each team specialty also has two sergeants, one senior and one junior. The weapons sergeants are experts on tactics and maintain the team's weaponry, such as rifles, machine guns, and rocket launchers. The engineer sergeants build and blow things up, and they also act as the team's supply sergeants. The medical sergeants are the Army's best trauma medics, but they can also treat common diseases, do dental work, and even provide veterinary care for farm animals. The communications sergeants maintain the team's radios and computers and keep the team connected to the outside world.

My team had studied the border region between Afghanistan and Pakistan for the past couple of months. The remote, wild tribal area in Pakistan, stretching five hundred miles along the Afghan border, has been lawless and violent for centuries. Today it is a breeding ground for jihad. Taliban and Al Qaeda militants hunkered down there to use the area as a launching pad for attacks against Afghanistan, and as a training ground for terrorist attacks worldwide. It is an area of Pakistan the government doesn't control and it is off-limits to the U.S. military.

We knew the major players and could occasionally tell the good guys and those just riding the fence from the bad. We plotted the Taliban's routes in and out, identified probable hideouts and ambush sites. Our Special Forces company, in conjunction with a brigade from the 173rd Airborne, had nearly shut the Taliban down in Kandahar Province during our last rotation eight months ago, and I prayed for the same successes this time.

After a few minutes, the plane finally stopped taxiing and the Air Force crew chiefs who'd loaded the plane opened the rear cargo door. They were dressed in tan flight suits and heavy body armor.

"Okay, Captain," Zack, my weapons sergeant, said sarcastically, chuckling as the crew chiefs waddled about trying to get the cargo ready to unload. "So we're on a ten-ton plane carrying five tons of fuel flying four to six hundred miles per hour. The absolute last thing you need to worry about is a bullet."

"I know Zack, I know," I said.

Zack was new to the team, having arrived during the early summer, but you would never have known it. He was burly, with a stocky build and a barrel chest that would have suited a UFC fighter. He fell in with Bill, the team's senior sergeant, and the two of them made a damn good pair. You can always tell who the pipe hitters are, and Zack fit the bill to a T. He was rough, young, brash, and annoyingly honest. He could most likely kick your ass, and he knew it. His thick black hair made for a great full beard, and I had already pondered the scope of his capabilities when in civilian clothes among the Afghans. My guess was that he could easily disguise himself physically and would work well with the team in dicey circumstances. Zack handled guns like professional drivers handle race cars. They were to be guarded and protected until it was time to use them. Then, when the time is right, you bang the living shit out of them for all they are worth. Zack knew he could repair or replace them later, but when they were needed, he knew how to apply them for their intended purpose and get every mile per hour out of them. He was Bill's protégé and they trained hard together. Bill turned Zack into a top-notch weapons sergeant, while Zack kept Bill on his best game. Between the two of them, anyone we ran into on this trip stupid enough to engage the team would pay a dear, dear price for his recklessness.

Zack was single, and several of the married team members lived vicariously through him. Women loved him and he never went without a lady on his arm. Zack was not cocky—okay, maybe a little—but it is not considered cocky in this culture if you can back it up. Zack always tested himself, rigorously, physically and mentally. Whether it was physical team events, marksmanship, drinking beer, or a Sudoku puzzle, Zack would come in first or die trying. His career was just beginning, but his mental toughness would continue to be sought after through the years. Watching him, I often wished I was fifteen years younger and twenty pounds lighter. Zack was the training partner to push you where you didn't think you could go. I kept that little secret tucked away in my bag of tricks. If I ever needed a square peg smashed into a round hole, I knew Zack was the guy to do it, and that it would please him greatly. I would have loved to have traveled the world with this extraordinary young man, kicking people's asses who desperately needed it. He didn't take any shit from the other team members, even though he was a new guy. If Zack didn't know how to do something, you only needed to give him a month and he'd be doing it better than you.

With the cargo ready, the broad gray hydraulic doors opened and the cool temperatures we had enjoyed at altitude quickly gave way to the stifling heat waiting outside the aircraft. Afghanistan smells like an open sewer running past a pine wood fire. Every head on the team literally sank, almost in unison.

We were back.

As the engines shut down, trucks began to pull up to the rear of the aircraft. The vehicles were dirty, banged-up Toyota Hilux trucks, the Afghan equivalent of a Toyota Tacoma compact pickup. The crew chiefs quickly snapped off the huge chain supports and rolled the pallets out of the back of the plane to the waiting forklifts, which lumbered forward and began to hoist the pallets of supplies out of the bowels of the plane. The pallets contained everything from weapons and ammunition to office supplies. Piled high on one pallet were boots and uniforms for our Afghan National Army soldiers. We had seen how poorly the Afghan soldiers had been equipped on the last rotation. This time each of us brought all his spare gear from home: boots, uniforms, belts, socks, hats, load-carrying equipment. I, and many others in the unit, had personally purchased additional gear for them. We knew what they needed and wanted to be sure they had it. All of it was critical for the fledgling Afghan Army.

I climbed out of the back of the plane and hit the concrete of the runway. My knees ached from being trapped inside. It had been six months since I'd left Kandahar Airfield and I took a quick survey. It was built in the 1960s about ten miles southeast of Kandahar city by the United States Agency for International Development (USAID) as a base in case of war with the Soviets. The Soviets invaded Afghanistan in 1979 and used the airfield themselves. Army Rangers seized it in 2001 and it became the United States' main hub in southern Afghanistan.

A senior sergeant from the tactical operations center greeted us on the tarmac and tracked each pallet as it was unloaded, checking it off on his clipboard. With the last pallet finally secured on a flatbed truck, we were ready to head out.

Bill pointed out the team's trucks. He had come to the team halfway through our 2005 rotation. A former platoon sergeant in the Rangers, he had taken only a few days to get up to speed. Now the team sergeant, the senior supervisor, he kept the team on track with training and tactical planning. Bill answered to me alone and was as good a noncommissioned officer as anyone could ever hope for—the guy who could be a friend to the soldiers, yet maintained their respect as the senior NCO. Raised in a poor rural community in White Settlement, Texas, he joked that his family was a living *Jerry Springer* show. He was a vivid, wiry Dallas Cowboys fan with a taste for top-shelf bourbon, and when not on duty he kept the team in stitches for hours. For men like Bill, combat was an extension of their personality. He could go from easygoing team member to head disciplinarian (or asshole) in less than a second if the situation called for it. But when it came to work, no one knew tactics and weapons better. He kept the team leaning forward, ready to take on the next challenge at all times. To say Bill was competitive would be an understatement. When he first joined the team he had been a physical stud—he could easily outrun any of us, do more push-ups, pull-ups, and sit-ups, typical Ranger stuff. He quickly learned that no one in SF gave a flying shit about running fast. A team member must be able to do three vital things in combat, all of them in full equipment and body armor: fight, carry a fully equipped wounded soldier, and carry a rucksack uphill. Most of us were Rangers. We *never* left a fallen comrade on the battlefield, ever. After several team lessons in the combatives pit, Bill figured it out. Soon after that he was attending daily workout sessions in the weight room. I think he liked the brawn and it stuck. He had put on nearly twenty pounds of muscle since the last rotation.

Climbing into the truck, I asked the NCO from the TOC for an update.

"Sir, it is pretty complex," he told me. "You'd better get the briefing from the boss."

Bill leaned over. "It can't be good if you have to go get the briefing," he whispered.

The special operations compound is a short ride from the airfield. We drove through the gate, past the guard shack, and were dropped off in front of our barracks, a hastily built plywood building. We threw our gear onto our bunks, which consisted of cheap, thin mattresses on ramshackle metal frames taken from the old Russian barracks.

The supply pallets were being delivered to a gravel field nearby, and we headed over to inspect them. Bill decided to stay with the team and make sure all the gear was accounted for while I went to the TOC for the brief. "Captain, I'm going to get a feel for the place. I'll catch up to you later," Bill said. Exploring the camp didn't interest me. I was eager to get the intelligence briefing and check in with my commander, Lieutenant Colonel Don Bolduc.

Rounding a corner, I ran into Bolduc and an old friend, Lieutenant Colonel Shinsha, the commander of the Afghan Army's 2nd Battalion, 3rd Kandak. Short, lean, and fit, Bolduc lived off some kind of inexhaustible energy source. Even this early in the morning, he was firing on all cylinders. He liked being around the soldiers in his command and used his time with them to get up to speed on what was happening in the field. It wasn't lip service, like some commanders. He really wanted to know what they thought, and he commented often that the input and information helped him make decisions. Bolduc himself had enlisted and became a sergeant before attending OCS. The mission always came first, but he valued his soldiers and took care of all of us. He treated everyone in the battalion, from his operations officer to a mechanic in the motor pool, as a professional.

In my fifteen years in the Army, I'd never had a better commander. Bolduc understood the importance of details and, like a chess master, his command of the big picture made him lethal. He seemed to know what the Taliban, ISAF, coalition, and even his own team leaders were going to do before they did it.

In the years between 2002 and 2009, there was no centralized national military strategy for Afghanistan—none. A strategy refers to a plan of action designed to achieve a particular goal. An overarching strategy for any conflict unifies and directs all of its elements to work toward the execution of that strategy, facilitating the accomplishment of the intended goal. In the absence of a strategy, military organizations, especially ones composed of diverse multidimensional and multinational forces such as those in Afghanistan, operate in an unsynchronized fashion, never accomplishing or achieving their intended goals.

If a unified strategy was out there during those years, it was invisible to us, and we populated the battlefield more frequently than any other unit. We received ever-changing directives from commanders that were based on their professional and personal leadership style, not necessarily around a cohesive, nested strategy that forced everyone in the battle space to work toward accomplishing the same set of goals.

The first and fundamental requisite for establishing a strategy is to know exactly what the end state needs to be. This is no small task. In Special Forces, we understood it was paramount that a stable and secure national government be established in Afghanistan and that that government had to provide for the security of the people and meet their basic needs. If the national government would not or could not meet the needs of the people, the insurgency would interfere or even try to meet these needs, thus creating a massive division among the people and their society. Once the end state is determined, the means to achieve it must be identified. To reach our desired end state, we needed to establish and accomplish a certain set of achievable goals. Defining what those goals were for ourselves allowed us to establish a series of objectives and accomplish them one by one.

Recognizing these inherent shortfalls in strategy and in the conduct of warfare, the members of our Task Force 31, or TF 31, and its commander did our best to establish a strategy by defining the desired end state, determining a series of goals, and then deciding on the specific objectives that needed to be accomplished to achieve those goals. The commander then directed the integration of all subordinate units under his command to abide by this strategy. He also ably recruited ISAF and coalition support by building rapport with the unified commands of southern Afghanistan, the Afghan National Army, and the local governmental officials. This small strategy created by an SF task force would be nested and synchronized with the overarching national goals of the United States and the fledgling government of the Islamic Republic of Afghanistan. Now, at least, we had a plan that reflected what the bigger picture should or would look like and we worked feverishly toward implementing it. This was a mere micro picture of what needed to be established across the entire country.*

A simple Thai proverb says it all: "How do you eat an elephant? One bite at a time."

The following is the direct guidance we received from the 1st Battalion, 3rd Special Forces Group (1/3 SFG) commander on all SF operations to be conducted in Afghanistan in 2005–06:

> Your operations must be intelligence driven, decentralized, full spectrum operations designed to have the best long term effects against the enemy and on the populace. All operations must be led by Afghan National Security Forces (ANSF). Your kinetic operations must have a non-kinetic effect built into the plan. Everything that we do affects the populace and we must ensure that our operations are conducted in a manner that gains the support of the populace. All of your operations must have a Civil Military Operation (CMO), Information Operation (IO), and Humanitarian Assistance (HA) component and capability and all post kinetic operations must be followed by a meeting with village elders to explain the purpose of the operation and to legitimize the Islamic Republic of Afghani-

---

* Shortly after taking over as the commander of all ISAF and coalition forces in the country in 2009, General Stanley McChrystal addressed the lack of a unified national strategy in Afghanistan. It took him less than a year to establish, synchronize, and direct its implementation, completing the macro (big) picture.

stan (IRoA). This will go a long way in gaining the support of
the local populace and will mitigate the enemy's IO plan to
discredit IRoA and coalition force operations.

Whether it was training in the United States or conducting operations in a war zone, Bolduc clearly articulated to all of his subordi-
nates what he expected to be done. He wanted them to have no
doubt what to accomplish in the execution of their orders—and also
in the absence of orders. There would be no ambivalence. Love him
or hate him, the men knew what to expect. The following are ex-
cerpts from the desk-side brief that was personally given to all of his
soldiers:

Leadership Philosophy: Understand where we have been; focus on the present and plan for the future. Everything has a
triangle which encompasses three major points. Discipline,
Competence and Trust comprise the first triangle.

Trust was the base of the triangle. We were expected to be able to
look in the mirror, not out the window. Confidence and familiarity
with even the smallest tasks established this. Competence was next.
There was always an expectation to focus on the fundamentals, understand the psychology of war, and do the right thing. The final and
most crucial ingredient was discipline; discipline in yourself and in
your soldiers. To Lieutenant Colonel Bolduc, discipline was not
about power, it was about the judicious use of authority and responsibility. Special Forces had a boatload of both.

Command Guidance: You will Pressure, Pursue and Punish.

We were expected to conduct the preparation and training for war
as skillfully as we would execute operations themselves during war.

During deployments we would often find ourselves passing this concept on to our ISAF and coalition counterparts. It is not hyperbole to say that we were expected to go anywhere, anytime, anyplace, and be prepared to do damn near anything.

Next to Shinsha, Bolduc looked like a kid. Shinsha is an absolute bear of a man, with a round face, huge hands, and strong and broad dark Tajik features. Unlike most Afghans, he wears a thin, well-groomed beard that he says is just long enough to keep the Pashtun tribes off his back.

I had barely gotten the words "Good morning, sir," out of my mouth when Shinsha recognized me. He came straight over and threw his arms around me. I am not a small man by any stretch, six foot one, but he easily picked me up in a bone-crushing hug and feigned two kisses on both cheeks. *Holy crap,* I thought, *he may have cracked a rib or two.* Bolduc, understanding the importance of our relationship, winked and walked off.

"It is good to have your long beards back in Afghanistan," Shinsha said. "Long beards" is a nickname given to Special Forces by the Afghans, a mark of respect in its comparison to the beards of their elders.

I was truly glad to see him. He and I had a long history. We'd fought together in 2005 and 2006 and had broken the back of the Taliban in Kandahar Province. Shinsha would proudly boast that "the Taliban could not stop to piss in Kandahar Province without us showing up that year." Unbeknownst to him, this statement was essentially true. Captured Taliban had said much the same. He jokingly referred to the Taliban as *"shuzzuna"*—women—in Pashto.

We'd spent many hours talking strategy and learning each other's languages over strong green and black tea. He still spoke only a smattering of English, and my Pashto was equally as bad. Since we were just out of earshot of the commanders, I asked him how things were going in Kandahar.

"What is the situation, my friend?" I asked in broken Pashto.

"No, no, no things good here in Kandahar," he said in heavily accented English.

Shinsha never minced words and painted a bleak picture. Taliban fighters were operating inside and outside the city and more fighters arrived daily. The Special Forces units that replaced us after our last rotation focused most of their efforts doing night raids and did not have sufficient time to build rapport with the population. This was not their fault; the directive to move only at night came from higher headquarters. Shinsha said the Taliban now dominated the daylight hours. I knew and respected members of the other Special Forces group as both friends and professional colleagues, but Shinsha's news worried me.

Last year we had rarely encountered resistance inside the city except for suicide bombers. We had run across the Taliban on patrol near mountain passes, but rarely in the city. When Shinsha's battalion had completed its training, we immediately started raiding Taliban safe houses. Eventually, the raids grew into full-scale attacks. My team hit targets up until the week before we rotated out. The constant pressure had driven the enemy deep underground or out of the province altogether, and we had passed our strategy to the incoming replacements. Eight months later the Taliban resurgence was obvious to everyone. Their progress was steady and methodical. Fighters based in the villages around and inside the city now attacked the ISAF coalition and measured its response. I wanted to know how all of our work had been reversed.

Winning a guerrilla war means getting out in the hinterland and not just showing, but convincing the population that your side is the winning team. Working by, with, and through the local population and indigenous forces is not optional. It is the essential key to success. Moving away from that holistic approach represents a fundamental breach in counterinsurgency operations, leading to major setbacks. For whatever reason, the pressure had not been kept on the Taliban rurally; the focus had switched mostly to raids and operating exclusively at night. We couldn't afford to take this approach anymore.

Shinsha and I agreed to meet later, and I hustled into the headquarters. The first thing I noticed when I walked in was the memorial wall. The list of our fallen soldiers now almost reached the floor. I stopped and ran my fingers across the names and closed my eyes so I could see their faces and hear their laughter. I fought back tears for my friends. It happened every time I came back.

Farther down the hallway, an eclectic assortment of dozens of modern rifles and rocket launchers hung side by side along the wall. Most were taken from weapons caches or dead enemy fighters. As on the memorial wall, I noticed a few new additions. But I put aside my nostalgia when I got to the door to the tactical operations center and keyed in the new pass code.

The TOC looked like the bridge of a starship. Several large screens displaying Predator feeds filled the main wall, with an even bigger screen that tracked every unit in southern Afghanistan. Everything was monitored by TOC drones, soldiers who buzzed around the room or huddled over laptops. Most of the time, they sat facing their monitors on a raised semicircular platform that resembles an altar. Each soldier, dressed in brown T-shirt and desert uniform pants, had a specific job. One might work supply requests while another coordinated aircraft and another coordinated artillery fire. The whole room revolved around the battle captain, who acted as the conductor of the orchestra of war.

The planning and intelligence office sat off the right side of the main room. I walked over and knocked on the door. Trent, my unit's intelligence sergeant, met me with a somber look on his face and led me to a seat.

Maps and pictures of possible targets covered every inch of the wall. A large table cluttered with laptops and intelligence reports ran through the middle of the room. Intelligence analysts sifted through radio intercepts, satellite pictures, and tips from Afghan locals, trying to build a clear picture of what was going on in southern Afghanistan.

Trent's assessment of the situation didn't differ much from Shinsha's. "This place is about three months from going under," he said.

He outlined a series of setbacks. When we left Kandahar after our last rotation, the Taliban were afraid to come into the city, and we seemed to be one step ahead of them. Now we were outnumbered and losing ground fast. By the end of the brief, I felt sick to my stomach. The sickness quickly turned to anger. My team now had to fight for ground we had already taken. Kandahar was the prize— strategically vital to both us and the Taliban.

The third-largest city in Afghanistan, Kandahar has been fought over for centuries. Since the time of Alexander the Great it has stood at the crossroads of trade routes to five major cities: Herat and Gereshk to the west, Kabul and Ghazni to the northeast, and Quetta in Pakistan to the south. With its airport and extensive network of roads, the city served as a center for the mujahideen resistance during the Soviet invasion and was the one-eyed Taliban leader Mullah Omar's hometown. When the Taliban captured it in 1994, it became their capital.

"Trent, please tell me exactly what the hell happened in the six months we were gone," I said.

"Seems the enemy moved in too fast and we lost a lot of the rapport we had built with the civilians and leadership," he said sharply.

It was our job now to rebuild it and keep the Taliban from reclaiming its power base.

Chapter 3

——

PICKING A FIGHT

Wars may be fought with weapons,
but they are won by men.

—GENERAL GEORGE S. PATTON, JR.

H eading back to the hut to brief the team, I saw "Ole Girl"—the
same truck that I had been using in Afghanistan since 2005.
Brian, my communications sergeant, had given her the name.

This truck and I had a rough history. She had taken more than her
share of bullets and shrapnel and I quickly matched some of her
battle scars to mine. Slowly and smoothly, I ran my hand along her
hood. I glared at a bullet hole just below the front windshield. The
year before, my team had gotten caught in an ambush near the Pakistan border. I didn't notice the hole until after the fight. I pulled out
my Sharpie and retraced the faded words "MISSED ME BITCH" I
had written then to commemorate another close call.

For me, Ole Girl symbolized American strength. She was big,
powerful, and dependable. In her belly, she carried some of America's finest warriors to battle. Her antennae flew a three-by-five-foot
American flag so that the enemy could see who was coming for
them. She was a force to be reckoned with and my comfort blanket.

On my way back to the hut, one of the battle captains from the

TOC stopped me. The team we were replacing had arrived from Kandahar to pick us up and escort us back to the firebase. Shef, the other SF team's leader, stepped out into the blinding sunlight. He looked rough, tired. We'd gone through OCS together almost ten years ago and traded places at the same firebase earlier in the year. The past rotation had been hard on him and his team. They'd lost two good men in a valley outside the city. I could see that the loss of his teammates had taken its toll.

"Shef, I am so sorry to hear about your guys," I said.

"Thanks," he said, looking down. The tears welled up in his eyes.

He needed some breathing room. I knew in my gut that Shef had been handed a shit sandwich on that mission. We agreed to meet later to plan for the convoy back to the firebase.

While I had been getting the update brief, Bill had taken charge. He sent part of the team to draw medical equipment and ammunition and inspect our trucks. The rest broke down the pallets from the aircraft while Bill went to meet with the embedded tactical trainers (ETTs) who would be attached to the team. I met him over at their headquarters.

Mostly National Guard soldiers, ETTs spent their whole tour mentoring Afghan Army units. The trainers helped plan missions, made sure the Afghans had the right supplies, and served as a bridge between the Afghans and their Western partners.

The ETTs had a huge poster of the Dallas Cowboys cheerleaders tacked to the wall of their bland, plywood-walled headquarters: white vests, tight shorts, big, um, smiles. I paused to admire the Texas handiwork, and then rapped heavily on the wooden door. "Come on in," yelled someone from a back room.

Bill sat on one of three threadbare couches arranged in a horseshoe around the television in the center of the room.

"Sir," he said, "this is Chris and Sean. They will be attached to us for this rotation with our ANA unit."

Both men were from the Oregon National Guard and couldn't

have been more different. Sean's massive six-foot-three-inch frame made him look more like a lumberjack than a soldier. I could imagine him in a red-and-black flannel shirt and wool hat, swinging an axe. His partner, Chris, was slighter and looked small next to him, but Chris had the look of complete focus. I got the sense immediately that he knew exactly what he was doing.

I asked both soldiers, point-blank, their opinion of the situation in Kandahar. They exchanged looks before responding. I knew instantly what would be said, but I listened anyway: Taliban fighters were in Kandahar in greater numbers; they operated practically in the open and our coalition partners didn't stop them. By now it was beginning to sound like a broken record.

That night, we finally got moving. My team would be operating from the same firebase as on our last rotation, so we knew the route, or so we thought. Just after dark, we checked our gear, lined up the trucks, and headed toward the main gate, which was guarded by coalition soldiers. Some of our Afghan National Army soldiers were waiting for us at the gate's massive entrance. Remembering us from the previous rotations, they jumped out of their trucks, arms open, their faces bright and their smiles huge. Several rounds of hugs and back-slapping later, we were finally ready to drive out of the gate. I was glad to know that the rapport we had built with these men had stood the test of time. I was feeling good for the first time since our arrival. We locked and loaded all weapons and the convoy began to move.

Shef's team took the lead. It felt really good to be out again. The leash was off. But I was concerned that the route would take us south of the city through an area we had previously tried to avoid.

Go with it, I thought, *be flexible.* It was Shef's show.

The main road was quiet and there was very little traffic. Unlike in America, Afghanistan is dark, pitch-black. There are very few streets, let alone working street lamps. Few of the houses or buildings in the city have lighting other than hearth-style campfires inside. Even with our night-vision goggles on, I could barely see beyond the main road.

Three miles later, we came across the first ANA checkpoint, set up at a bridge that crossed a broad, dry riverbed. The ANA had built two machine-gun nests out of sandbags on either side of the crossing. We came to a slow stop and an ANA soldier came out from behind the sandbag wall, hands in the air. He had no weapon and looked rattled. "Don't continue down the road," he warned us.

"Whew, this guy may have pissed his pants or worse," one of the soldiers on Shef's team said over the radio.

At least he didn't leave his post, I thought. Some discipline is better than none. The Afghan soldier told Shef that about an hour earlier a dark Toyota Hilux truck had approached with its lights on, blinding him. When it got close, six men with AK-47s jumped out. Shoving the muzzles in his face, they told him the road was closed and they'd attack anyone who didn't obey. Then they stripped him of his rifle, took the little bit of money in his pocket, and loaded the truck with ammunition.

We cut our primary lights and relied fully on our night-vision equipment. Touted as a new alternative to traveling through the center of Kandahar, the road took us south of the city through the slums, a place for the dregs and homeless and now a haven for Taliban fighters. It was also a primary drug-smuggling route, and caution was the watchword. We had gone into this area a year earlier to hand out medical supplies, and even then we'd been warned to be very careful.

The convoy wove its way through the maze of compounds. The rutted dirt roads reeked of sewage. Piles of garbage, some several feet deep, ran along the compound walls. The dark, hidden alleyways and streets made me nervous considering the prevalence of suicide bombers in Kandahar city. We knew too well how suicide bombers operated. They hide in the black corners, behind walls, and in traffic-congested streets and attack like cowards, killing indiscriminately. To them, killing dozens of innocent people just to wound one of us was acceptable.

The bombers usually wore white and shaved their heads. Captured Al Qaeda training manuals say that followers are allowed to break all their religious laws and betray their beliefs to put themselves in a position to attack us. For our enemy, the rule book is something they make up as they go along. No wonder my hair is turning gray.

"What the hell are we doing, Captain?" Bill called over the radio. "This is a perfect ambush area, and known enemy activity to boot."

"Sit tight, boys, and let's see how it plays out," I responded. The team hated situations like this, when they knew I was just trying to be positive on the radio. We all knew Bill was right to be concerned.

We turned a blind corner. The L-shaped road was lined with mud walls for more than 150 feet on both sides, with a heavily wooded area just beyond the walls providing an escape route for attackers. It was just the spot I would have picked for an ambush. In the glow of our night-vision headlights and spotlights, the group of twenty or so men waiting around the corner looked like a Taliban recruiting poster, dressed in the traditional all-black turbans and dark olive clothes. We had been going so slowly, and without our primary headlights on, that they never saw or heard us coming. They initially looked puzzled, but quickly realized we were a military convoy.

Some immediately threw their hands in the air and some hid their faces. Most just stood there, stunned. The hasty call came over the radio to be ready for a fight. I didn't see any weapons, but that didn't mean they weren't there. Several Taliban ran for the cover of a nearby irrigation ditch. Someone requested permission to open fire. I almost said yes, but before I could respond an ANA soldier jumped off his Ford Ranger truck and swung his AK violently, flashlight in hand. The rifle struck a Taliban square in the face and he fell onto the dusty road. The ANA soldier screamed at the Talibs to go get their weapons and fight like men. The Taliban sat or huddled, hissing and sneering like hyenas, gnashing their teeth, making hand gestures toward the Afghan soldiers. After all my time in the country, I couldn't believe what I was seeing—it was medieval. The hatred on their faces could not be disguised. This was the enemy we all sought, up close and personal—and without weapons. We could not do a damn thing about it.

The Talibs didn't move. The Afghan soldier quickly searched several of the better-groomed men, then swore at them one more time and hopped back in the truck. Those who were well groomed were likely the subcommanders, or were tribally affiliated with those who had favor among other Taliban commanders. The rougher-looking members of the group had probably just been brought across the desert or smuggled across the border in a vehicle trunk. As long as they were unarmed, we couldn't touch them. It was the ultimate frustration of legitimate counterinsurgency.

Shef gave the order and the convoy slowly moved on, toward the city and away from the group of Taliban. I really, really wanted to move faster, to get the area behind us as soon as possible.

About twenty minutes later we stopped. The TOC called over the radio and warned us that the group of Taliban we had run into had their weapons now and were talking about a new ambush site in intercepted radio calls. But we weren't far from the firebase and I was beginning to feel comfortable again. We got under way again and not long after, we made the final turn toward home, Firebase Maholic.

The convoy movement taught us several lessons. First, the Taliban now operated openly in the city and at night without fear. Second, their ranks were being reinforced with new personnel and supplies. Third, they had little fear of the ANA checkpoints.

But it also taught the Taliban their own lesson. Someone different had returned to the battlefield.

Chapter 4

———

WELCOME BACK

If you know the enemy and know yourself, you need not fear the result of a hundred battles. If you know yourself but not the enemy, for every victory gained you will also suffer a defeat. If you know neither the enemy nor yourself, you will succumb in every battle.

—SUN TZU

It was three a.m., but Juma Khan and the other ANA soldiers, about thirty of them, were too pent up to sleep. They boiled chai and wandered around the firebase, waiting. The word of our arrival had spread rapidly among the Afghans after I had called the base to tell them we were on our way. The "long beards" of 1st Battalion, 3rd Special Forces Group—their *rora*, their brothers—were coming again to fight by their side.

Ours wasn't the typical relationship. As had been made clear to us on numerous occasions, Afghan soldiers historically distrusted ISAF and other coalition forces because of their perceived lack of commitment and capricious attitude toward the country and its people. We were inherently different. We ate, slept, lived, and breathed with the Afghan people as if we had done so all our lives, immersing ourselves in their language and culture. It was not a perfect fit, but we tried in earnest to show respect and still project the power of the United

States. Respect goes a long, long way in Afghanistan; you have to give it to get it. The ANA regularly expressed their respect for us because we did our best to abide by their customs and culture. This was reassuring, considering what was regularly being projected in the media. We were, after all, at war. My team and our ANA-partnered units worked cohesively on how to operate jointly among the Afghan people against the Taliban. Fighting the foreigners such as Al Qaeda was a different story. The Afghans understood that it was better to help the Americans fight than to get between them and their enemies.

It was comforting to see the glow of the firebase as we turned onto the paved road that led to its gates. It sat on a plateau and had a commanding view of the northern half of the city. As we got closer, I could see shadowy figures in the high concrete guard towers set at intervals along the stone walls, providing welcome additional protection from the rockets and mortars that occasionally fell. It took a few minutes for our eyes to adjust to the camp's low-level lighting as we traveled through the front gate. The Afghan guards, trained by civilian contractors, looked professional and were well equipped. I felt safer here than at Kandahar Airfield. This was like coming home.

The ANA surrounded our trucks as we rolled into the motor pool, patting the hoods, clapping, and dancing, their dark faces lit by brilliant smiles. *This is what it will look like when we kill bin Laden,* I thought. The Afghans reached into the truck and pulled me out, into their giddy midst. *Crap, I'm gonna have to dance,* I thought. I hated doing stuff like that—I would hear about it for days afterward from my teammates. And someone always had a camera. My e-mail would be clogged with images of my face pasted on the bodies of belly dancers, break-dancers, and other imaginative surrogates.

The dancing led to chai, and soon everyone on the team had a scalding cup in his fist. From the center of the crowd, I saw Juma Khan.

Juma Khan had enlisted as a private in the ANA and worked his way quickly up through the ranks. Unfortunately, he was illiterate like most Afghans and couldn't be promoted higher than sergeant, no matter how brave he was in battle. He smelled like a campfire and wore a white T-shirt and loose-fitting pants. Barely five feet tall and one hundred pounds soaking wet, he always led his countrymen from the front. I looked down and noticed his pair of worn, white Nike sneakers, a gift from when I'd first met him. He refused to replace them.

In 2004, he had been left for dead after his militia unit was ambushed and an improvised explosive device (IED) sheared off parts of his face and mangled his legs. An American Special Forces medic found him next to the flaming remains of his Hilux and kept him alive. After numerous surgeries to repair his face and months of physical therapy he returned to the firebase. I thought of him personally and professionally as a miniature soldier with a Goliath-sized heart.

The family reunion gradually wound down, and we all turned in. After a few hours of sleep and breakfast, the teams shuffled into the firebase's version of the TOC for the handoff brief.

Each firebase had its own tactical operations center, which functioned just as the TOC in Kandahar did, but the similarities ended there. If Kandahar was a starship, then the firebase TOC was like a wooden glider.

Rather than dozens of people buzzing about the latest and greatest in automation, projectors, screens, lights, and computers, the firebase had two computers sitting on mismatched desks along one wall. The radios were neatly organized and positioned along the opposite wall for quick removal or destruction in the unlikely event we got overrun. A projector—one of only a few on the base—sat on a table in the middle of the room, pointed toward a painted wall that served as the screen. A hodgepodge of chairs and tables of various shapes and sizes served as a conference area. Locally made mats and threadbare rugs in ornate reds and greens kept the dust and dirt down. It wasn't uncommon to see an occasional mouse or rat run across the rough-hewn log rafters.

Members of both teams—the outgoing and the incoming—filed in and quickly claimed all the chairs. It paid to show up early because these briefings could take a long time and late arrivals had to stand. Critical for maintaining continuity, the handoff brief was basically show and tell. The outgoing team went over everything they knew about the area, the enemy, and the Afghan Army units assigned to the firebase.

A good handoff can make or break the first few weeks of a deployment. This one started with a thud. Just as Shef took the floor, the power went out and the room went dark.

"Well, some things haven't changed," someone cracked.

The base was on the Kandahar city power grid, so we, like the locals, were at the mercy of the ancient Soviet generators and years of neglect and incompetent upkeep. While we waited for the generators to kick back on, I wondered if the people were grateful for the limited power they did get. It was more than they got under the Taliban.

Compared to the other five bases, ours was sprawling and spacious. Once the Taliban's presidential palace, construction on it had begun around 1996, the year the Taliban took control in Afghanistan, and took about three years to complete. Osama bin Laden had built the compound for Taliban leader Mullah Omar, and Kandahar residents still call it Omar's compound. Special operations forces took it over in 2001 and called it Firebase Gecko, after the lizards that patrolled the walls.

It had a double-wide fireplace in the cafeteria, three catfish that lived in a two-tier fountain, and a swimming pool for when it got too hot. We had room to build a looping five-mile dirt track around the perimeter and even a shooting range for us and the Afghan soldiers.

Our backup generators finally kicked on and the power returned.

Shef started the brief by introducing Ron, the Air Force joint tactical air controller (JTAC), who nodded at us. He was a big stick in the room, with the power to save our asses by calling in air strikes. In his early twenties, he seemed quiet and reserved behind his thick, dark beard. I made a mental note to sit down with him after the meeting.

The brief rolled on as Shef went over key leaders, targets, and areas in and around Kandahar. Then he started to talk about Operation Kaika. Three months earlier, Shef had led his team and a company of ANA soldiers into the Panjwayi district south of the city. The team had received reports that the Taliban were forcing Afghans out of the villages in the district. Besides being the Taliban's hometown, the district was Kandahar Province's breadbasket because it encompassed the wide Arghandab River valley, which holds the primary water reserve and provides the most fertile and sustainable crops in southeastern Afghanistan. Pomegranate groves, corn, wheat, and marijuana fields, and grape vineyards mingled with the country's biggest cash crop, poppy. At harvesttime, the valley is filled with endless fields of flowers. The poppy sap, mixed and processed into heroin, fuels the Taliban insurgency, and the district supplies insurgents and Afghan government officials alike with cash. Afghanistan's main highway and numerous secondary roads flow through the province, creating a network of routes between Afghanistan and Pakistan. During my last rotation, my team could move through Pashmul, a Panjwayi subdistrict, without incident. There hadn't been much enemy activity there. But when Shef pushed into the district hoping to capture Taliban leaders, his team was quickly surrounded and had to fight its way out.

Shef lost two Americans and three Afghan interpreters during the mission. My guys stared at the floor as he described it. No one looked up. No one wanted to ask questions for fear of sharpshooting the operation or playing armchair general. It was a clearly understood, unwritten rule.

The brief broke a few hours later. Each of the teams' specialists met separately to review their piece of the base. The weapons specialists checked on the ammunition. I followed Shef out. I wanted to know more about Panjwayi and Operation Kaika. How had a rotation, which on paper went well, gone to shit over one operation?

Shef seemed worn down as we walked across the hall to his room. His bushy beard and tanned skin hid it, but you could tell that the rotation had aged him. As we walked, he said most of their missions had gone extraordinarily well. His voice sounded confident, but his tired, bloodshot eyes told the real story. I had to know what happened in Panjwayi.

"How did they move into the area under our noses with such force?" I asked him, spreading several large maps out on the table in his room. "I need to know more about Kaika. It looks like they might be planning something in there, and I need ground truth."

He paused for a second and looked me in the eye. The upbeat Shef I had known for almost ten years was gone. "Stay out of there unless you go in with an army, because you're going to get hurt. I've been reporting the buildup of large numbers of Taliban in there and no one's listening," he said flatly.

Operation Kaika had started off well. Shef and his men moved on foot to the compound of a suspected Taliban commander and took it. But when night fell, a large Taliban force attacked from three sides with machine guns and rocket-propelled grenades. Shef said he had Taliban fighters close to breaking through, but a steady stream of machine-gun fire and mortars beat them back. Luckily, no one was seriously hurt, but the ferocity of the assault surprised Shef and he called ISAF for a quick reaction force (QRF). The QRF launched but was not given the authority to cross a critical bridge leading into the contested area. The help never came.

"The ISAF units got to the Arghandab River but would not cross," he told me. Even saying the words seemed to put a bad taste in his mouth.

Time, I thought. Time is the most valuable asset you have on the battlefield, and it can never be replaced. He lost critical time waiting for that unit. Surrounded in the valley, with no help on the way, they tried to counterattack. Shef's team located a compound the Taliban used to stage the attack. Master Sergeant Thomas Maholic volunteered to clear out the compound with twenty Afghan soldiers.

As they moved to attack the compound, Maholic split his men into two groups and dispatched Staff Sergeant Matthew Binney, a medical sergeant, to set up a machine gun to cover the attack. Binney took an ETT and nine Afghan soldiers with him and set up the machine gun. Maholic quickly cleared the compound, but a large Taliban group counterattacked and surrounded both his and Binney's groups. Based on intercepted radio transmissions, Shef learned the Taliban's intent was to capture the Americans alive.

Every time Binney and his team came over the radio, Shef could hear intense fire. Finally, Binney's team moved through a hole in a mud wall and stumbled into a group of Taliban fighters. Binney and his men reacted first with furious fire and hand grenades at close range. Shef said the Taliban got close enough to Maholic and Binney's men to yell insults and threats.

Exposing himself to throw a grenade, Binney was hit in the back of the head. Confused and temporarily blinded and deaf, he groped for his weapon and bearings. When he regained his wits, he organized an attack on a Taliban position, but Staff Sergeant Joseph Fuerst, the ETT, was hit in his left leg by a rocket-propelled grenade. Binney tried to drag the trainer to safety and was also hit. The bullets shattered his left shoulder and upper arm.

Shef had his own problems, as the Taliban began a wave of attacks on his compound. Between assaults, Shef said he moved from position to position, rallying his men and monitoring Maholic and Binney's situation at the same time. His truck was covered in spent machine-gun shells. I tried to put myself in his shoes.

When he heard about the wounded, medic Brenden O'Connor

volunteered to lead a group to reinforce Maholic and treat Binney and Fuerst. O'Connor fought his way out of the patrol base with eight Afghan soldiers, an interpreter, and another Special Forces soldier. He led the small relief force along a wall that provided cover from Taliban machine-gun fire and rocket-propelled grenades. When he got to the end of the wall, O'Connor realized that the wounded soldiers were two hundred feet away across an open field covered by three Taliban machine guns.

Apache gunships had come in and were flying overhead. Shef said he tried to get them to cover O'Connor, but the Taliban fighters were dug into thick-walled mud huts. Bullets were tearing into the dirt and shredding the grass.

O'Connor realized that he couldn't get low enough to avoid enemy fire because of his body armor. He quickly took it off and tossed it aside. Inch by inch, he made his way across the fire zone, somehow managing to stay a fraction lower than the hundreds of Taliban machine-gun rounds. He told Shef afterward that he couldn't help thinking all the way across how the instructors at the Special Forces medics course would have roasted him if they were watching. They always hammered into their students not to go after the wounded because their skills were too valuable to risk them getting injured. Let the wounded come to you.

Fuerst had already lost a lot of blood from the gaping wound to his left leg by the time O'Connor reached him and Binney. O'Connor got a tourniquet on the leg immediately, but there wasn't time to do much else. The Taliban were closing in. The medic picked Fuerst up and hauled him to a pump house on the edge of the orchard. He stashed the ETT in a shaded area and scouted out the pump house, hoping enemy fighters weren't waiting. He climbed over the six-foot wall into a small dirt lane, where he found some Afghan soldiers and their advisor. O'Connor went back over the wall and brought Binney, and then Fuerst and two Afghan soldiers, back to the other side.

Once everyone was in the lane, O'Connor started to tend to the wounded seriously. Breaking out his medical gear, he discovered that the 120-degree heat had melted the glue that kept his IVs together. His gear was a mess, but he did his best to help Fuerst and Binney.

Throughout, Maholic had rallied the defenders in his nearby compound, ignoring the withering fire as he raced from position to position, and inspiring them to fight harder against the relentless waves of Taliban fighters barraging them with machine guns and rocket-propelled grenades.

Virtually surrounded, Maholic spotted a Taliban fighter moving down an alley near the compound. As he exposed himself to shoot the fighter, Maholic was mortally wounded. Galvanized by the master sergeant's example, the Afghan Army soldiers rallied and beat back the Taliban fighters.

After nightfall, O'Connor led the relief force back to Maholic's compound. When he got there, he found out that Maholic was dead, and he immediately took over the defense of the position.

"They needed that leadership. Up until that point, they were in disarray, just trying to hide and survive," Shef said. "When he showed back up with the wounded, he provided that. O'Connor provided that leadership that was needed."

They evacuated the wounded by helicopter as Shef called in air strikes. Fuerst ultimately died from his injuries.

Shef's team had changed the base's name a month before we got there. It was now called Firebase Maholic.

After telling me the story, Shef needed a break. I could see that he was still fighting the battle in his mind. There was a lot I needed to digest. We agreed to meet later, and I went to check on the team and supply situation.

I couldn't shake Shef's story. For starters, the battle told me two things: the Taliban had good advisors, and I probably couldn't plan on using the ISAF, the NATO units that now owned southern Afghanistan, in a pinch.

★   ★   ★

The handoff took several days. On the third day, we focused on the
ANA company at the base. Reconnecting with them was an important part of the process because we would soon be fighting side by
side. Standing in formation in the middle of our dusty firebase, wearing old green camouflage U.S. Army uniforms, the Afghan soldiers
looked like a ragged bunch. But the excitement of our arrival hadn't
worn off. "Positive motivation can go a long way on the battlefield,"
I told Bill. He just laughed. Always the pessimist, he spat, "Wait and
see how they do under the noon sun when they're tired and thirsty."

It was hot, really hot, even for August, but the Afghans performed
remarkably well in the first drill. It started with an ambush of a disabled ANA truck. The Afghans had to recover the truck and then attack a compound where enemy fighters were hiding. As they raced
to the compound and quickly cleared the rooms of imaginary fighters, my team followed close behind, taking notes. The Afghan soldiers knew what to do and moved with confidence. It impressed me
and meant they were one small step closer to working us out of a
job, an advisor's ultimate goal.

Overall, I liked what I saw. Bill, on the other hand, had a list of cor-
rections.

"Rome wasn't built in a day," I told him.

He let out a skeptical laugh and shook his head. "This sure isn't
how they started either," he noted, rounding up the Afghans and
sending them through again.

During the exercise, I noticed that Ron, the JTAC, had come out to
watch. I took the chance to introduce myself again. We talked about
the last couple of months and operations with Shef's team, and he
wasn't afraid to point out shortcomings such as problems with ISAF
support structure. That was the type of candor every commander
needs to hear from his men. I liked him immediately.

As the sun set, Bill and I sat outside with cups of strong coffee. The cloudless sky was bright with sparkling stars. With no industrial pollution or competing light sources, looking at the stars in Afghanistan is awesome, but the spectacle was lost on us. Our minds were still foggy from the long trip over and the struggle to get acclimated to the hot weather and altitude. I was exhausted and knew I would stay that way until I boarded the plane to come home.

"You know, Bill, Afghanistan looks like Texas," I said, poking fun at his home state.

Before Bill could respond, we heard the heavy whistling of the first rocket and threw ourselves to the dirt. Willing myself as flat as possible, I heard the rocket hit in a flash that looked like hundreds of sparklers. Red-hot shrapnel shot out across the tarmac. The second rocket landed just outside the compound's walls.

Soviet-made 107-mm rockets. The Soviets brought in countless numbers of these lightweight, three-foot mini-missiles during the decade-long war in the 1980s. Now they were buried or hidden in caves all over the country; the insurgents fired them using timers and wooden launchers from the backs of trucks or straight off the ground. The wooden launchers are crude, just wedges of wood cut to different angles to provide optimum trajectories. But they work.

After a few minutes, someone hollered, "All clear." Dust and the heavy smell of explosives hung in the air.

Bill and I went to the TOC to see if anyone had been injured. Bill got a head count. We were short one person—Steve, our junior medic. His room sat near the tarmac where the rocket hit. My heart began to pound. Had he been on the tarmac? If so, why was he out there? Had shrapnel pierced the sandbags around his hut or penetrated his room?

We sprinted through the narrow, mud-walled hallways toward Steve's quarters. His door was shut, and there was no answer when we pounded on it. We shoved it open to find him lying on his bed, peacefully asleep. He was wearing earplugs and didn't even flinch when the door burst in.

Steve was our newest team member. He had arrived a few months before the deployment and breezed into our team room at Fort Bragg with bleached white hair and the dark tan of a surfer. He chain-smoked cigarettes and looked like a scrawny version of the Marlboro man compared to the other team members. Normally, they would have considered his laid-back demeanor and easygoing attitude a sign of weakness. But the unspoken rule on a team is never make the medics angry, ever. Unlike the ranks in most other sectors of the military, those working in the medical field can personally make your life miserable, by way of "losing" your medical records, threatening proctology exams, and finding myriad other opportunities to hit you where you live.

Despite his warm, youthful smile and comforting demeanor, some on the team thought Steve had a habit of becoming nervous when conducting medical training, giving an IV, or negotiating other stressful situations, and they dubbed him "Shaky Steve." Most, including myself, thought he was just young, maybe intimidated by his status as the youngest among a group of seasoned, driven veterans. We would soon learn that we were all wrong, dead wrong. When treating the wounded, even under the worst conditions, Steve had nerves of steel and the hands of a surgeon. He would display a flowing fountain of emotional calm and that easygoing smile during horrific situations where others would have folded. He was invaluable in dealing with the local Afghans. He could treat the most frightened child, deliver a baby, and gain people's trust with a warm, youthful smile and comforting manner.

At the moment, Bill's manner was far from comforting.

"What are you guys doing in here?" Steve asked, half asleep and expecting a practical joke as we rousted him out of bed.

"What are you doing?" Bill screamed, mostly out of frustration. "You know after an attack you've got to come up to the TOC."

"What attack?" Steve responded as we left to continue on our rounds.

My heart rate slowed as we got to the ANA area of the base. No one was hurt and we headed with the Afghans out to inspect the crater. Squatting next to the new hole, Dave, our senior engineer, was digging in the dirt, well into his impact analysis. Shrapnel had gouged the earth around the crater, and he pulled out dozens of razor-sharp metal shards.

"It came in from the north," he said, studying the pattern of the impact. "They probably meant for it to hit near the TOC, in the middle of the living quarters, but missed."

It was our first stroke of luck.

Chapter 5

BINGO RED ONE

Regard your soldiers as your children, and they will follow you into the deepest valleys. Look on them as your own beloved sons, and they will stand by you even unto death!

—SUN TZU

After a full day's meetings, we dressed in our best uniforms and joined the Afghans for the traditional feast we threw after a team exchange. It showed our appreciation and helped build the much-needed rapport that's essential in combat. Warm light spilled out of the biscuit-colored hut and Afghan soldiers loitered outside. As we walked through the door, we were assaulted by smells of roasted and grilled goat, stewed squash, carrots, hot peppers, and tons of rice. Plates of flatbread, fresh onions, cucumbers, and tomatoes crowded the rest of the table.

More than two hundred Afghan soldiers crammed the room. Dirty, smiling, with bad teeth and ad hoc uniforms, they all stood erect when we walked in. Lieutenant Colonel Shinsha came forward, gave me a perfect salute, and then turned to face his men. He opened the festivities with a short growl of a speech, introducing my team as the guests of honor and lauding us for helping to free their country from the Taliban. The gratitude of a freed people is humbling, and

I thought of what it must have been like for those soldiers during World War II who liberated Europe.

After the speech, the Afghans lost no time in mingling with us. Old and new faces passed in front of me shaking my hand, hugging me, firing off greetings in short Pashto bursts, and urging us to sit and eat. Across the room, I saw the familiar, scarred face of Ali Hussein, a lieutenant in the Afghan Army. The last time I saw him he was being loaded onto a medevac helicopter. I hurried over. He reached out to shake my hand and I saw his eyes were misty.

He seemed upset and dismissed the other soldiers standing around us, almost angrily. Suddenly I wondered if I was actually in for a tongue-lashing. I'd been pretty hard on him the previous year.

When we first met during my last rotation, his men had openly mocked him. He was short and frail, and it was known that his tribal ties with the Hazara and a hearty "donation" had secured his commission in the army. On patrol, he looked scared and unsure. Wild things like soldiers and dogs can smell fear, and his Afghan soldiers had little confidence in him.

After a handful of missions, I couldn't stand it any longer. Leading men into battle was not for the meek, and I wanted him to understand the gravity of his position. At night, he'd come to my room and we'd go over chapters from the Ranger handbook. We'd review how to patrol, ambush, and clear rooms of enemy fighters. I berated him for every mistake and miscalculation. Within a few months, he confidently set off to lead his men on a long patrol into the Ghorak Valley with my SF team.

It was late 2005.

We were departing an area where we had just conducted an operation. My truck was in the lead as we carefully navigated down a wadi, a dry creek bed, near the border of the Helmand River valley. The anti-tank mine was well concealed among the smooth gray creek stones, and we missed it by a few inches. One single second later, Ali's truck hit it. I was leaning out of the truck looking for mines when the explosion blew off my headset and sheared off the front half of his Ranger truck. The shrapnel killed several of his men and sliced Ali's face open to his skull. We evacuated him and I figured that he'd retire after his wounds healed.

But he hadn't. When Shef's team was surrounded in Panjwayi, Ali refused to leave Fuerst, the wounded ETT. He beat back several attacks by the Taliban. When they tried to bribe him to give up the American, he traded insults with them. If Ali was the warrior Shef claimed he had become, then I wanted him as an ally. Standing there at that feast, I waited to see if he intended to give me a taste of my own medicine first. After he dismissed the nearest soldiers, he turned to me and said in accented English, "You my captain, you my commander. I want die with you. You make Ali man. My family have honor now because Ali is man."

"I hear you are a lion now, brother," I said, shaking his hand.

I threw my arm around his shoulder, and we started toward the table. Ali called over Shamsulla. This was turning out to be a real family reunion. Shamsulla, who went by his nickname Taz, was an American Ranger trapped in an Afghan body. I stood staring at the two of them. Taz had definitely been hitting the weights. He too had put on muscle while we were gone. I brought him over to Bill, who broke into a huge grin as I reminded him of some of Taz's exploits.

Taz became infamous in 2005 for two incidents, the first at a checkpoint near Kandahar city that we'd set up to look for roadside bomb makers. After several hours in the hot sun, I had decided to pack it up. Any Taliban fighters in the area had probably heard about the checkpoint and avoided it. I watched as a beat-up gray Toyota sedan bounced along the road toward the checkpoint, trailing a dirty dust cloud behind it. Suddenly the driver stopped, threw the car into reverse, and roared backward. Taz was operating a hidden rear security position in an abandoned hut. The road was too rough for the Toyota to get up any real speed, and after seeing the car turn around, Taz and two other soldiers took off running in pursuit. Partway to the car, Taz stopped and fired a burst from his AK-47 into its engine, bringing it to a halt. With his weapon at the ready, Taz approached the driver, who cursed him, calling him a dog. Suddenly, Taz, mad with rage, dove into the car. The other Afghan soldiers started screaming at us to come. My team sergeant, Willie, and I raced to the car, weapons at the ready. I heard two muffled cracks and then Taz squirmed out of the window covered in blood and bits of brain matter. He was smiling.

The driver had tried to pull a pistol, and during the struggle it went off, most unfortunately, two times under the driver's chin. Oops. In the trunk of the vehicle, we found AK rifles, ball bearings, wiring, mines, and blasting caps. All were common components for IEDs—roadside bombs. Needless to say, the car's passenger was more than willing to cooperate.

The second event occurred two weeks later. Around midnight, Taz banged on my door. Snatching my pistol, I followed him to one of the ANA barracks rooms. One of the team's interpreters, Hik, was lying on the mat, bloody. He had gone to the bazaar with his father to buy supplies for the soldiers and was stopped at a checkpoint by the Afghan National Police. The ANP were known throughout Afghanistan for being corrupt, untrained thugs. They wanted a bribe, and when Hik refused, they threatened him and his father. For his loyalty to his father, the police thugs beat him and punctured his lung.

We took Hik to the team's medics' shed, where they started patching him up while I went with Taz to the ANA compound. There I found all of the ANA armed and clustered outside a small storage building. Inside, the two ANP thugs had been dumped on the dirt floor of the shack, bound into human balls lying in the fetal position.

After the terp had staggered back to the camp, Taz had gone to the checkpoint, beaten the corrupt police officers, tossed them into the back of his truck, and taken them to the shack, but hadn't killed them. Our classes on civil society and human rights were partially working. It took several days of negotiations between the ANP and the ANA, but we finally convinced Taz to release the two miscreants. The bigger lesson was that Taz had taken the ragged group of ANA, formed them into a unit, and taught them absolute loyalty, albeit Afghan style, by going after the corrupt guys who'd hurt the terp.

All too often people get wrapped up in the popular Hollywood action version of what we do and forget that the Special Forces were created not just to destroy things, but to work within foreign cultures to turn their soldiers into a functioning army.

I'd studied sociology in college and have been fascinated by foreign societies, cultures, and languages since I was a boy. I also grew up in the mountains of North Carolina, where hunting, fishing, and the outdoors are a way of life. Special Forces scratched all of my itches. My career started when I enlisted in 1993. I served with the 25th Infantry in Hawaii before earning my commission. I served with the 82nd Airborne Division during my first rotation in Afghanistan. I'd learned a lot from the 82nd Airborne, especially leadership and how to build unit cohesion. I got a glimpse of Special Forces in Kandahar on that rotation. Their missions—learning the language, respecting the culture, and fighting as guerrillas on the enemy's ground—appealed to me. I realized then that I wanted a bigger challenge.

Now that challenge meant forging the ANA into a fighting force that could handle the resurgent Taliban. Since arriving, I'd heard nothing but bad news. The account of Taliban fighters almost overrunning Shef's team, and Shinsha telling me that the Taliban moved openly along streets where they once feared taking even one step, obsessed me. We were five years into the fight. This shouldn't be happening.

I was trying to focus again on the celebration when a heavy hand fell on my shoulder. It was one of the soldiers from our firebase's TOC.

"Sir, come with me now," he said. Shit, another good meal wasted.

I excused myself and headed for the TOC. I remember thinking about the scene in the movie *The Green Berets* when John Wayne is interrupted during his dinner with the code word "Tabasco." The code word was for an emergency situation. Whatever the TOC wanted now, it was not good and not scripted. The only thing missing was the code word.

The TOC was alive with frantic radio calls for assistance. I could tell from the accent it was not a Special Forces team. An ISAF unit had been ambushed—in a big way, from the sound of it.

"Have you heard from KAF or the TOC yet?" I asked the radioman.

"Sir, they're waiting for you to call on the satellite phone," he said.

I picked up the bulky black phone and headed for the rooftop to get a clear signal.

"This is 31. Put me through to the boss," I said. Bolduc got on the line moments later.

"An ISAF unit has gotten themselves in a pickle and I want you to be prepared to assist them," he told me. I asked him if we should wait for an execution order or just go immediately.

"Stand by till I can get you a clear picture," he said. "I'm not going to send you into a bad situation if I don't have to. Get your kit ready as a QRF."

By the time I got off the phone, Bill was at the TOC. I told him we were the QRF for a Canadian unit that had been ambushed. "Tell the boys to get their kits, weapons, helmets, body armor in the trucks quietly." Bill disappeared into the darkness. Back in the TOC, I got on one of the computers and requested an update. I needed to come up with a plan and had lots of questions.

Where was the ambush? *22 kilometers from Kandahar.*

How many Canadian soldiers were wounded? *Unknown.*

How many enemy fighters were in the area? *Best guess, between 25 and 40.*

By the time the team filtered into the TOC, Bill and I had developed two courses of action. We could go to the exact site of the ambush and assist the ISAF unit from there. Or we could estimate the direction of enemy movement and ambush the ambushers. We were fully prepared to maneuver behind the enemy and kill those savages where they stood.

With no permission yet to go out, my guys sat around the table and listened to the radio as casualty reports came in.

"They're just sitting there, Captain," Bill said.

"Their call," I said. "They're a professional army and they know the rules. If they're in contact and can't move to a safer location or assault the enemy positions, then they'll have to eat it till we get the word to launch."

The voice on the other end of the radio was shaky. No one was assisting them, and they weren't doing well at assisting themselves.

"They sound like they're in the hurt locker," Dave said, meaning they were in a bad way.

"Probably so," I said, praying that we could go help them.

Maybe twenty minutes ticked by, feeling like hours. I was running through the multiple options. I thought about the ISAF units who had listened in when Shef's team was in heavy contact. "Fuck it," I said. "Let's go. I'll deal with the repercussions later. We won't leave them out there without help."

Clearly relieved, my teammates moved toward the door. We headed for the motor pool and loaded the trucks. It felt good, really, really good to be back in my seat. I could hear rounds slamming into the chambers of the heavy guns. The radio crackled with more situation reports. Things were getting worse—more wounded, more incapacitated vehicles. I loaded an ammo belt into the machine gun mounted to my side of the truck. The GMV's engine rumbled to life. This was one hell of a start to our 2006 rotation.

"Let's go boys," I said into the FM radio as the trucks crawled to the garage exit.

Juma Khan came up to my window, clinging to an AK-47 and a

vest of ammunition. "I want to go," he said. I'm not sure whose smile was bigger, his or mine.

"*Wali na,*" I said—why not?—signaling him to hop into the back.

Then, over the radio, the Canadian voice said, "Bingo Red 1, this is Bingo Red 7. We are clear of the ambush. We have numerous casualties and are twenty kilometers from Kandahar Airfield."

Our vehicles ground to a halt. Bill sauntered over to my truck.

"I don't think they've moved far, Captain. The Taliban must have run out of ammo."

"We can go to KAF and get the real story," I said.

The trucks were running, the plan was set, the radios were up. I just needed the launch order from Bolduc. He finally gave an order, but it wasn't the one we wanted: "Stand down."

I didn't like it but I did it. I trusted Bolduc, and if the mission was a no go then it was a no go. Disappointed, we rolled back to the motor pool and unpacked our kit to return to the celebration.

The next morning we started our intensive training cycle with the ANA. Under the freshly risen sun, we did calisthenics and ran around the five-mile track we'd built just inside the base's walls. Besides keeping us in shape, the routine forged a bond with the Afghans and allowed us to identify our problem children. Those who couldn't keep up got the most attention.

I took the officers, including Ali, under my wing. The rest of the team worked with the sergeants and soldiers. Bill and I focused the training on three areas: moving, shooting, and communicating— the basics of combat. We'd worked with some of these soldiers in the past, but before I took them into harm's way I wanted to know what I had.

Like everything in the Army, we trained in three phases. Crawl. Walk. Run. After the morning's workout, we had breakfast and met back at the range for the "crawl" phase. Basic marksmanship started with the weapon's zero. If the sights didn't align then it was impossible to hit the target. It should have been a simple exercise. Instead, it took us all morning because many of the Afghans had lost respect for their weapons. Instead of maintaining them, they got lazy and banged the rifles around or tinkered with the sights. Every aspect of discipline has to be maintained.

During the break, our team, under Bill's direction, worked on our own marksmanship skills with a "stress shoot," which is a race against the clock. Bill set up a series of targets that forced us to move in full kit and hit targets while changing magazines or switching between our rifles and pistols among numerous firing positions. The winner got bragging rights, a source of great pride on a team of wiseasses. Before the competition started, we all got to run through the course once to get a feel for it and to eliminate excuses.

The course was about half a football field wide and an equal distance long. The range extended far beyond the barrier walls and made a slow rocky climb to the base of the adjacent mountain. The ground was flat, gumball-sized gravel offering some stability, but not much. During the day the stones acted as a mirror, reflecting the heat of the midday sun onto our baking bodies.

There were several types of targets. We had plywood barriers to shoot around, over, under, and through. Bill added a pile of chairs, a GMV, an ATV, and a junk car. The first targets were a mix of steel pistol and rifle silhouettes, flat plates in the shape of a human head and shoulders that fell when struck. The other targets were commercial cardboard targets depicting menacing faces or hostage situations, increasing the difficulty level.

I watched my team practice the course meticulously and methodically. They made it look easy despite their cumbersome body armor.

Bill started the competition. As the team sergeant, he set a high standard. He raced from behind the Humvee to the pile of chairs. *Ping. Ping.* His direct hits reverberated across the range. He reached the final target, transitioned his now spent M4 to the side, and smoothly drew his pistol. Within seconds, he was standing at near point-blank range of the final target with a tight cluster of shots on the target's chest, an empty pistol in his hand.

When he was finished, he walked the course with each of the team members, calmly coaching them through it.

"Slow is smooth and smooth is fast. Relax, feel the trigger. Squeeze, don't jerk. Keep your eyes on the target," he coached as we moved from mark to mark. "Change magazines without taking your eyes off the target. Transition to your secondary weapon, don't look, know where it is. Know where your magazines are. Everything must be muscle memory."

Bill knew that in a close firefight the steady, consistent shooter would come out the winner every time. Bill was consistent with everyone when it came to training, even me. There was a standard you were required to achieve. You fail, you go home. It was that simple. I loved these courses. They were some of the best combat training you could get. I had done well in the past and I was anxious to see how I would do now.

Shouldering my rifle, I looked down the sights and dropped the first target. Trotting to the next mark behind some plywood, I again zeroed in on the target and heard a familiar ping. Two for two. My internal clock counted the seconds. My body went into autopilot while I controlled my heart rate. Sweat ran into my eyes, and all too soon, my lungs heaved and gasped for breath in the high altitude. Ending a few minutes later, I holstered my pistol and waited for Bill to grade me.

"Middle of the pack," Bill said. Even if I did well, Bill didn't hand out compliments.

Steve was the last shooter and got most of Bill's attention. He seemed rattled at the finish line and after Bill counted up the hits, he had the lowest number. Dejected, Steve told Bill he needed to re-zero. In one motion, Bill took Steve's weapon and fired two rounds into the steel target two hundred meters away, knocking it down. He walked over to the weapons table and grabbed a shotgun. "At least with this, Steve, you won't have to aim," he said, with that familiar smirk. Steve took it in stride, but I knew I'd see him later practicing on the range when no one else was around.

Our company commander, Jared, had arrived at KAF and had spent the last day or so getting briefed up on a massive operation. He was in charge of several Special Forces teams, including mine, and wanted to read me in on the details. I arranged to get him a helicopter over to the firebase for a short visit to get us up to speed on the mission.

Before we left KAF, I'd heard rumors of a big operation. But I hadn't wanted a piece of it. I envisioned a room full of commanders from half a dozen coalition countries sitting around a table trying to create a plan, all of them convinced they were smartest. But based on our running into the large, defiant group of fighters on the convoy to the base, plus the rocket attacks, plus everything else I'd been hearing, they sure needed to do something—and soon.

Ever since Operation Anaconda, Special Forces teams had rarely taken part in large-scale operations, especially those involving conventional units. During Anaconda, in March 2002, troops from the 101st Airborne Division and 10th Mountain Division planned to block enemy escape routes, but the whole mission crumbled when some Special Forces and the fledgling Afghan militia made contact with hardened Al Qaeda fighters in Gardez in the bitterly cold Shahi Khot Valley. The end result was that there were critical mistakes made by all parties and some Al Qaeda and Taliban leaders escaped. The 10th Mountain and 101st Airborne didn't communicate with the Special Forces teams much after that. For our part, we had received so much blame for that operation that it was not worth the effort to participate in others.

The fallout crippled Afghan relations with conventional commanders, who now defined the Afghan militias as unreliable. So Special Forces continued operating on their own, "by, with, and through" the indigenous Afghan forces. As a result, we had built critical relationships and a structure to develop the Afghan Army. Over time, the conventional commanders began placing more and more emphasis on partnering conventional forces with the fledgling Afghan Army. We were with them to make sure they succeeded. Now I learned from Jared that Bolduc saw this new operation as a chance to really show ISAF and the world that the Afghan Army could do its part. It was our job to make sure his intent became reality.

I put out the warning order to prepare to support an ISAF operation, much to the chagrin of my team. We had been at the firebase only a week. They wanted more time with the Afghans. Our ANA soldiers needed more training to make sure everybody knew the basic battle drills. We needed more sergeants and officers to lead the soldiers. But most of all, despite knowing some of them from past rotations, we needed to renew and continue to build our relationship. We needed a level of trust that could sustain the pressures of combat.

I let everyone know we would be leaving for KAF in twenty-four hours. The damn mission had not even been formally announced, but I had to get the Afghans on board. We held a team meeting in the small mud TOC, and almost all the comments started with, "But Captain . . ." We had no choice but to make the mission work, so we called a chai session with the Afghan leadership in their compound.

Shinsha, the Afghan commander, and Ali Hussein, my scarred protégé, came and joined me and Bill on the floor of their main mud hut, which was used as the ANA headquarters. Over boiling-hot tea, I started by channeling my best football-coach-before-the-big-game speech. I played heavily on the centuries-old unwritten tribal code of Pashtunwali, an ancient ideology that governs the actions of Pashtun tribe members. They believe that when they die, they will be judged by their god, Allah, by however closely they have followed the Pashtunwali code. I hammered home the blood feud with the Taliban (*badal*), the duty to honor the family (*nang*), the love of the Pashtun culture (*dod-pasbani*), and their sworn oath to protect it (*tokhm-pasbani*).

"Will your people remember your names? Do you want to live under the heel of Taliban rule again?" Then I bellowed, "You are the Lions of Kandahar! You are the protectors of southern Afghanistan! We have fought and bled with you many years. Will you not fight with me now?" My Afghan comrades, dressed in fatigues and sitting cross-legged on the floor, seemed fixated on what I was saying.

"No country has ever helped Afghanistan like America. Did we not help you defeat the Russians?" I asked.

Then I told them this was their chance to get *badal*, or revenge, for what had happened to Shef's team and heal an open wound. That's what they desperately wanted. Narrowing their eyes, they grunted and nodded.

Ali turned to Shinsha.

"*Wali na?*" he said.

Now came the hard part. We had to figure out how to tell them about the mission without giving up too much detail. I figured we could give them just enough information to shape their ideas into plans we had already made, making them think that it was their plan. If it was their plan they would keep it quiet, knowing that a slip of the tongue would tip off the Taliban. Loyalty in Afghanistan can be bought, and we knew the Taliban had spies in the Afghan Army. Hell, we knew there were Taliban at the firebase. We just didn't know who they were. I explained that none of the soldiers could leave the base, all the weapons needed to be locked away, and all cell phones and the barracks office phone had to be confiscated.

Shinsha asked us to leave. He wanted to talk with his commanders dispersed around the room. He knew I spoke some Pashto; this was his subtle way of being polite. We ducked out of the hut. When we returned, they agreed to join the mission and to all of my requests.

We ended up with a volunteer force of almost sixty soldiers and nearly ten solid leaders out of more than one hundred ANA. The rest of the unit was getting ready to go on leave.

In the meantime, Jared had talked again to Bolduc and knew a little more about the operation. The planners back at KAF wanted us to block Taliban escape routes out of the district, which I preferred to tagging along with a Canadian unit for the whole operation. We would need to sneak into the district to retain the element of surprise and initiative.

Briefed on the basics, and with the Afghans ready, I approached Jared about the trip back to KAF, where we would be brought into the complete plan for the operation. Jared had commanded my team several years earlier when he was a captain and remained in good standing with the unit—he got the "wink, wink, nod, nod" from the operators when they heard about his return. He stood six feet tall and was in good shape. Although he was an avid runner, he also lifted weights and his build was far from the average buck-o-five runner stereotype. Personable, confident, with strawberry blond hair and a fierce red beard, he was a welcome returning addition to the deployment. The million-dollar words that astute men picked up in their work with high-ranking officers sounded strange in his thick West Virginia accent. He, like many field-grade officers at that time, had only one rotation in Afghanistan (some had none), but he made up for it by being smart, easy to work with, and open to suggestions from his team leaders.

Not long after Jared's return, in true Charlie Company fashion, all of the detachments had demonstrated their support for him by attaching their team stickers to the bumper, window, and tailgate of his red Chevy 4x4 pickup truck, along with other vehicle adornments thoughtfully selected in honor of his well-known fondness for hunting. Intertwined among the parachutes, swords, skulls, and arrows were stickers attesting to an affiliation with PETA, anti-gun slogans, a colorful rainbow, and a "Vote for John Kerry" swatch.

Jared was housed in the base commander's room I had occupied the year before when there was no company commander on that side of the compound. He made a point of telling me how very much he appreciated my fixing up the room for him. I refrained from noting that the joke was on him. The room was directly across from the operations center. His room would be the first stop for every issue and every question anyone had. Seldom in years past had I had a complete night's sleep.

In any event, it was only fair. I and another team leader, Matt from ODA 333, also known as 3X, had played several good jokes on Jared in the past, most recently a dinner we and our wives had shared at a nice Japanese steak house. That night we told the owners that it was Jared's birthday and we wanted to make a really big deal about it. When the time was right, the owner broke out the party hat and had the entire staff sing him "Happy Birthday," along with the rest of the restaurant for good measure. Jared wore the hat and went along with all of it to keep from insulting the owner and everyone else, despite the fact that it was nowhere near his birthday.

Jared was a good commander and had a real concern for the soldiers and their well-being. I liked that you could get into very heated debates over issues with him and things never got personal. That was what made Jared an exceptional officer. He understood everyone had a voice and a perspective or opinion. He also understood that at the end of the day everyone wanted to do the right thing.

An in-depth planning session began over routes and execution for the convoy movement back to KAF. We agreed to leave that night and go through the city, instead of around it. Traffic would be light and no American units had been down the road for months, which we hoped would throw off the Taliban. Speed was also good security against car bombs, and we knew we could hustle on the paved road.

By nightfall the GMVs, masquerade jingle trucks, and ANA pickups were lined up at the gate. The jingle trucks derived their name from the hundreds of dangling bells, chimes, and decorations that ring out for good luck from local trucks as they lumber along rutted dirt roads.

Brian started our truck and looked at me to give the order to move. Brian and I had served in the same units before Special Forces and went through the Special Forces Qualification Course together. Needless to say, when Brian became available for selection to a team, I fought hard to get him, and he joined the team not long after I did in 2005. Brian knew me. It was not a secret that I would never follow my men into combat, I would go first everywhere, unless my team sergeant said otherwise. I couldn't stomach the idea of one of my men being hurt or killed when I should have been out front for him. Brian believed in that philosophy as wholeheartedly and as deeply, if not more so, than I did. I think that's why he soon made sure he was the driver of the lead truck, my truck. He analyzed every trail, road intersection, and ditch as carefully as any of his beloved NASCAR drivers would study the day's track and took infinite precautions all along the way. On many occasions I have personally attributed my survival to him and his finely honed instincts for keeping us alive in that truck.

During his off-duty hours Brian lived for NASCAR. He knew the drivers, their statistics, the tracks, all of it. I think he was drawn to the challenge of individual competitiveness and the technical expertise it required. He lived simply, but he was very complex and technically adept. I admired and appreciated him for everything that he was. He had his own workshop at the firebase, which looked like a super-villain's lair with antennas, handsets, and cables covering the little table. If we weren't on a mission, he was in there tinkering, building "stuff the Army should have." He treated everything as a no-fail event. When it was time to communicate with others, you did it, period.

Brian was the team's senior communications sergeant; if he set up your radio, you knew it would work. But as key as that role was, Brian was much more than just my senior communications guy; he was a close advisor and friend. Between Brian, with his lean build, reddish hair, and freckles; Smitty, our intelligence sergeant; and me, you would have thought we had an Irish team. Brian could not grow a beard to save his life, but with his mustache and soul patch, he reminded me of Doc Holliday in the movie *Tombstone*. He was, in a word, meticulous. He was also was my version of MacGyver. He could take gum wrappers, a Coke can, a AA battery, aluminum foil, and electrical tape and make a radio that would work from the two ends of the earth.

We liked to joke about Brian's likely formative years in an old woman's home because he was so anal. Everything had a place on Brian's planet and it better be put back there, properly, if he even let you borrow it in the first place. Lord help you if it wasn't. Despite that, Brian was one of the most easygoing members of the team. Yet he had a ruthless streak when it came down to the art of "business."

As I said, I had a Super Bowl–caliber team. Brian is the best communications specialist I have ever seen in my fifteen years in the military. He took his job and responsibility to move, shoot, and communicate to another level. He and Smitty were a deadly combination in any room takedown.

A simple man, Brian was never distracted by the normal worldly allures of fancy cars, motorcycles, money, or women. Like most of the guys, he was a deeply devoted family man. He took his family as seriously as he did his job. It was a trait that I held in the highest regard and encouraged other team members to emulate.

Our gypsy caravan entered the sleeping city through a section of the bazaar. During the day, all the shops were crowded with people and overflowing with everything from hanging meat and carpets to household goods. At this hour, the market was deserted, and the numerous shuttered shops were good cover for anyone watching our movements. The cars, trucks, donkey carts, and burned hulks of old

Soviet military vehicles parked along the road provided easy places to hide roadside bombs.

My night-vision goggles allowed me to peek into doorways and backstreets as I scanned for danger. Small white dots from our rifles' laser sights traveled from alleyway to alleyway and darted along the buildings. We could see the Afghan National Police checkpoint ahead and flashed the infrared (IR) signal to them. I had no trouble making out the Afghan policeman's broad grin under the green glow of night vision as we passed. He gave us the Hawaiian shaka, the familiar thumb and pinkie hand signal.

We rolled into the first straightaway and as soon as the last vehicle passed the police checkpoint, Brian floored it. The support company mechanics, huge fans of NASCAR, had manipulated the governors so our trucks could accelerate and maintain incredible speed with their supercharged diesel engines. I felt safer traveling fast, especially as we approached a particularly nasty section of the city known as IED Alley.

About 70 percent of all suicide bombers and IEDs hit along this stretch of road inside Kandahar. Just seeing it made my butt pucker. Scars from the attacks pocked the pavement. Big, deep holes that could easily shatter an axle or bust the trucks' suspensions forced us to slow down. If we could just make it through this stretch and reach the city outskirts, we should be okay.

As we slowed to avoid a pothole big enough to swallow our truck, the radio crackled a warning: "Motorcycle at three o'clock!"

I spotted the bike running parallel to the convoy on a side street. Suicide bomber? Or a tail to help his buddies set up an ambush? It was two a.m., so it was unlikely he was out getting milk.

Bill came over the radio and said the motorcycle had shot down an alleyway toward the convoy. I tightened my grip on my rifle, ready for the motorcycle to cut out into our path. A warning burst from an Afghan soldier's AK-47 broke through the rumbling of the engines. I just caught the back of the bike as it darted down the alley away from the convoy. Maybe the rider was just a civilian who wasn't paying attention and now had to change pants. If he had been a suicide bomber, he would have kept coming.

We crossed under the concrete arches that reminded me of the McDonald's logo, which marked the official entrance to the heart of the city. I finally exhaled as we reached the dark highway leading through the city and picked up speed. There are no bright street-lights lining the avenues of Afghan cities. Power lines hung in a thick crisscross above the dusty road. The squat tan buildings passed by in a blur as we raced toward the airfield. We soon saw its bright lights glowing in the distance.

We neared the bridge where the Taliban patrol had disarmed the guards two days earlier. The convoy came to a rolling halt and I asked the ANA soldier if there had been any trouble. He shook his head no. He had his weapon and there were now two other guards joining him.

We drove through the first Afghan security gate on the north side of the base, where the Afghan Army had a compound. The guards greeted us with smiles. The jingle trucks peeled off as we continued deeper into the airfield. The coalition gate was protected by menacing sandbagged machine-gun nests and two concrete towers bristling with machine guns. My truck slowed and I waved to the guard. No response. The gate stayed closed, which was strange. We were in clearly marked American gun trucks.

"American. Open the gate," I yelled to the ISAF guard.

A voice on a muted bullhorn ordered our Afghan soldiers to surrender their weapons and move into the razor-wire containment area where Afghan workers and drivers are searched before starting work on the base. *What?*

"Hey, partner, what's the problem here? We're Americans and they're with us!" I was completely confused. We were American soldiers, in American uniforms, riding in American gun trucks, and we were being denied entry to the very base that the United States had seized and established. These Afghans weren't civilians—they were Afghan government soldiers accompanying a Special Forces team. I wasn't going to put these Afghan soldiers in a containment area like common criminals or pets to wait until we returned. I got out of my truck and walked toward the guard.

"Hey, partner, what's the problem here?" I repeated.

The guard took a step back behind a small concrete barrier and moved his weapon to the low ready position.

"What the *fuck* are you doing?" I growled.

I demanded that the sergeant of the guard come out and talk with me. No one responded. Now I was really getting pissed. I could see them on the phone following their long list of protocols, trying to get their superiors on the line. Finally, the sergeant of the guard came to the window of the bunker and demanded—not asked—that I surrender my ID card.

Fishing it out of my shirt pocket, I held it up. "Come out here and get it!"

Not surprisingly, he didn't budge. Fed up, I went back to my truck and called the TOC on a radio channel that every coalition unit in southern Afghanistan monitored and announced that ISAF soldiers had detained my team, including my Afghan soldiers, at the gate. Dave's voice from the turret whispered, "Easy, Griz." Griz was a nickname Matt from 3X had given me for moments such as this.

The battle captain in the TOC came back a moment later. "Stand fast. We will deconflict."

I held my tongue. Leaning against my truck, I suddenly felt like laughing. In the last few hours, we had raced through downtown Kandahar and avoided roadside and suicide bombers, only to run up against an immovable object—this damn gate. We were about to kick off a massive combat operation with this same force. *Some teammates,* I thought. I hoped this wasn't an omen of things to come.

After five minutes, a truck arrived at the gate and broke up the staring contest. A member of our unit went into the guard shack, and when he came out, the sergeant of the guard nodded. The guard opened the gate without a word.

As we drove past, the sergeant of the guard gave us the finger.

Chapter 6

OPERATION MEDUSA

*It is better to live one day as a lion
than a hundred years as a sheep.*

—ITALIAN PROVERB

On Lieutenent Colonel Bolduc's first rotation, he built a door with a cipher lock in the wall between the Special Forces compound and the Regional Command South compound. He did it intentionally to open up communications and build rapport with ISAF, since southern Afghanistan was NATO territory. In return, he got to use a side door straight into Brigadier General David Fraser's office. Shortly before we got back to Kandahar, he made use of that access. Passing between the compounds, Bolduc walked into Fraser's well-furnished office. He wanted to shake hands, look the boss in the eye, and test the water.

The Canadian general commanded all coalition troops in southern Afghanistan. The two men had met and gotten along well during Fraser's last rotation, when Fraser, then a colonel, worked on the Canadian staff. When Bolduc came in, Fraser got up from behind his large desk and joined him in a small sitting area. Pictures of NATO troops in Afghanistan and mementos from the Canadian army made up the decor.

An aide brought in coffee and the two men discussed what was planned to be the largest NATO combat operation in history. Fraser explained that within days of his taking command from the Americans in early August, between three hundred and five hundred insurgents attacked a Canadian element in Panjwayi. The Canadians killed several dozen enemy and didn't suffer any casualties, but the attack sent ripples through the command and made it clear the nature of the fight had significantly changed. The Taliban no longer attacked in small groups but in mass. That meant the counterinsurgency fight the Canadians had prepared for was out the window as long as the Taliban controlled the area. That was where Operation Medusa came in. Medusa was intended to destroy the thousands of insurgents who had gathered outside of Kandahar in Panjwayi, the Taliban's heartland.

"Hey, boss, I just want to lay out the groundwork and make sure I get your guidance," Bolduc said, pulling out a packet of printed PowerPoint slides. He never brought more than ten slides to a meeting with Fraser in hope of keeping it tight. Simple.

The plan relied on three of his teams to lead the Afghan Army on a reconnaissance mission and attract the attention of the Taliban. Make them turn on their radios so that the Canadians could track the location of the leaders in the valley they would be attacking. The teams would move into Panjwayi from the Red Desert—the Registan—and catch the Taliban off guard. Bolduc knew the Canadian army was the main element, but this got his men in the fight and got the Afghans in the lead.

Fraser reviewed the slides and quietly listened to the Special Forces commander. Taking out his gold pen, he initialed the slides, giving Bolduc the green light. Bolduc left the meeting and called Jared.

By the time I arrived at the special operations compound in KAF that night, my nerves were fried and my head throbbed. The ride, except for our encounter with the ISAF guards, had been a milk run, but it still rattled me. I had forgotten the peaks and valleys that your mind and body experience when you're exposed to combat stress. Everybody remembers the cool parts and forgets the headaches, the sleeplessness, and the nerves.

We parked the trucks at the motor pool, locked the radios and weapons in the arms room, and headed over to the chow hall for breakfast. In Kandahar, we knew we could get a good meal no matter what.

The dining facility near the compound's gate looked like every other stucco building in southern Afghanistan. But if Napoleon was right that armies march on their stomachs, Sergeant First Class Redd kept us going at one hundred miles an hour. The senior cook, on his fourth rotation, not only managed the special operations chow hall in Kandahar, but kept the firebases in southern Afghanistan stocked. If you didn't have it, Redd would go and get it. Once, a shipment of steaks went missing, and Redd flew to Germany, put a knot in someone's ass, and came back with the missing steaks, plus some.

"What's happening, sir?" he asked as I pushed open the door to the dining facility. It was how he greeted everybody.

"Livin' the dream, Redd," I said, smiling at the smell of fresh bacon and eggs.

I had followed my guys into the chow hall. I always ate last to make sure they got the best selection of food. Loading up with eggs, bacon, and coffee, I noticed Bolduc finishing up his breakfast. He saw me, too, and came over to my table after greeting my team.

Lieutenant Colonel Bolduc expected his detachment commanders to come by and see him whenever they came to Kandahar Airfield. It was not negotiable, ever. He wanted to talk with the men and get their perspective on what was going on in the field. A passionate and dedicated leader, he often solicited new insights on a problem or situation or suggested a new strategy in the course of deep, detailed discussions. He let us operate as we were designed to, independently and autonomously, to achieve strategic effects on the battlefield for the United States.

Bolduc had been part of the first Special Forces units inside Afghanistan and had dealt directly with the Afghan resistance, militias, and Al Qaeda. He prized comprehensive knowledge and experience as integral elements of leadership. As uncompromising as the cold in his native Northeast, where he grew up collecting maple syrup on his family's small farm, it was out of the question for him to accept anything less than the real thing. He was famous for certain traits that could rub team members and staff officers alike the wrong way—a stubborn insistence on multiple rehearsals under multiple timelines, for instance—but more often than not, what were initially regarded as Bolduc's "quirks" came to be understood as small glimpses into what "correct" looked like and were ultimately adopted as standard procedure. Point-blank, loved by some, hated by others, he was without a doubt respected by all, and, as I had personally experienced, he was a commander who would sacrifice his career to protect his men if they were in the right.

Bolduc asked about the ride in, thankfully not about the mix-up at the gate, and welcomed me back.

After breakfast, I walked over to the TOC. People buzzed about and there was palpable tension in the air. Radio calls burst out of the speaker system. A Special Forces team was in a hellstorm of a firefight. A soldier had been killed and several wounded. I walked over to the battle captain, who was feverishly working on getting aircraft support. Without looking up, he turned one of the computer monitors so I could see it. The computer showed the team's location on a map overlay and the numerous enemy positions. I nodded and walked around the half-moon-shaped table to an empty seat and scanned the status board. Medevac was en route. Two sorties of attack aircraft were inbound. No resupply was scheduled. I phoned the operations sergeant down at the supply company and asked if the bundles of ammunition were prepared so they could be pushed out of a helicopter.

Just as I sent a runner down to the company with a list of the requested supplies, Jared and Bolduc walked out of the conference room. Jared tilted his head, motioning me to come into the room. I tilted my head at the battle captain, meaning I wanted to stay and help there. Jared shook his head no, and I got up to leave. As I passed, the battle captain winked, acknowledging his appreciation. In this business, you put everything aside to help those in need.

A number of high-ranking Australian, British, Canadian, and Dutch officers were sitting around the table in the conference room, which was meticulously laid out with nameplates for all the senior officers. I sat in a row of seats behind the massive table.

"This is where the minions sit," I muttered to Jared as he settled into the seat next to me.

Bruce and Hodge, both fellow detachment commanders, sat down next to us. Hodge was older than I was, with a head of receding silver hair, and reminded me of Mr. Burns from *The Simpsons*. I had known Hodge from the Special Forces Qualification Course, and I liked working with him. We had served together in Hawaii when we were both just sergeants, and he knew me as well as my teammates. He and I simply wanted to serve our country with as much autonomy as possible.

Bruce was new to the unit and on his first deployment to Afghanistan. A Georgian who spoke with a soft southern accent, he'd been an armor officer in Kosovo and Iraq, where he was wounded by a roadside bomb that had delayed his Special Forces training. A cautious and methodical commander, he was a welcome addition to the team.

An Australian operations officer started the brief. I've been very fortunate to work with the Aussies throughout my entire career and on all my rotations to Afghanistan. I'd always liked and admired the way they did business. No bullshit. No politics. Get to the frigging point and get it done. This officer was no different. "Right, mates, in seven days we will be conducting the largest operation since the invasion of Afghanistan and in the history of NATO. Two mechanized Canadian battle groups will lead the assault, with an American infantry battalion securing the right northern flank. You Special boys will seal the south and block the escape," he said.

Code-named Medusa, after the mythological Greek female with hair of serpents, the operation focused on encircling the Panjwayi district. A frontal attack was unthinkable. The district was sandwiched between the Arghandab and Dori rivers, which run northeast by southwest through the province, and was littered with irrigation ditches, bunker-like grape huts, and thick fields of grapes and marijuana. In a decade of fighting, the Soviets never conquered it.

"The main effort will be the Canadian Mechanized Task Force conducting a clearing operation from northeast to southwest through the entire Panjwayi Valley," the Australian officer continued. "We need you boys to infiltrate, stir up some trouble to draw enemy attention to the south, then occupy blocking positions and report all enemy intelligence to ISAF HQ. Bolduc has convinced us that you can play a vital supporting role, and we hope you can fill that gap."

The plan called for us to look at areas of interest and report on what we saw. We were given timelines, radio frequencies for the other units, and the areas they wanted us to watch. Big operations were the toughest, especially ones involving several different countries. There were a lot of moving parts, different operating procedures, and of course politics, which increased the chance of mistakes. And in combat, something always goes wrong.

Bruce, Hodge, Jared, and I glanced at one another, silently working on our list of questions. On paper it looked straightforward, but we seriously doubted they were prepared for contingencies. Hodge and I began to raise our hands. Bolduc, his hand on his lower jaw, looked me right in the eye and shook his head. The message was loud and clear: This was an ISAF operations order; we were to be in receive mode only. So when our coalition partners finished, all we did was shake their hands and smile.

Bolduc raised a finger at us and we knew to give him a moment and wait outside. Once the conference room was empty, he took us back inside and gave us the real brief.

"All right, men, I did not intend for that to turn into a six-hour interrogation," he said. "That's why I stopped you. They wanted us to play a much different role in the operation, but I sold them on this. We all know this will be a significant undertaking with them trying to use mechanized forces in an underdeveloped urban environment. We will take this piece and this piece alone. Make it work."

I headed for the huts and found Bill waiting for me. My face gave away my skepticism. "Well, boys, wait until you hear this," I said as I pulled out the map and showed the team the basic concept of the operation. No one liked the operation, but they were professionals, so they grumbled under their breath and got to work pulling together all the equipment. We didn't have much time.

My team would depart in twenty-four hours with Jared's command team and Hodge's team. Bruce, who was still missing some of his teammates, would be the quick reaction force. They'd link up with us later. Paul, the intelligence sergeant from Bruce's team, came up with the idea of driving to our target area through the Red Desert. He had the infiltration route mapped in his head and knew the Taliban would never expect us to come across that forbidding terrain.

Our route would take us southeast, away from KAF toward the Pakistan border. Then we'd turn due west and cut into the Red Desert. From the desert we would head north and come out in the underbelly of southern Panjwayi. Once we got there, we'd recon our areas of interest, probe enemy positions, link up with the quick reaction force coming in a more direct route from Kandahar, and occupy blocking positions on the southern border of Panjwayi while the Canadians cleared the valley. To meet our deadline, we had to cross the entire red sand desert in four or five days. The desert had an area of several thousand square kilometers. That was a big challenge, but with air-dropped supplies and some luck we could do it.

Our planning meeting broke around lunch. Jared asked for a driver and communications guy for his truck because he didn't have enough men. I reluctantly gave up Jude, our junior communications sergeant, who had worked closely with Brian.

Jude had joined the team the previous year and immediately immersed himself in Brian's tutelage. I knew he couldn't be in better hands as he learned the team's ropes and would hit the ground running with us. He was a quick study, and while he lacked Brian's tenure, he shared his deep familiarity with a wide array of radios, antennas, and encryption devices, and he did his job with the same precision. Quiet, unassuming, well educated, Jude came from a middle-income midwestern family and had chosen the military over the family business. Average in stature, with clean-cut hair, he reminded me of a banker or a Wall Street broker—someone who could easily blend into the urban business world making the type of salary we all dreamed of. The convertible sports car he drove stood out like a beacon amid the rows of 4x4 pickup trucks, Jeeps, and Harleys in the unit parking lot. I hadn't been sure at first what to make of him or how he'd be accepted by the other team members. Once again, I would be humbled to learn that all green hatters were chameleons and that Jude could be counted on as a willing participant when so-called better men faltered.

On the rare occasions when Jude said something, it was either really funny or really profound, usually the latter. You never saw him coming, but when he did it was good, and I admired not only his reserved attitude, but also his precise, logical judgment and clear vision—he could always size up a situation and know where it was going. He was selfless, and he was a good teammate because he took care of himself as well as he looked after the team. He maintained a rigorously healthy diet and usually drank V8 or some fruity, juiced-grass concoction, which was an ongoing source of concern for those of us desperately trying to destroy our livers. We voted him the guy most likely to order a drink with an umbrella in it.

In his own unique way, Jude was different from everyone else and yet the same. He was himself and that was his strength—he was as vibrant an individual as you will ever meet and, to his credit, just as humble. He always saw the good in others and never took credit for himself, nor did he feel the need to compete with other teammates over things he considered childish. He didn't have to. Within weeks he would display superhuman courage and strength that came from a hero's heart—the stuff legends were made of. But I had no doubt even at the outset of our mission that Jude—and all of us—would be deadly effective on this rotation.

Jude shared that he and his girlfriend had gotten engaged before our departure from Bragg. He was clearly excited, although he tried to restrain himself. I could only smile. The team had relentlessly aggravated him about not getting married. I congratulated him and truly meant it, but the leader in me wanted to make sure he had covered all his bases.

"Do you have your insurance up to date, and is your fiancée on it?" I asked. Several friends of mine had been killed without having updated their paperwork to include their fiancées or wives.

"I have all the proper documentation, Captain," Jude said, sounding like a good banker. "Bill has the copies."

He was on top of it, as always. I was reminded again of what a superior addition to the team he was going to be on this deployment, and I hated to let him go to Jared's team.

Bill and I headed straight back to the hut to iron out details with the team before we had to brief back the whole plan to Bolduc. Smitty, the team's intelligence sergeant, gave us a detailed brief on what to expect. We weren't going up against your average Taliban. These groups had been taught in Pakistani madrassas, probably by Al Qaeda or foreign-trained fighters, and would not flee the valley at the sight of NATO armored vehicles.

I never said so, but if Smitty had an idea, it was going to get serious consideration. In addition to his intelligence expertise, he was the team's ad hoc psychologist. He would often answer a question with a question, irritating some and perplexing others: "So, you say you're angry. What do you think makes you angry? Is it your fault? What could you do to not be angry?" He was the devil's advocate in desert camouflage. There was a greater goal behind his approach, though. Like a big brother, Smitty always discussed the pros and cons of every detail with the team in order to come to a collective decision, and there was invariably a lightbulb moment when the questions sank in and the rest of the team got it. He could gently make the team see their own shortcomings and motivate them to retrain or fix the problems internally. He was my greatest force for team cohesion. His comfortable, easy demeanor around fellow team members was based on a deep foundation of trust, and we all took pleasure in his friendship.

Born in the mountains of Virginia, Smitty had a southern drawl that poured smoothly across the ears like fine bourbon across the palate. When I wanted a reminder of home I'd go talk to Smitty. Growing up in a small town meant a life where everyone knew everyone, and their business. Four days after graduating from high school, Smitty walked into the recruiter's station with his diploma in hand and joined the Army. He was a master of field craft, having grown up with little and spending much of his youth in the woods. Smitty had a public education but was Army trained and it showed—he had been collecting experience for sixteen years and shared it generously with others. His quick common sense propelled him to the top, above the typical bravado exhibited by other SF operators. He did not talk crap (unless he had seen it or done it), and he had a nose for bullshit like a Tennessee bloodhound, detecting it or matching it like no one else, as the situation required, character traits he valued and honed from the example of earlier, more experienced warriors. Very few lies slipped past this supremely experienced SF soldier. Fun-loving, with a zest for life and a sense of humor that defused the worst situations, Smitty had the air of a latter-day pirate, which his dirt-red hair and suitably menacing beard only amplified. Never one to go without a Jedi mind trick, and unpredictable at best, Smitty was the type of guy who would shave his head and grow his beard extra long, imitating the Taliban just enough to get in the head of prisoners and make them wonder just who in the hell they were up against. He was perfectly suited to his role as our intelligence expert, and I couldn't imagine the team without him.

The team rounded out the rest of the plan—how and when we'd get supplies, the radio frequencies and call signs we'd use. Next, we prepared contingency plans. This was the real meat and potatoes of planning. As we broke up into groups, Riley and Steve, the team's medics, pulled me aside.

"Sir," said Riley, "we have a recommendation. We know of a soldier who would be perfect for this mission." His name was Greg, and he was attached to a civil affairs unit, but he was Special Forces qualified and in fact had been one of their instructors at the Special Forces medical school. That got my attention. "No one knows trauma better than he does. If this thing gets messy that far away, he'll come in handy," Riley said. I agreed to talk with him.

The groups continued to drill down on every detail. What was our route? How long would it take to get there? How much fuel would we consume if the trucks carried double the basic load of ammunition, three additional passengers, and three times the amount of fuel we needed? How much fuel would the ANA require? How would we evacuate casualties?

We'd been working for about an hour when there was a knock at the door.

"We're busy. Go away," Bill said.

"It's Greg," the visitor said.

I folded over the maps and documents; there was no sense divulging classified information if he didn't end up going with us. Greg came in and stuck out his hand. He had a strong handshake and a humble demeanor. In this business, humility is usually accompanied by confidence and focus. I liked him. But I waited for Bill's response.

"Where have you been, and what have you done?" Bill asked.

Greg had spent nearly two decades with Special Forces teams and had taught at the renowned Special Forces medical school. Bill was impressed, nodded yes, and walked out of the hut. I told Greg to sit down and opened the map. He was a true country boy from Tennessee but clearly far from naive. Just past his middle thirties, he was in excellent shape. He reminded me of most of the people I grew up with.

"I'll tell you up front, I have concerns about this operation. I don't have a good feeling about it at all. I would prefer that you not go," I told him. Greg hadn't trained with the team. I didn't know his strengths and weaknesses. He didn't know our operating procedures and had never worked with our Afghans. We didn't have a chance to do detailed planning, didn't have time for rehearsals with·the Afghans, and we hadn't discussed what would happen if the Canadian operation didn't go as planned.

"This could get bloody," I told him, "although it appears as if our part of the mission is going to be a cakewalk."

"There's no such thing as a cakewalk," Greg said. "Unless you tell me otherwise, you couldn't keep me from going."

That was the right response.

"Can you handle a .50-cal heavy machine gun?" I asked.

He grinned. "Like a broom." I had to smile.

I told him to get his kit and see Bill for his truck assignment. Normally teams don't accept any latecomers, but Greg knew what I knew—you can never have too many Special Forces medics on an operation. Plus, Bill approved, and Greg came highly recommended from operators. Finally, he had the experience, and we could use his expertise in case this thing got ugly.

We continued to plan for the next four hours and met again with the other teams to confirm everything. With the detailed planning done, we had about sixteen hours to get ready to leave. While Bolduc and Jared briefed Fraser's staff, we concentrated on the vehicles, radios, and weapons. We packed and repacked our kits. We configured the trucks and loaded them with as much ammo and fuel as we could fit.

Dave, our engineer, ranted and raved about the weight in the trucks, his "girls," as he always called them.

"Captain, the girls are too heavy. We need them to be lighter," he protested. "At this rate, we'll be out of fuel way before our first scheduled resupply."

"What's your solution, then?" I asked.

"Strip off any excess armor plating and equipment," he replied. We'd gotten only a few of the air-conditioned and fully armored trucks that the units in Iraq had, so we'd made our own modifications. After five years of war, many of the trucks had *Mad Max* style armor and plating to protect against roadside bombs. Dave didn't care if he looked stupid; he just wanted to be right.

Dave had been quickly promoted to senior engineer, and with his sharp tongue and quick wit he made fast work of senior operators looking for an easy score. A midwesterner from Ohio who knew how to handle himself in every situation, he was a chameleon in human skin, a wild card—the joker in the pack. A century ago, he would have been a gambler in the Wild West. He could charm the pants off a woman and win all your money while making you feel good about losing it. He knew how to play the game and had the cynical attitude of one who has seen much and keeps it to himself, unless you are foolish enough to say something he disagrees with. Dave did his job because he loved it, not because he owed the Army an obligation. He was the guy every team hopes to have. At barely six feet, he wasn't all that imposing, yet he was solidly built. Some men are connoisseurs of wine, art, cars. Dave was a connoisseur of pizza. He'd eat pizza that was two days old before he would eat regular food, and he had even attempted to make pizza out of military rations—Meals, Ready-to-Eat, or MREs—or the local Afghan food, which had prompted whispered discussions at tribal meetings.

Dave came to the team at the beginning of the last rotation and had combat tenure. He was young, smart, and a fast learner; he didn't have to be told something twice to know it and put it to use. Before a patrol in 2005, he asked the interpreters to teach him some simple commands—stop, get out of the way—and he practiced them in the turret as we drove. Later on, I heard him screaming the same commands at nearby drivers as we made our way down the street in Kandahar.

As an engineer, he was an artist and would spend endless hours working feverishly on a structural project. He loved details. What kind of materials to use, the length, width, the temperature, density, humidity, barometric pressure, weight, etc. It didn't matter if it was a dog house or a bridge, Dave could build it. It didn't take long to figure out why he loved building so much. His real passion was demolition.

"You can't enjoy destroying things if you don't know how to make them," he would say.

Dave absolutely, positively, with all his heart loved to blow things up. A massive explosion or complete destruction was not his forte. No, not Dave; that would be too easy. Too crude. A good partial destruction was usually his goal. It denied use of the object to the enemy, then, later, Dave could rebuild it again and put it to some other use.

When Dave was finished with the trucks, the plates and excess parts were piled in a heap in the motor pool. He'd managed to remove hundreds of pounds of armor that would have bogged us down in the sand as well as burned excessive fuel. Now we could meet our scheduled resupplies. It made me a little nervous to see even the smallest piece of protection lying in the dust, but we had no choice. We needed the trucks and the guns they carried into the fight more than the little bit of armor we were leaving behind.

That night, we lay in the hut drenched in sweat, wide awake. After a while, Bill started quizzing us about the mission.

"Greg, what's the distance from the entry point to the exit point of the desert?"

"Two hundred seventy-five, two hundred eighty-five kilometers."

"Steve, how far to the first turn off of Highway 4?"

Silence for several seconds, then Steve said, "Did you forget already, Bill?"

The hut erupted with laughter. I tried to hold back, but couldn't. The tension broken, Bill continued to question the team until a few drifted off to sleep.

Bill and I remained awake.

"What do you think?" I asked.

Bill sighed. "I don't like it, any of it. There are too many things that can go wrong. ISAF will get mauled in their armored vehicles because they can't maneuver. There's too much cover and concealment for the enemy in an urban fight."

Bill had fought in Iraq and knew urban combat very well.

"Okay, sir, check this out," he went on. "The intelligence said that there were probably four hundred Taliban fighters in that valley, right? Intelligence is close, but never spot on. What if there are more? Four hundred fighters, that's a lot, and I mean a lot, of people trying to kill you. We will have to be on our A game for this. Besides, what if we run into a fight way out there in the middle of that godforsaken desert? No cover. We could keep the Taliban at bay for a while with our heavy machine guns and grenade launchers. But we can't move at night. The Afghans don't have night vision. If we move during the day, we'll slow-roast in those vehicles and be exhausted by nightfall, losing our edge."

He wasn't even convinced that we'd stay in our blocking positions.

"I'll bet you a case of beer the Canadians get into trouble and we have to go in there to help. The boys will be exhausted by the time the fight starts and when it starts, it will go on for a while. I mean weeks," he said. "ISAF is not planning on taking enough dismounted infantry to clear that huge valley. Somebody is gonna have to do it. Who do you think is gonna get volunteered?"

I dredged up the old adage, "There is a Thai proverb that goes like this: How do you eat an elephant?" I asked Bill.

"How the hell would I know?" Bill said. "I wouldn't eat that nasty thing."

"One bite at a time," I said, smiling. We both laughed and got about an hour's worth of sleep.

The whole hut rattled when the guard pounded on the door. Bill shot straight up. "Get up," he bellowed. "The sooner we get this started, the sooner it will be over."

Then he cut on the overhead lights, blinding everyone in the room. I felt for my boots and we all shook off the grogginess. Most of us headed to the chow hall to grab some Red Bull energy drinks or coffee. I found Bolduc and Jared pacing around the assembly area, talking.

With caffeine under their belts, the team started to check their equipment again. I went over to the ANA huts to wake them up so they would have time to make some chai and get ready to leave. But by the time I got there, the Afghans were up and moving and the chai kettles were on the blue, red, and gold propane tanks.

Shinsha was expecting me. I wished now that I hadn't had that Red Bull, because I knew I was going to end up drinking a whole pot of tea with him.

He shooed his men away and we sat down on the cheap woven mats and each filled our right hand with doughy bread. You always eat and shake hands with your right hand, because in a culture mostly devoid of toilet paper, you can guess what they have to do with their left.

"I want you to make some words for the soldiers before we leave," he said. "Some are scared and I cannot convince them of our success. I am afraid they will leave when the fighting starts and go back to their villages."

"No problemo, amigo," I said.

He looked perplexed.

I grinned. "I would be honored. But we need to get going." I needed to get back to the team, but I'd make sure to talk to the Afghans before we left.

As I rounded the corner building, I could hear the Special Forces gun trucks warming up. ANA trucks were arriving and taking their places in the convoy line. The ANA were almost never on time or prepared, but this time was different. This was their mission and their fight.

Hodge's team would be leading the operation to the Red Desert, and I felt very comfortable with that. I said good morning to some of his men, who seemed a lot like mine. When I reached my team, I got the word that Bolduc wanted to say a few parting words. There was the usual groaning, but if it made him happy, so be it. We gathered around.

"Gentlemen, tonight you embark on one of the most important missions ever in the War on Terror and in support of the government of Afghanistan," Bolduc said. "Let me be clear. If we fail, Kandahar could fall in several months, so there is no pressure."

That brought smiles from the group.

"You are well prepared for this. Remember who you are, where you are from, and why we are here. God be with you."

I remember trying to let it sink in. I remember thinking these men were some of our country's greatest heroes and I got to serve with them. I looked around trying to memorize faces, because in a few days some of these men might not be with us.

When Bolduc finished, I needed a minute alone. I told Bill to gather the team and the ANA at my vehicle and walked to the hut. There was no one inside. I got down on my knees, folded my hands, and prayed. I prayed for the safety of my men, and for the guidance to make the right decisions, and for strength. I prayed for my family and the families of my men. I prayed for the United States and for victory. It was what I always did, but this time I prayed harder. I had a bad feeling. Something told me nothing would go as planned.

When I got to my truck, the Afghans seemed apprehensive. I gathered everybody close.

"My brothers," I said, "tonight we depart on a mission to destroy the Taliban. It will be difficult. The mission will be dangerous. You have fought with me in the past. You know we will not leave your side until death. Think about how you feel right now. I would rather die on the battlefield today, as a free man, knowing when I went before God that I did all that I could for my people, than die many years from now, old in my bed and living under the foot of a tyrant. We are the Lions of Kandahar!"

By the end of my speech, the Afghans were excited, and I hoped no one would fire his weapon in the air. They stood straight, proud. Ali Hussein pumped his fist. He got it. We broke the huddle, and the Afghans returned to their trucks, ready to go. Even Shinsha looked taller.

Dozens of soldiers came out of the darkness to wish us luck. Each handshake and slap on the back had an air of finality. We wouldn't admit it, but it was a last good-bye between brothers and friends. Finally, Jared called the TOC and requested permission to leave. Bolduc's steady voice crackled over the radio.

"Talon 30, this is Eagle 6 actual, permission granted, Godspeed."

Chapter 7

——

RAT LINES

The journey of a thousand miles begins with
one step, and a lot of bitching.

—UNKNOWN

W e had traveled no more than a mile off the main road when
a series of infrared flashes up ahead brought the convoy to a
halt. Something was up. Scanning with my night-vision goggles, I
saw several Special Forces soldiers jump out of their trucks. The rest
of us waited and watched. The snowy images wearing helmets and
body armor moved forward, hunched over with weapons at the
ready. They communicated only with hand signals. It was cool to
watch, even for me. Finally, after several minutes, the all clear was
given. They had rounded a blind turn and discovered a bunkered
fighting position with a heavy machine-gun mount inside. Fortu-
nately, it was unmanned.

The ride so far had been uneventful. The convoy had slowly pulled
out of Kandahar Airfield and headed toward Pakistan, hoping to
keep the Taliban, with its prying eyes, guessing. Only every third
truck had its lights on. As soon as we got to Highway 4, which runs
east toward the border, we split into three separate, smaller groups,
keeping enough distance between us so that anyone observing

wouldn't suspect a large force. The lights on our gun trucks were disguised with tape or disabled to make the vehicles look like civilian vehicles from a distance.

The paved highway proved to be the last luxury of the mission. After a while, we dipped into a dried riverbed that took us deep into "Indian country." The lights from a far-off jingle truck peeked from behind a bend. We watched it appear and disappear regularly as it picked its way through the deep, craggy wadis. After the truck was gone, there was nothing. No compounds, no buildings, no signs of life, only endless dirt roads and fields.

As we climbed up the hills, our lead element reported that the jingle truck we'd observed earlier had disappeared into the ten-foot-tall crop fields. Marijuana. We had stumbled upon hundreds of acres of marijuana. This was as dangerous as being in Taliban-held territory. The drug smugglers had no loyalty to either side and hated both for disrupting their business. The reason for the odd placement of the machine-gun nest was now obvious. Normally, we would have destroyed the bunker. Shinsha wanted the machine-gun mount, but he understood when I explained to him that to preserve the secrecy of the operation we would leave everything in place. We didn't need any eyebrows raised. We called the TOC and reported the location of the bunker. If any coalition force was attacked in this area, the U.S. Air Force would ensure the lethal nest was given proper attention.

On a ridgeline, we took a break and allowed all three groups to link up. We watched and waited to make sure the enemy wasn't onto us before pushing up a steep, winding road. It was treacherous and narrow and definitely never meant for broad, heavy vehicles. I remember thinking that Dave's jettisoning of the armor had probably worked out for the best. Now we just had to pray we didn't hit a mine. The Russians emplaced more than ten million mines during their decade-long duel with the mujahideen. They left another three million during their hasty departure. I didn't think of them as a likely threat now because we were in the middle of the Taliban's infiltration routes—which we called rat lines—from Pakistan, and they would have been cleared. But mines would definitely be a concern in Panjwayi.

We traveled through the remainder of the night and into the morning. At dawn, Afghanistan offered up its real beauty—the sunrise. Even in this forsaken place, seeing the flaming red sun break over the dark blue mountains was beautiful. The fingers of sunlight spilled over the horizon, reminding me of the power of light. Some bacteria, when exposed, die. Too bad we couldn't just shed light on the Taliban and be done with them.

As the sun crept higher in the sky, it illuminated the lushness of the bushes and crops. Caramel-colored ribbons of water cut through the middle of the terrain. Most of it came from natural springs farther north in the mountains. For the five years before the U.S. invasion in 2001, Afghanistan had been in a severe drought. But soon after we arrived, it rained, a lot. Record amounts. Call it divine intervention or climate change. The fact was, when we got to Afghanistan, so did the rain, and it became a bargaining chip we used to meet with local leaders and village elders—they believed we brought the rain with us. It gave us a chance to build the relationships that we then used to root out the Taliban. It also partially revived agriculture near Kandahar, Afghanistan's breadbasket. Based on the size of the marijuana fields, things had continued to improve.

We drove on through the morning. That afternoon, we finally stopped on a hilltop to let the overheating ANA Ford Ranger pickups cool down. They weren't designed to take the beating that rocky landscape dished out. Barely existent roads—sometimes just a set of tire tracks in the dirt—wove like drunks through wadis and around hills. It also didn't help that the Afghans drove the trucks like rental cars with no care for their condition. These occasional stops allowed Hodge, Jared, and me to reconfirm the route and adjust our timeline, but they also made it impossible for us to hold our schedule. We were still miles from the desert, which would be even more unforgiving.

To make up the time, we flirted with changing our movement intervals to the early morning hours and late evening, when the heat wasn't as bad. The team members had been rotating who took turret position in each vehicle, which was nothing more than a miserable slow roasting. Our only fear was that driving these roads in the dark would lead to a broken truck.

In the end, we got the same result in full daylight. A couple hours after our last stop, the call came over the radio that an ANA truck had died. It went down next to a riverbank, as its overheated motor seized up. Walking over to Jared's truck, all I could do was shake my head. Jared looked frustrated.

"It's a marathon, not a sprint," I said.

Bill was standing nearby and asked Jared if he knew how to eat an elephant.

"I wish all you philosophers on 31 would shut the hell up," Jared jokingly barked.

Then he called in to the TOC in Kandahar and requested a replacement truck with water and fuel. We had too much gear to crossload the dead vehicle's cargo onto the other trucks. The TOC got us a replacement truck, but also needed to arrange for a helicopter to fly it to us. The Special Forces do not have any helicopters of their own, strange as that may sound, so we have to borrow them from other units and are dependent on the owners' schedules and priorities. Most units were really, really good at supporting us when they could. The major problem with helicopter lift assets arose when we received time-sensitive information on targets. Special Forces has a solid intelligence network, but bad guys don't stay in the same place too long. When we need helicopters fast to go after someone, more often than not they aren't available.

We finally got word that the helicopter would arrive in two hours, and we started to tow the disabled truck to a makeshift landing pad in a flat area between two irrigation ditches, having stripped it of ammunition, weapons, and equipment. We had it halfway to the landing zone when the familiar chugging of rotors echoed across the valley. The birds were early. Shit. Jared sent out the landing team to mark the landing zone (LZ) with purple smoke, as Afghans and Americans alike converged on the broken vehicle, manhandling it across the remaining irrigation ditch. I went to the LZ with the off-loading party to prepare to remove the new vehicle.

The whirling CH-47 Chinook—a huge dual-rotor cargo helicopter —touched down, sending up a massive cloud of loose gravel and dirt that penetrated every crevice and pore. As the ramp on the bird dropped, its crew chief gave me a thumbs-up. An Afghan soldier raced up the ramp and dove into the window of the truck sitting in the helicopter's belly. I climbed into the truck bed, over the cab, and onto the hood so that I could guide him out.

The engine roared to life as the Afghan turned the key and floored it. I screamed *"AROM SHA!"*—Slow down!—at the top of my lungs and held on for dear life as the truck shot from the belly of the helo. The driver hit the brakes just as the rear bumper cleared the ramp. I hopped off and gave the driver an earful, but it couldn't have gone better if we had rehearsed it. The helicopter crew chief just stood there, the cable still in his hand, a stunned look on his face. I gave him a thumbs-up and rode off with the ANA.

We needed to move fast. The pilots don't like to stay on the ground for long. I told the driver to load up all the equipment and went back to help the crew pushing the dead truck toward the helicopter. After several false starts, we got it lined up. Drenched with sweat and caked with dirt, we set our feet for the final push up the ramp. That's when I noticed that the machine-gun mount was about to slam into the roof of the helicopter. I gestured to the GMV crew on the hill, and someone raced down with the tool kit from his truck. I tried several wrenches on the large bolt before I found the correct size. I cranked on one nut, no movement. God, I wished I had some WD-40. I scrambled on the top of the cab to gain some leverage and pushed the wrench until the bolt loosened. Jared hopped in the back with me, and like a NASCAR pit crew we cranked off the rest of the bolts. I threw the mount clear and everyone pushed the small truck into the belly of the Chinook.

I helped the crew chief tie the truck down with cargo straps, and then he gave me a thumbs-backward gesture to beat it off his helicopter. I scrambled off just as the bird's engines let out a high-pitched whine and the massive Chinook leaped into the air. Within fifteen seconds, it was disappearing into the crystal blue sky.

Our sideshow with the trucks had used up the rest of the day. Jared decided to stay put until morning and see if the Taliban had any surprises for us. It was a good move; we needed some rest. He also started rotating which team took point. It would be my team's turn tomorrow.

There's a saying that you've never lived until you've almost died. You can only get that from being out front, facing the unknown. You're the eyes and ears for every man behind you. Losing focus is a matter of life and death. You have to identify every danger, from an IED to an ambush. If I could choose, I would rather be hurt or killed than have it be one of my men. I felt very comfortable with Brian, Dave, and me in the lead, and we made good progress the next day. During breaks we worked on the vehicles and prepared for the next movement.

I usually took the last guard shift at night because I was always up late anyway trying to send our status reports. This normally took a while because we had to share satellite bandwidth with other units talking to the base. Finding a gap in the traffic always took some time. That night, it was after midnight when I finally shut my eyes for a few hours of sleep. I woke at about four in the morning to the usual tug on my foot. I cut on the propane for my handheld coffeemaker, and I began to conduct the normal checks on the ANA guards. I returned to a piping-hot pot of coffee and started to wake the rest of the team for "stand to." It was a rule we dared never break.

During the French and Indian Wars, Major Robert Rogers wrote twenty-eight rules for his company of six hundred handpicked Rangers. "Stand to" was developed from rule 15: "At the first dawn of day, awake your whole detachment; that being the time when the savages choose to fall upon their enemies, you should by all means be in readiness to receive them." Rogers's rules have since been adopted and rewritten by the 75th Ranger Regiment. When in the field, without fail, every day before sunrise we packed up our kit and pulled security for thirty minutes before and thirty minutes after the sun came up.

When no attack came, we loaded up and continued to move along the narrow dirt trail that came and went on the map. We dropped into a series of deep ravines that were full of high grass and water. Far off to the side at the bottom of a ravine through a gap in the grass, I noticed something distinctly out of place: a stick about four feet tall with a piece of red cloth tied to it. It looked like a linkup marker for Taliban coming across the border on foot. The Talibs would often infiltrate on foot, undetected, and then meet with a "mule," or vehicle, that would take them to a safe house.

I stopped the convoy and radioed Jared. We moved the vehicles off the trail and Brian and I got out. As we made our way toward the marker, Dave watched the high ground above us from the truck with the heavy machine gun and Ron scanned the ravine floor with his rifle. We skirted the trail and approached from the east, cutting through the thick grass. I could feel my heart pounding away in my chest. Slick hands. Dry mouth. I could hardly swallow. As we got close to the narrow opening in the grass, I gave Brian the hand signal to stop. I could see the small piece of red cloth that marked the entrance to the meeting area.

I held up my fingers to my eyes, silently telling Brian to keep an eye on the tall grass just in case someone walked out. Then I studied the ground and saw fresh footprints—both boots and sandals—spaced about a man's stride apart. It looked like maybe six or seven sets. I signaled to Brian that I could see something inside. Creeping to the opening, I slowly inserted the barrel of my rifle between the blades of grass and gently swept them to the side. Ahead lay a small, circular opening in the reeds of the sandy riverbed. Several yellow water jugs, some still partially full, littered the area. The clearing was wet from the morning dew, but I saw several dry spots about the size of a mat or blanket where it looked like someone had slept. Nearby, a spot as big around as a truck tire was bone-dry.

Brian came closer and softly tapped me to let me know he was there. I placed my hand on the tire-sized spot. Warm. The fighters had covered their fire without putting it out. Digging down a few inches with my knife, I found the smoldering ash. Dave whispered in the headset that he couldn't see us anymore, let alone cover us. I took a knee and put my hand behind me, signaling that I was coming out. Brian nodded and turned toward the truck. As he did my eyes caught a glimpse of movement over his left shoulder. I carefully raised my rifle. Looking through my scope, I saw four men—one of them carrying a weapon—on a ridge three hundred meters away.

I fired.

The round smashed into the rocks at their feet, too low to hit the lead Talib. I focused on the second Talib, who was now running at full sprint. I fired twice, trying to lead him a little. Brian saw him too and fired. We raced back to the truck and called Jared. They'd heard the shots and Hodge's team—Team 26—came up fast. I set up firing positions while 26 moved up to pursue. The Afghan soldiers were right there.

I watched 26 skirt the low ground and move up and over the small crest where I had seen the Talibs. Not far past it, they ran across a group of Kuchi tribesmen, nomads with strong ties to the Taliban. The Kuchis have survived several invasions—the British twice, the

Russians, and now us—and consider it all a minor inconvenience. Over the radio, Hodge reported that the nomads were claiming there were no Talibs on the hill and the team wasn't finding any blood trails. I had gotten excited and jerked the trigger. Bill would be all over me about it.

While 26 searched around the hill, the interpreters finally got the Kuchis to talk. Hodge radioed to tell me they admitted the men were Taliban, but they had run off when the firing started. There must have been a recent crossing and the fighters had linked up with guns, but not trucks.

We were already running well behind schedule because of the truck breakdown, so we collected as much information as we could from the Kuchis and started moving again, now with a real sense of urgency. The infiltration route was awfully well populated for late August. The summer heat should have been keeping Taliban fighters at home, yet they were moving north. This was extremely unusual, and all the commanders agreed that we needed to change the route and get to the safety of the high desert.

Maintaining radio silence as we drove, we kept watch for Taliban fighters, who were now undoubtedly watching for us. After several hours of driving, we reached the last remaining obstacle to the high desert and safety—a fast-running stream. It was a classic ambush point and good hiding spot for IEDs. But the biggest problem was a mud pit forty yards wide that the ANA's Rangers couldn't cross. We stopped the convoy and had the ANA drivers put the trucks in four-wheel-drive low.

"Don't gun it," Bill told the lead driver through an interpreter. "Just let it glide through the mud."

The Afghan nodded and, grinning from ear to ear, floored the gas pedal. The truck sloshed into the mud in four-wheel-drive high. It made it across but dug a massive trench right through the middle of the pit. Bill screamed at the driver, who was jubilantly pumping his arms up and down in victory. In his mind, all he had to do was get across. The next driver took off without warning, before we could explain things in more detail. The ANA truck raced into the mud and just barely made it through.

We decided to stop the next ANA vehicle and send a GMV across. We knew the hefty GMV would make it with little effort and could tow vehicles across if necessary. But as the first GMV started moving, another ANA truck darted in behind it, and it immediately got stuck and sank in the mud. This crossing was going to take much longer than expected.

Of the sixteen vehicles in our patrol, we still had four more ANA vehicles to get across and all nine of the GMVs. My team was pulling security on the bank and staying low in the vehicles. Several more GMVs crossed and joined the teams pulling security on the far side. One of the last GMVs tried to winch the small Ranger free from the clutches of the mud but only managed to get itself stuck, too.

Riley, our medic, sat in the back of his truck scanning the rocks. That's where he spotted a black turban and dirty face with a scruffy beard peeking out, right where he was pointing his M240 machine gun. The M240 fires a bullet the size of your pinkie finger and can punch through nearly three-quarters of an inch of steel.

The sound of the machine-gun burst sliced through the noise of the straining engines, immediately accompanied by sporadic AK fire from both sides of the river. The rounds slammed into the young Taliban fighter's head, and his body rolled out from behind the rock. The endless ranting of mullahs from the mosques in Pakistan and the foreign fighters in the training camps had driven the guy to try and steal a glimpse of the infidels. Curiosity killed him.

Another fighter popped up out of a small ditch nearby, weapon in hand. Riley cut him down before he could get away.

I called Riley for a report.

"I just killed two assholes hiding behind a rock. Light fire from our side," he radioed back.

As the team medic, Riley provided the team and our Afghan soldiers with all our care. You didn't go to Riley for a stomachache un-less you wanted to be called a sissy or worse. But if you were lying in a pool of blood, Riley was the first person you wanted kneeling at your side.

Riley's personality was, let's say, multidimensional. Like Bill, he was from Texas, the small town of Tolar, where the cattle vastly out-number the people and his high school graduating class numbered thirty-two. He had enjoyed the vast freedom of the open plains since he was a teenager, with a near frontier upbringing that kept him busy raising livestock and roping cattle. Just short of five foot ten inches tall, he was as wide as two men and had the strongest, heaviest hands on the team, obviously from his youth of handling horses and other men. He was most comfortable in cowboy boots, a T-shirt, and jeans and would have happily gone on patrol in that clothing if I had al-lowed it. I could imagine him in a long duster, dismounting a sixteen-hand quarter horse and sauntering into a bar, spurs singing, shotgun in hand. Riley was a free spirit and as wild as the horses he kept and the state he came from. I was willing to endure his turn-of-the-previous-century antics on and off duty for one simple reason: loy-alty. Having Riley on the team was like having a brother around full time. He was never without a smart-ass answer to a question and was always ready to back up his statements with a brawl. That being said, we could be in the thick of a team feud, but outsiders best not make the mistake of messing with any one of us when Riley was around.

A life of backbreaking farmwork had honed Riley's tendencies when it came to force. This I used to great advantage as my team pursued our country's goals. I could and would ask Afghans nicely one time and one time only for anything. If my politeness was taken for weakness, I would send in Riley. Whatever technique he applied, he did so without hesitation, usually resulting in a smiling Afghan returning to me hat in hand, ready to do what I asked. Soon word got around and I only had to ask the one time. This job and Special Forces in general were a perfect fit for Riley. While methodical in the clinic, he was a fierce gunfighter fueled by natural rage. He wore his emotions on his sleeve and preferred to be on the front of stack ready to kick in the door and lay waste to the enemy. If you wanted to take ground, put Riley in the front. The problem was, he was too valuable to sacrifice. His job was to keep everyone else alive.

As the senior medic, Riley never forgot his absolutely critical responsibilities. He was charged not only with providing medical assistance to the Afghans, and training the medics for the ANA, but most important, with keeping team members alive until they could be medically evacuated from the field. These things made for a heavy rucksack of burden, but Riley had big shoulders. His ability to practice medicine in the worst of circumstances was inspiring. Once, he got word that one of our ANA soldiers had been wounded in a firefight. The nineteen-year-old arrived in the small triage room with a huge gunshot wound to the chest. The ISAF medic and nurse had already given up on him because they couldn't get a chest tube inserted to inflate his lungs so he could breathe. Riley arrived, dropped his trauma bag, and went to work. He had the chest tube inserted and the patient stable and breathing on his own in minutes. It would be one of many instances where Riley would back up his brash demeanor to the hilt.

Riley continued to fire all around the rocks and up into the wadi to suppress enemy fire. Taliban fighters on the opposite side of the river began firing back, thinking that their ambush had been sprung; in response, all the machine guns and grenade launchers on the GMVs opened up. For the second time that day, I heard Jared call, "Troops in contact!" over the radio.

The remaining GMVs raced forward across the mud. Jared's truck stopped just long enough for him to jump in, and then all the Americans were across except for my team and the GMV stuck in the bog. The Taliban fire began to die down.

Across the river, two trucks dashed back to the edge of the mud, tossed towing straps to the sunken GMV, and easily freed it. Jared ran

to Shinsha and told him to get all of his equipment off the stuck
Ranger. Under sporadic fire, the ANA formed a line and heaved backpacks and ammo to another truck. Finally, with everyone else on the
far side, Jared ordered my team across, too. Brian grinned as the massive Goodyear tires slung mud in all directions. We roared past the
waiting trucks and once again took up the lead.

A significant ambush never materialized. Once we moved through
the kill zone, the Taliban fighters stopped taking shots and our machine guns went quiet. There were no more targets. Overhead, Air
Force jets covered our escape. Jared called in an air strike on the
Ranger we'd left behind to prevent the enemy from digging it out
and using it. We couldn't afford to have Taliban fighters in possession
of an official Afghan Army vehicle, parading around in it as propa-
ganda. As the bluish gray sky gave way to darkness, we saw the flash
of a precision bomb striking the vehicle. If anyone had been trying to
pillage it, they were dead.

We were down a truck, but we made good progress after the mud.
We set up a small base on the ridgeline on the cusp of the Red Desert, content with the day's accomplishments.

Chapter 8

———

A CAT-AND-MOUSE GAME

In war, only the simple succeeds.

—FIELD MARSHAL PAUL VON HINDENBURG

The warm water felt good as I poured a small amount of it over my eyes. It ran down my neck, soaking my already wet T-shirt. The blazing sun had baked us during the day, but as it dipped below the mountains the heat was giving way to a cool breeze at the edge of the desert. I swigged warm water that would have felt better in a shower instead of in a water bottle, swishing it and spitting it out to get the dust and grime from my mouth.

We had covered about ninety kilometers, had a truck successfully airlifted to us, and been in two small firefights with no one injured. A busy three days. On top of that, the Taliban had to be wondering just what the hell we were up to down here.

"Not bad," I said to Dave.

"Yeah, no problem, sir," he said dryly. "Now we just have to cross two hundred kilometers of some of the most unforgiving terrain on the planet, sneak into the enemy's sanctuary, establish blocking positions, and wait for the ISAF to push the Mongolian horde into our tiny element."

"How did you become so cynical?"

Dave cocked an eyebrow and looked down at me as he finished cleaning the heavy machine gun.

"I've worked for you for two years, Captain."

In that moment, I wished I could stay in this job for the rest of my career.

Jared came by and said we should get some quick rest. We needed to be off the ridge before the sun came up. I went to pass the word to Hodge and Team 26.

Hodge asked, "So, Rusty, how did you miss that Talib today?"

"Guess I didn't take my Geritol," I said.

He laughed.

"What about yourself?" I shot back. "I'm surprised at your age that you can see that far, much less think you can hit a moving target at over three hundred meters."

"Yeah, but I didn't miss today. You did."

Hodge was right. I had reflex fired instead of taking the time to line up the stadia lines in my optic sight and lead the target. I would not let that happen again, ever.

Bill set up the guard shifts while I went over to check on the Afghans. The fight had left me keyed up. There was no way I could rest. Plus, I knew the ANA broke out the chai every time we stopped. When I got to Shinsha's truck, the blue propane flame was licking the black bottom of the brass pot and I could hear the water rolling to a boil.

Shinsha was in good spirits. His men, who seemed as fired up as I was, scurried around their trucks making the tea, smoking, or making a mess. As soon as I sat down, the Afghans started making fun of my Pashto, which I speak with a western North Carolina accent. I could say a few words and phrases and knew enough to get my point across in a pinch, but I needed an interpreter for the heavy lifting. Still, the tea was hot and sweet and an hour passed before I headed back to my truck to take my guard shift and relieve Smitty.

I settled into the turret of the truck, picked up the thermal imag-

Crossing the Red Desert (August 24–31, 2006)

① Kandahar Airfield, home of the ISAF and coalition contingent. Starting point for Operation Medusa.

② First contact with Taliban made in riverbed during infiltration. Units turn west into the Red Desert.

③ Interdicted military fuel trucks smuggling ammunition and weapons into Panjwayi.

④ Discovery of the Taliban training camp and weapons firing range.

⑤ Unit heading northwest to the aerial resupply point.

100 miles

Afghanistan

Detail Map

Detail Map

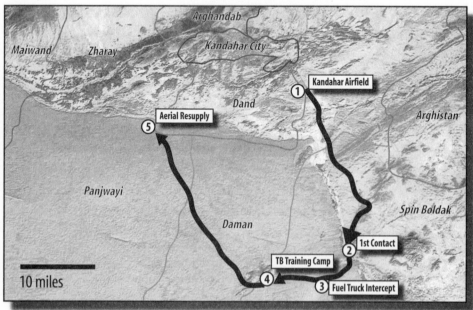

10 miles

ery scope, and took a look around. Nothing. Not even a stray donkey or camel herd. Under the dying light, the smooth, rolling surface of the desert flowed away out of sight. After such a long day, I enjoyed the few hours of quiet. It gave me time to collect my thoughts, which soon drifted back to my family. I did the math and figured out it was still afternoon in the States. I could see them in the kitchen. I wondered what they were having for lunch.

Just after midnight, I began to wake the troops. The Taliban would eventually come looking for us. Leaving at night allowed us to get a good head start, and the morning breeze would blow sand over our tracks. Since the Afghans didn't have night-vision goggles, Special Forces soldiers jumped into the driver's seat of the Afghan trucks. We headed out into the open desert. The rugged trails and riverbeds that caused your back to ache for days were behind us. I checked my map and compass. We were cruising at a good clip, despite our worn and dated equipment.

As reassuring as it was to be back in Ole Girl, she was ancient by military standards. Afghanistan is murder on trucks. Busted axles, blown tires, and punctured hoses are common on the rock-strewn landscape. Ole Girl was a first-generation GMV. She hit the ground in 2003 and for the last three years had never stopped bouncing along the wadis and dirt tracks of Afghanistan. She lacked any of the advanced armor and electronics that were so prevalent in the new trucks, but those were all headed to Iraq.

Most conventional combat units had the newest Humvee models with an onboard tracking system called the Force XXI Battle Command, Brigade and Below, or FBCB2. The system let commanders navigate and see all the other units on the battlefield through a satellite uplink. Dubbed a "force tracker," it showed the positions of friendly units and trucks on a digital map. The operator could click on the icons and not only tell their location but the type of unit as well.

Brian, Ron, and I had to MacGyver one out of my laptop, a GPS, and some scrap metal. Brian and Ron figured out a way to hook the GPS to the computer mapping system and put an antenna in the back so we could track our position. I built a mount out of a piece of old aircraft aluminum and several yards of sticky Velcro. It looked like it sounds, but it worked. That was the difference between Special Forces and other units: We could improvise. But after six years at the tip of the spear, we shouldn't have had to.

In the distance, I saw lights. They flickered on the horizon across the vast wasteland. I took a closer look through my monocular. From the number of lights, it looked like several trucks or cars, but I couldn't tell how many. I called Jared and recommended that we set up a checkpoint and see who was driving out here.

Jared agreed. Hodge, listening on the radio, pulled out to our right flank and set up to cover us. I radioed all the vehicles and ordered the teams to attach an IR chemlight, a small glow stick that can only be seen through our nods, to the rear of the trucks. The lights would let us identify friend and foe should any shooting start.

When we stopped, Bill jumped out and scouted out a low, sandy trough in front of the oncoming vehicles to put two of the ANA trucks into. Then he moved his truck to the right side, creating a barrier and funneling the headlights into the ANA trucks. Taking his cues from Bill, Brian positioned our truck off to the left. To Bill's credit, the checkpoint was well established in a very short period of time. I called Jared and told him that my team was set. Hodge called in and everybody was in position. Then we all flashed our IR lights— like the glow sticks, they could only be seen with nods—to make sure everybody knew where everybody was.

The plan was simple. Hodge was covering us. Jared, Shinsha, and the others were set up nearby, ready to be the cavalry if things went south. I felt like one of those spiders waiting for my prey to fumble past in the darkness and fall into the trap. The headlights slowly drew closer. At one point, they stopped. Light and sound carries over extremely long distances in the open desert, and I feared we'd been spotted. But soon enough the lights started toward us again.

We could hear the rumble of their engines. Too loud to be trucks, I thought. It wasn't jingle trucks or busted up pickups. I called over to Bill. He was thinking the same thing. Hodge couldn't see the vehicles, only four sets of lights. But he agreed with Bill that the vehicles sounded like tanks or armored personnel carriers.

I radioed Jared and asked him to call the TOC and see if ISAF had any units in the area. "I don't know what those are," I said, "but we may have our hands full out here."

I could hear Jared radio back to the TOC as I called Bill again. "Bill, get your anti-tank weapons out and ready!"

He was already ahead of me. He'd ordered the gunners to switch to API, armor-piercing incendiary rounds. The interpreters went to the Afghan trucks and gave the same order. Bill also told the Afghans with RPGs to shoot the last two vehicles in the convoy if the American gunners opened fire. Finally, he told the GMVs' rear gunners to "scratch their backs," or spray the turrets and chassis when the crews exposed themselves.

The lights were a half mile away and the ground started rumbling. It felt like a small earthquake.

"Wrap it up, Bill," I called to him as I hopped out of my truck. I pulled the Velcro strap that held an AT4 rocket launcher inside my truck and cradled the weapon in my hands.

The spring-loaded front and rear sights flipped into place and I set them for a range of 150 meters. As the lights got close, I noticed that the group was in a staggered military formation with equal distance between them. Taliban fighters didn't operate this way. Who the hell was coming at us? Lost Pakistanis? Al Qaeda? Mullah Omar and his bodyguards? Whoever it was, they were in for a shock.

"You ready?" I called over the radio to Hodge.

"Always," he said.

The convoy made a slight right turn around a sand dune and started straight toward us. I clutched the AT4 in my hands, waiting to shoulder it.

"Holy shit! Captain. Look right ten o'clock. Now!" Brian said.

Snapping my head in that direction, I felt a dead cold chill run straight down my back. In the green glow of the nods, thirty or forty men, several hundred meters away, were walking right toward us, backpacks on their shoulders.

What was going on here? What had we stumbled upon?

"Dave, you keep looking straight ahead. Bill, you take over the ambush! We may have dismounts to our left," I called over the radio.

I set the AT4 gently down on the floorboards of my truck, grabbed my M240 machine gun, and swung the swivel mount over the hood. Pressing my shoulder into the buttstock, I leaned into the gun and centered the front sight post on the far right group of dismounts.

"You take far right and I'll start from the left, working our way to the center," Brian said.

The rumble of the engines rolled over us like waves as the vehicles got closer and closer. My finger gently touched the trigger, ready to cut loose with my first burst. I slowly flipped the safety off and settled my cheek on my left hand, gripping the stock in anticipation of the recoil.

"WAIT, wait, wait," Brian said.

As the dismounts got closer, I could finally see that they were camels and their handlers, just passing nearby. Snapping the M240's safety back on, I snatched the AT4 just as the headlights arrived.

"Captain, we have four very heavy movers, not armor, how copy?" Bill said.

The ANA moved up the road, switched on their searchlights, and stopped the massive vehicles. Several motorcycles that had been traveling with the convoy took off in all directions. Scouts. If the truck drivers tried so much as to argue with the ANA, we'd light up all four vehicles with gunfire. Several Afghan soldiers maneuvered carefully around all sides of the trucks, preventing anyone from exiting. The ANA squad leader cautiously approached the lead truck's driver's-side door. I heard him tell the driver to cut off the vehicle. Apparently the driver said something the squad leader didn't like. The ANA leader reached into the cab and suddenly the driver came flying out, headfirst. One of the rear vehicles started to back up. An Afghan soldier jumped up on the running board and rammed his AK barrel into the driver's chest.

The vehicles were giant military fuel trucks. They'd been covered with decorations to make them look like traditional Afghan transport trucks, but I knew exactly where they came from. I radioed Jared.

"Sir, we have four heavy movers. Tankers camouflaged to look like jingle trucks. They are Iranian-type military vehicles headed for Pakistan," I said, noticing the Farsi writing on the trucks.

The message was short and to the point. The TOC monitored our frequencies, and I was sure that the last message had started secure phones buzzing at the command headquarters for all military operations in Afghanistan.

The ANA pulled the drivers and passengers out of the cabs. No one wore a uniform, but the trucks were definitely military vehicles and these guys were most likely soldiers. The ANA separated the drivers and started questioning them as they squatted in the dust. All of them stuck to the same story: they were supposedly stealing fuel in Iran and selling it in Pakistan. By crossing on the outskirts of the Registan Desert, they avoided paying Afghan taxes. The problem was that there are no Afghan taxes.

"Captain, we got diddly shit here," Bill said over the radio. "Whatever cargo these guys had they dropped off and were headed back."

Fuel trucks without a drop of fuel, clearly military, with drivers who seemed to be soldiers. It just didn't add up, but I needed more than gut instinct to go any further.

One of the ANA squad leaders came up and asked if they could burn the vehicles and leave the drivers in the desert. They wouldn't last long this far from the nearest village. The issue of whether to kill prisoners was one of the scenarios we'd worked through rigorously during Robin Sage, the Special Forces culmination training exercise in the forests of central North Carolina, as were many of the dilemmas we faced in Afghanistan. It was one of the best training exercises in the army. Thanks to Robin Sage, I had no question as to my response.

"We can't go around killing enemy without weapons," I told him. "If we do, we're no different than the people we're trying to defeat."

That wasn't the answer he was looking for, but he concurred because I was the commander. In his mind, war was a vicious cycle and all about survival. If your enemy lived, he could fight you another day. Before I could go on, Jared called me on the radio.

"Thirty-one, this is 30."

I ignored his first call, but he called again. Jared wouldn't have bothered me if it wasn't important.

"Thirty, this is 31. What's up?"

"Be very cool," Jared said over the radio, and in three words I got the message.

We were being watched by a Predator unmanned drone from high above. Jared had been tipped off by someone back in Kandahar. But why would anyone bring an asset onto the site and not tell us? We were being spied on by someone, and whoever it was, they didn't want us to know they were there.

I called Bill. "Wrap it up."

"Stand by," he said. A minute later he walked up and thrust a Pakistani military identification card into my hand. One of the drivers had hidden it under the dashboard of his truck. I turned it over, checking it under my red light. It was valid. Since before the war, the Pakistani Inter-Services Intelligence directorate had had strong ties to the Taliban. The ISI regularly gave them sanctuary and helped them cross the border. This was a smoking gun.

I called Jared and asked him what he wanted us to do with the guy. Did we risk falling a day behind schedule to detain these guys in an attempt to slow aid pouring over the borders?

We decided to just keep the ID card and took pictures of the drivers, passengers, and trucks. The Afghan soldiers tore into the trucks but could not find the access to the empty fuel tanks. We had to let them ride off, hopefully with their tails tucked firmly between their legs.

It later became apparent that they were not smuggling fuel, but munitions. With this regular supply line exposed, the Taliban would end up cut off.

Chapter 9

———

THE RED SANDS

We will either find a way or make one.

—HANNIBAL

The mountain looked like a rotten, jagged brown tooth sticking out of the sand. The closer we got, the more we picked up Taliban chatter on the radio. A commander, watching our dust plume grow closer, started to describe our convoy in detail and finally ordered his fighters to hide.

Jared sent David's team to the south side of the mountain and I took my team north. The plan was to recon the area and meet on the opposite side. Along the way, we'd watch for fighters and make note of any possible cache locations, fighting positions, or areas the Taliban used as observation points. But we weren't planning to get close enough to wind up in a fight.

A path in the sand led to the mountain, passing about a dozen compounds along the way. Shinsha agreed to send an ANA squad into one of the compounds. We covered them from the trucks as they quickly moved in. We could see fresh signs of life—water jugs, trucks, clothing, and even dogs. But the compounds were missing one thing: people. No children came running out for candy. It was lifeless and eerie.

After several minutes, the first Afghan soldier came back out. He shrugged his shoulders and looked confused. The squad leader came to my truck and described the inside. The place looked lived in, he said, with sleeping mats on the ground and dirty pots and dishes, but no people. Shinsha ordered his men into another compound. Same story.

I didn't want to waste any more time, so we loaded up the troops and headed north. As we passed the compounds, the Taliban began transmitting again. Taliban checkpoint 17 was losing sight of us and checkpoint 18 had picked us up. We followed the path into a lazy right turn that ended in a twenty-foot sand berm. It looked as if the desert ran straight into the mountain, the dust collecting up against its base. The trucks groaned as we forced them up between the berm and the rock ledge of the mountain. Slowly we climbed like a ship up a huge ocean wave until we finally crested the berm and half drove, half surfed down the other side.

As soon as the last truck got over the berm, the Taliban chatter reached a fever pitch. *"Allah akbar! Allah akbar!"* crackled out of the radio's speaker. Victor, my terp, said the Taliban were setting up an ambush down the craggy rock trail. I stopped the convoy. It was time to recalculate the risk. We had not come to get caught up in a firefight. The cliffs around us were so steep we couldn't raise our machine guns high enough to return fire and so narrow that we'd be traveling in one line like ducks in a row, easy prey for a well-coordinated ambush. We turned around and skirted the berm again. Now heading south, I focused on several large, flat rock faces with dozens of impact marks.

"Hold up, Brian. Bill, do you see that?" I asked over the radio.

"Sure do, about one hundred meters up from the desert floor," he said.

"Correct. Now, look around."

The ground was scattered with brass casings from weapons and plastic booster containers for RPGs. I called Jared.

"Sir, I don't know what you have up there but we have just discovered a Taliban training camp. We could not continue because there was significant chatter and the terrain was too restrictive. The compounds we saw on the way in were housing and we just now found the weapons range."

Brian hit the accelerator and I took down a ten-digit GPS grid coordinate. Jared's response came back seconds later and didn't need repeating.

"Get out of there now."

We hit the accelerators and raced back to the convoy. My truck came to a rolling stop next to Jared's and I jumped out with my map. Spreading it out on his truck's hood, I showed him the camp. He took the dog bone—our nickname for the similarly shaped radio handset—and reported our findings to Kandahar.

In four days, we'd run across a remote training camp, been ambushed at a river crossing, found an infiltration site used by soldiers coming across the border, and gotten a line on supply routes between Iran and Pakistan. I caught a glimpse of Lieutenant Ali raising his eyebrows when I told Jared about the camp. That summed it up for me. We were smack dab in the middle of the Taliban's superhighway into Panjwayi.

Jared finished on the radio and gave us the sign to move out. I watched as the team climbed into the trucks. The heat waves rolled freely across the horizon, causing even the most physically fit to slump. Everyone had heat rash on their shoulders and backs—our skin, soaked in sweat, rubbed against our body armor and became inflamed. Our pores were clogged with salt, oil, and dirt. Dragging my body armor on and off felt like having glass ground into my skin. I gritted my teeth and threw my armor over one shoulder and then the other.

Slumping into my seat, I looked back and watched Victor hop out, spread his prayer rug by the rear tire, and, using a bottle of water, quickly rinse off his hands.

"Come on, it's time to go," Dave said from the turret.

"It is my duty to pray. You can wait," Victor said, pulling off his vest.

"We are getting ready to move and move means move. We'll give you time to pray when we make the next stop," Dave said sharply, growing weary of the lackadaisical attitude from the team's new employee.

Victor said nothing. In his early twenties, he was stocky for an Afghan from the predominant Pashtun tribe, with only scruff for a beard, which he nevertheless cultivated because it made him feel manly. He walked away from the truck and began to unlace his boots.

Our former interpreters had been killed during Shef's rotation. Victor and the other interpreters were vetted by a contracting company. Once approved, they were randomly assigned to teams. The good ones, like my old interpreters, became part of the team. The bad ones bounced from one unit to another. Victor got bounced to us when we arrived.

Victor had shown little interest in praying five times a day up to this point, so it was obviously a ploy. He wanted a break. I was also afraid the other terps would see him and want to take a break too. But Victor knew he had us over a barrel. How would it look to the Afghan soldiers if we threw him into the back of the truck instead of letting him pray? I told Dave to relax and traded the unscheduled break for future rapport.

For the next few minutes, I watched as Victor faced the Ka'ba shrine in Mecca and alternated between standing ramrod straight behind his rug and prostrating himself, knees, forehead, nose, and palms to ground, praying to Allah.

After about ten minutes, he finished. He took his time putting his gear back on and rolling up his rug. I followed as he walked back to the bed of the truck, where he was now starting to pull out an MRE.

Rapport was one thing, but his actions were now on the verge of jeopardizing the mission. We had a deadline to make. It was time for a lesson in unconventional warfare.

"What's up, man?" I asked, shooting him my best smile.

"I will now eat," he said.

"Okay, no problem," I said, managing to maintain my equanimity. "Would you like some water?"

"Yes," he said, warming to my newfound interest in his welfare.

I started digging in the back of the truck for a bottle of water. I could feel Dave's eyes on me from the turret.

"Hey, Captain, we got to go," he said through clenched teeth.

Victor opened the MRE and began to sift through the package, complaining about the selection. "This isn't a halal ration. Captain, I'd like another," he said, taking the water from my hand.

I pulled out my pocketknife and, with a metallic click, opened it and thrust it into the bottom of the bottle. The warm clear water ran out onto his hand and the desert floor. Victor looked at me, confused.

"Captain, why did you do that?" he asked.

"It's at least a week's walk out of here from this point," I said, keeping my voice calm. "Unless you want to start now without food or water you should get on the truck."

To reinforce my point, I slapped the MRE out of his hand. I wasn't going to be tested or questioned by anyone on the team, ever. My tolerance for bullshit was zero. "Get on the fucking truck now before I lose my temper," I barked.

I had dealt with enough drama for one day. Victor wiped his hands on his shirt, put on his ammo vest, and got in the back without saying a word. He had learned a valuable lesson the hard way. From then on, we'd ask nicely once. The second time brought consequences.

"Let's go," I said into the radio.

Ole Girl's engine roared as she crested a thirty-foot sand dune and started down the back side. From the top of the dune, I could see hundreds more, looking like sets of waves coming ashore. The GMVs easily crested the dunes, but the ANA Hilux trucks had problems. A few miles into the desert, the first call came over the radio that a Hilux was stuck. Jared and the others helped dig the truck out. Grabbing the Afghan drivers, we told them to lower the tire pressure for more traction. We also had them put the trucks in four-wheel drive or low. They all nodded in agreement, but as we pushed on it was obvious that they still weren't understanding the basic dynamics of this kind of driving.

One of the most austere environments in the world, the Registan is, for the most part, a sandy desert shot through with ridges and small, isolated hills of red sand as far as the eye can see. The sand ridges and dunes, reaching heights of between fifty and one hundred feet, alternate with windblown, sand-covered plains, devoid of vegetation and changing in some parts into barren gravel and clay. It looked like Mars.

Our progress ground to a near halt. It was like driving in rush-hour traffic in hell. The waves of heat shimmered off the dunes. We sat in pools of sweat. The heat rash on our backs and shoulders burned. I felt like a cookie slowly baking in the oven.

When the radio crackled again about another stuck truck, Dave screamed in frustration and grabbed the machine gun in a rage, shaking it violently. After a few seconds, he stopped, then leaned down from the turret, smiling calmly. "I am much better," he said in a pretty good British accent for a guy from Ohio.

At sunset, my truck got stuck climbing up a massive dune. The wheels started to sink. Brian dropped the truck into four-wheel low and gently pressed the brakes, trying to get the non-power-side tires to catch. No luck. I got out of the truck, shrugged my shoulders, and took a bow. The ANA roared with laughter. Finally, the big, bad Americans had gotten one of their trucks stuck, and they could take a break as they watched us dig it out. I looked at it as an opportunity. We had pushed them so hard and for so long that I figured this negative could be a positive. It was a way to humanize us.

That evening I boiled a pot of tea for the ANA. I'd picked up the strong black tea in the bazaar for just such an occasion. Grabbing the pot and a few glasses, I headed for Shinsha's truck. I poured tea for him and some of his men. They graciously accepted it, but I could tell it shocked them. Afghan commanders never make tea for their soldiers. But I figured that this pot would ensure that when an Afghan truck got stuck it wouldn't stay that way for long. We sat on the matted rugs in the desert and watched as the sun retired while passing handfuls of stiff unleavened bread among ourselves. I had two cups of chai and retired for the night.

I unrolled the drab green sleeping pad and removed my shirt and boots. I always slept in Teva sandals because I could fight in them and my boots and feet could dry. Ranger school preaches taking care of your feet, so I poured a bottle of water over mine to clean them. I took another bottle of water and tried to clean the grime, salt, and sweat out of my shirt, finally hanging it on my truck, where in this heat it would dry in just a few minutes. I finally laid my head down on my inflatable pillow. My wife had bought it for me, and I thanked God for the day she married me. I said my prayers and drifted off to sleep.

In what seemed like seconds, I felt a tug on my foot. Time to move. I packed up my mat, threw on my now dry shirt, and was almost ready to go when Bill and Smitty cornered me, looking grave.

"We have plenty of food but water is going quickly," Bill said, looking at a list of supplies in his log book. "We're going through a gallon or more of water a day per man."

"Captain, we need to get resupply in forty-eight hours. If not, we'll be in the hurt locker," Smitty said.

We marched over to Jared and filled him in on the problem. Studying the map and tracing our route into Panjwayi, we finally agreed to head for a bit of flat desert where a cargo plane could drop us pallets of water. Jude rigged up the satellite antenna so Jared could send up the supply request.

Hodge's team took the lead, and my team fell back to the end of the convoy. By the time the morning sun broke the horizon, we had hit a relatively flat plain and I estimated that by the end of the day we would cover more than fifty miles. Then I saw the hulking sand dunes in the distance. The highest dune looked like a man hunched over with his arms stretched over the horizon.

"You get a feeling the dunes are trying to keep us out?" Brian asked me.

"Seems like it," I said as Hodge came over the radio.

"Talon 30, this is Talon 26. We have to find a way around these dunes. Some of them are six stories high."

Jared ordered us to stop and do some navigation.

Throwing my kit in the front seat, I jumped out of the truck and stretched my legs. Suddenly, I heard the crack from an AK-47, which sent me diving into the scalding-hot sand.

"Get back in the truck, Captain," Dave yelled, as he sank immediately into the turret, grabbing his .50-cal machine gun and spinning quickly toward the direction the sound came from.

I did my best football scramble, pumping my legs as fast as they would go. Seconds later, the call came over the radio. We had a wounded Afghan soldier. I grabbed the first aid bag from behind the driver's seat and dashed to the ANA trucks behind us, where an Afghan soldier stoically cradled his hand. I saw pencil-thin streaks of blood splattered on the truck and all over the soldier's uniform and face, and I knew immediately what had happened. We had warned the ANA time and time again about putting their hands over the end of their AK-47 rifles. The weapon has a uniquely unsafe safety catch, and if left on fire, the rifle will discharge with very little pressure on the trigger.

I grabbed the Afghan's wrist as crimson blood ran down his arm and covered my hand. Despite having just turned his right hand into hamburger, he didn't yell or flail around. The bullet had splayed his hand open between the index and third fingers, with the wound stretching from his wrist to the top of his palm and the two fingers hanging loosely on silky white threads of tendon. I gripped his wrist tightly and placed my thumb and fingers against the radial and ulnar arteries to reduce the blood flow.

Steve arrived and dove into his kit bag for a compression bandage. Trying to salvage something positive out of the ugly accident, I had the Afghans gather around as Steve, with Victor's help, gave an impromptu class on how to dress and treat a wound. Steve pushed the open wound together and applied an entire roll of Kerlix and a pressure dressing to the impact site, Victor translating every step. The administration of intravenous fluids followed. When the class was finished, I chastised the ANA openly for being so undisciplined and causing us to lose a valuable soldier with such a stupid mistake.

I walked to the truck, washed my hands, and called Jared. The Afghan had to be evacuated. Jared called it in while my team set up the landing zone. Already short soldiers, losing one to something this unnecessary aggravated me. If the operation was going to work, we needed everyone.

Steve and Riley had the patient ready to move when the call came in over the FM radio.

"Talon 31, this is Mustang 11. Confirm grid and status of LZ," the pilot said.

"Mustang 11, this is Talon 31. No change to grid. Status is cold. Beware of blackout sand," I responded.

"Talon 31, roger. Inbound," the pilot said.

I could see the drab green Black Hawk helicopter on the horizon. It was just a speck, but it was growing bigger by the minute. Someone popped purple smoke. On descent, the helicopter's blades kicked up a massive cloud of sand and grit. I ducked my head and covered my eyes. I had no idea how they could see in that mess.

The medevac helicopter stayed just long enough for Dave and Riley to load the Afghan soldier, and then it shot from the desert floor into the sky again, leaving another huge dust cloud. Shinsha walked over and slapped me on the shoulder. He had such a broad smile it made his eyes squint. He didn't speak, but I got the message. We took care of his soldier. He expected this of me, and I would do nothing to lower his expectation.

Before he left, I told him about the emergency air drop. "We're low on food and water, so we have to make it last," I said. "No wasting water. No throwing away food. When it's gone, we'll have to go without."

Shinsha understood and promised to speak to his men.

On my way back to Ole Girl, I ran into Chris, the stocky mechanic from the support company that flew in with the replacement ANA truck. For the last several days, he'd kept our trucks running on duct tape and sheer grit. He repaired leaking hydraulic lines by cutting off the secondary lines and overlaying them on the broken ones. The radiators on a pair of ANA Hilux trucks ran out of water, so he filled them with water, urine, and whatever other liquid was available. To fix one of the trucks with a broken leaf spring and another with a broken steering stabilizer, he used five-thousand-pound nylon ratchet straps, intended for securing cargo, and cinched the parts together tight so that the trucks could keep moving. Whether we could fight with them was another issue.

"Captain, when these trucks get hot again, those straps will melt," he said. "Then it's back to the motor pool."

Jared decided to wait until morning to resume moving. I thought it was a good decision because we were tired and everybody was frustrated with the vehicles and the Afghans. The break allowed tempers to cool.

* * *

At first light, we took advantage of the cooler temperatures to make our final push through the desert. The pain from my heat rash was excruciating, and I began to seriously debate riding this last leg with my kit off. My rash was turning into sores. If the sores got infected, I'd need antibiotics and be forced to raid our meager supply, medicine that I knew we might need for more serious injuries. I packed a fresh dip of snuff, closed my eyes, took a deep breath, and swung my body armor on. Pain shot like an electric current down my back and across my shoulders. I tried to control my heart rate and blinked away the tears in my eyes. As soon as the pain passed, I swallowed a half-dozen Tylenol, got on the radio, and called for the convoy to move.

For days, I'd suffered through Dave's ear-splitting techno music. He'd hooked his iPod up to two Sony speakers on the turret. The enemy threat was low, and the music was great for breaking the monotony. Since he was in the baking sun all day, I'd allowed him to play DJ. But I couldn't stand his high-octane techno anymore.

"For fuck sake, Dave, do you not have anything else on your iPod?"

"I've already been through all five thousand songs. What do you want to listen to?"

I reached back and fished a small Pelican case out of my assault pack. I passed up my old first-generation twenty-gig white iPod, which I'd taken on three rotations and which had survived a roadside bomb blast and several firefights. It was a gift from a family friend. On the back, he'd inscribed, "One does not make friends. One recognizes them." The iPod had become a sort of good luck charm.

Dave plugged it into the speakers.

"What do you want to listen to?"

I told him to pull down the country road music playlist. The first song couldn't have been more perfect: the first few bars of "East Bound and Down" by Jerry Reed blared out of the speakers.

This is the Taliban prize: Kandahar City. It is the crossroads to the five most important areas in Afghanistan and has been since Alexander the Great. (© *Andrew Craft*)

Beginning a patrol.
(*U.S. Army*)

Crossing the Red Desert.
(Photograph by Team 26)

The Afghans enjoyed watching us dig out one of our vehicles for a change.
(Photograph by Task Force 31)

Dinner is almost ready: ANA soldiers preparing a sheep purchased from a local farmer.
(Rusty Bradley)

Up early, Jared identified the target compound where we found the communication site. *(Rusty Bradley)*

The target compound Jared identified after exiting the Red Desert. The large makeshift antenna was for a satellite phone. *(Rusty Bradley)*

The objective: Sperwan Ghar. *(Rusty Bradley)*

Interior of a grape-drying hut; the Taliban used these huts for bunkers. The buildings, some centuries old, had mud walls up to three feet thick. *(Rusty Bradley)*

The black-walled room where the Taliban left their terrifying message for the local villagers. Note the names on the wall and sandal marks on the ceiling. *(Rusty Bradley)*

Sperwan Ghar as we defended it during a counterattack. Note the vehicles lined along the southern wall. The Taliban had converted the V-shaped school and hill into a training camp. *(U.S. Army)*

Close fighting. The enemy got within half a football field of Smitty and Bill's truck. Note the smoking building from which they were engaged. *(Rusty Bradley)*

This picture was taken from the top of Sperwan Ghar during a lull in the fighting. It shows the prolific vegetation and landscape. *(Rusty Bradley)*

Dave waiting for another attack, as the sun goes down. He would not have to wait long. *(U.S. Army)*

Round two to the long beards: seven two-thousand-pound bombs going into enemy compounds after the ambush on September 3. *(Photograph by Team 26)*

Briefing Major General Freakley
two days into the battle. During his visit,
the 3X boys were borrowing his helicopters.
(U.S. Army)

It was nearly impossible to see
through the dense marijuana fields.
Doc is six feet tall; you do the math
on the size of these plants.
(U.S. Army)

This was Greg and Sean's GMV after the IED
strike. You can see there was nowhere to hide
from enemy fire, which made Jude's act
absolutely heroic. *(U.S. Army)*

Planning for our first push into enemy territory. Other Special Forces teams and reinforcements from the 10th Mountain Division had arrived. *(U.S. Army)*

Jared, Shinsha, and an interpreter named Jacob discuss options before assaulting Objective Billiards. Earlier, Jacob had heroically defended a wounded U.S. soldier. *(U.S. Army)*

Bill, Zack, and Jude receive their Combat Infantryman Badges from the battalion commander on September 11, 2006. *(U.S. Army)*

My ODA with the Air Force JTAC and ETTs on September 11, 2006. *(U.S. Army)*

Captain Rusty Bradley. *(Rusty Bradley)*

Chapter 10

THE NOTEBOOK

Do not touch anything unnecessarily. Beware of pretty girls in dance halls and parks who may be spies, as well as bicycles, revolvers, uniforms, arms, dead horses, and men lying on roads—there is nothing there accidentally.

—SOVIET INFANTRY MANUAL ISSUED IN THE 1930S

T he Kuchi tribesman, with about twenty camels in tow, came over the horizon. As he got close, I could see his weathered face and long black beard. His thin frame was covered in layers of robes, and he had a sizable knife, curled at the end, wedged into his belt.

"This guy looks like an extra from *Raiders of the Lost Ark*," I cracked.

Smitty called over the radio that through his binoculars he could see several large packs on one of the camels that appeared to be ammunition or mortar rounds. I didn't see a weapon in the tribesman's hands, but I knew the desert can play tricks on you. Hell, I had just seen a herd of camels that I took for enemy soldiers.

When the Kuchi saw the long line of trucks, he stopped, dropped his pack, and threw his hands in the air.

"I like this guy already," Bill said over the radio.

Steve, Smitty, and their terp, Jerry, went to talk with the man. He told them that his herd was part of a dowry from his bride. Steve and Smitty searched him and then asked to see his cargo. Without hesitation, he pulled out his knife and cut the heavy packs off the camel. The woven cloth bags tumbled to the sand.

Smitty rifled through the packs while Steve watched with his rifle at the ready. The bags were full of scrap metal, mortar fins and munitions casings, which the tribesman said he had collected at the training camp we had found near the mountain about a week's walk south. His story made sense. There was plenty at that camp to pick up. He smiled when Smitty offered him three bottles of water, glad to drink from our supply rather than his own. While he drank, Smitty took out a notebook and started asking questions. I stood off to the side by my truck.

"Seen anyone around here?" he asked, as Jerry translated.

"Several Hilux trucks."

"In which direction?"

"From the south, toward Panjwayi," the Kuchi responded, polishing off the last bottle.

No one innocent would cross this desert on a joy ride. I checked our position on my computer and GPS. We were almost out of the desert. I watched the Kuchi repack his load as we started again toward Panjwayi. Ahead of us, the contour lines on the GPS display converged, indicating more high ground to surmount.

After a few hours, we crested a hill and spotted a small cluster of multicolored tents pitched on a plateau. The Kuchi's future father-in-law. As we passed, the man greeted us and asked if we had seen his camels. He didn't seem too interested in the welfare of his future son-in-law.

"Typical father-in-law," I told Brian.

The plateau fell off into another series of rolling hills. When we at last surmounted the final one, stretching out before us was the lush green Panjwayi Valley. I called Jared to let him know we'd made it out of the desert and were near the drop site. Jared radioed back that another truck was stuck, so Brian, Dave, and I shut off Ole Girl, shed our gear, and handed out bottles of water like celebratory champagne.

Beyond us flowed a vast ocean of green vegetation. I could see the Dori and Arghandab rivers framing the valley on either side, an intricate network of hundreds of villages crammed with mud huts, grape fields, pathways, trails, and irrigation ditches. For a moment, I imagined how ancient travelers must have felt when they saw the valley after weeks of walking across the desert, but the feeling didn't last. The battlefield calculus was all too obvious. The Canadians were going to need more troops—a hell of a lot more. This wasn't a few remote villages. This was an undeveloped city.

"Good thing we don't have to clear it," Brian said, reading my mind.

Jared's truck pulled up next to mine, its radiator hissing, the cooling fan churning at full blast.

"Man, that sure is a sight for sore eyes," he said.

"Let's just hope we don't have to fight in it," I responded.

Victor hopped off my truck and pulled out several bottles of water and his prayer rug.

"What's the water for, Victor?" I asked.

"It is time for me to pray," he said.

We were close to the drop zone, but still short on supplies, which we'd been rationing for a day. I wasn't taking any chances until the pallets of food and water arrived.

"You can either drink that water or wash your feet with it," I said. "I don't care, but that's all the water we have left to share with you. Your choice."

He thought for a second and put two of the bottles back in the truck. Dave looked down from the turret and smiled. "Maybe he's a fast learner, Captain."

"We'll see."

Jared met with the commanders and we all agreed to wait until dark to approach the resupply site, so that we wouldn't compromise it. I spent part of the afternoon going over my gear. I had two pairs of socks and two T-shirts. My skin was raw because of the heat rash. I soaked an expensive Under Armour T-shirt in water and washed my chest and feet. My civilian boots were holding up, and it helped that they were a size too big. In this heat, my feet swelled badly. Army desert boots have a piece of leather that cuts across the top of your feet—and, when they swell, digs into them and cuts off circulation to your toes. You can't cram a soldier into boots and equipment made by the lowest bidder and mass produced for every soldier. It doesn't work that way and never has. That's why most special operations soldiers wear civilian hiking boots. It isn't because they look cool. It's because they work.

I grew up in the infantry and still remember the Ranger instructor's words of wisdom: "Listen up, girls, there are two things you will take care of as a grunt or you will not last long on the battlefield: your rifle and your feet. In that order." I put on fresh socks and slid my boots back on. They were tight, really tight.

Team 26 had volunteered to lead the way toward the valley and we got under way as the sun was setting. As Hodge turned the convoy off the ridgeline and into the riverbed, the temperature dropped at least twenty degrees, and we were soon soaked by the light spray thrown up by the tires and the water sloshing over the floorboards of the truck.

The convoy churned along in the shallow river for about a mile, until we converged on the drop point programmed into our computer maps. For once the map of the area basically reflected the actual ground. Our homework had paid off; the site was perfect. A large sandy drop zone was surrounded by a ridgeline that we could set up on, and that provided some concealment for the vehicles and a commanding view for miles. Bill set up sectors of fire that I plotted on a laminated tablet, later adding the Afghan positions that Shinsha showed me. The sector sketch was basically a diagram of the position and showed the machine guns' interlocking sectors of fire in the event a fight broke out.

With the area secured, we set up signals for the pilots. A night air drop could be more dangerous than a firefight. Once those pallets slid out of the aircraft, the only thing controlling them was weight, wind, forward throw, and gravity. One mistake and thousands of pounds of water and ammunition might land on our heads.

With the sun now gone and still several hours until the aircraft arrived, we decided that the ANA could go down to the river in groups of ten men at a time. The first five would bathe while the others secured the area. When the first group finished, they would switch. We needed to wash, too, and the medics—Steve, Riley, and Greg—talked about it, consulting cards they carried in their uniform pockets and checking the amount and types of medicines on hand. The river was full of microorganisms and bacteria.

Finally, Greg gave us the thumbs-up.

"Do it, but you have to dry your clothes in the sun to kill any remaining bacteria," Greg said. Riley added that we could soak the clothing in alcohol to kill most of the creepy crawlies if we had to move before it was light. I agreed to their recommendation and Bill sent the guys down to the river a couple at a time.

Nearby, Jared had some good news and bad news. He told me everything was on time and the Air Force was dropping more than twenty thousand pounds of water, fuel, repair parts, ammunition, medical supplies, and rations. Riley and Steve had also ordered boxes of baby wipes, rubbing alcohol, and rags to scrub the heat rash and sores. I could see Jared smile against the glow of his computer screen. The bad news was ISAF might delay the start of the mission. He didn't say why. It wasn't confirmed, and until it was, he was going to stick to the schedule. We had to be in position before they could launch the attack.

With only thirty minutes before the bird arrived, Jared, Hodge, and I separately confirmed one another's math and walked to check the drop markers and signals, a series of infrared strobe lights arrayed in a predetermined shape. Bill made sure the team was ready and everyone had their nods and "go" bags, small backpacks with food, ammo, and other essential equipment, just in case one of the pallets decided to fall on top of a truck.

The pilot's voice came over the radio.

"Talon 30, Talon 30. This is Archangel 51."

Jared reached for the handset. The MC-130 was inbound. The specially designed aircraft could fly in any weather and was made for low-visibility operations.

"Archangel 51, this is Talon 30. Go ahead."

"Talon, we have a few things for you. Are you ready for drop?"

"Roger that, Archangel."

Jared went through the checklist in his lap. The aircraft flew over us to confirm the drop site and spot the marker on the ground. It would have to make two passes to put the cargo out. The calm, cool air turned electric with tension. Brian sat at my truck on the trail edge of the drop zone with the signal ready. I could hear the heavy hum of the plane's four turbine engines closing in, and I caught a glimpse of the open tailgate on the aircraft.

"Talon 30. This is Archangel. We have you spotted. Half drop, ten bundles next pass. How copy, over?"

We were on our toes now. As the bundles came out, we had to confirm full chutes. If a chute didn't open, a one-ton pallet was crashing to earth. A few minutes later, the plane made the fifteen-mile circle over the drop zone. The crew confirmed its course and requested that we light the infrared signals.

"Talon 30. This is Archangel. Markers identified. Drop in ten seconds."

"Execute, execute, execute."

As quickly as the turbine engines roared directly over head, they were gone. I could hear the muffled popping of parachutes opening.

Brian shut the signal off. I scanned above: one, two, three, six, eight, and ten. Ten good chutes. I contacted Jared and Hodge on the radio.

"Roger, we confirm ten chutes," I said.

The massive square platforms creaked and swayed as they drifted down directly in front of us, and we felt the *crump* of their weight hitting the earth. Jared reported all ten pallets were touchdown.

"Bill, give me a status," I called over the radio.

"All good here, Captain, including ANA." I still held my breath. We were only half finished. The MC-130 was approaching again. Without a word, Brian cut the markers on when he heard the engines.

"Talon 30. This is Archangel. Markers identified. Last drop in ten seconds."

"Execute, execute, execute."

Again the roaring engines were followed by the popping and whipping of the chutes. One, two, four, seven, nine . . . nine.

"I count nine only nine," I said, my stomach in a hard knot.

"Shit, I don't see it," Dave said.

"Neither do I," said Brian and Bill simultaneously.

Jared spotted the two-thousand-pound pallet a few seconds later. It was a hanger—a pallet that comes out late or is hung up on something and breaks free to fall cleanly to the ground. I heard all the pallets hit the ground and finally relaxed. Jared called the bird and thanked them for a perfect drop. I had conducted dozens of these aerial resupply missions in my career, but none had gone this well. Almost every one of the pallets had landed upright and literally right in front of us on the dry side of the riverbed. I stood on the edge of the ridge and looked down directly at the top of a cargo pallet twenty feet below.

"Thank you God," I said quietly. I knew we were being protected and cared for.

"Amen, brother," Bill said.

Now we needed to move fast. The busy work had to be done to break down every pallet and distribute the supplies. We knew what we had ordered, but sometimes the bundles don't get loaded, or they break or get stuck in the bird. Bill and Jeff, 26's team sergeant, decided to unload the most critical supplies—ammunition and fuel—first, so that they, at least, would be secured if we got into a fight and had to leave the area. We were down to only a little more than a basic load of ammunition, about two hundred rounds each, but the resupply brought us up to a full double load. Since we are such a small unit, we have to gain fire superiority quickly, which requires the fast expenditure of about a third to a half of our stores. The enhanced loads were very welcome.

Next, we started on the fuel. We hand-carried twenty fuel cans to the fifty-five-gallon drums on the pallets and filled each one using a hand crank. The work took us all back to Special Forces selection, the first step in becoming a Green Beret. During one of the exercises, you have to carry fuel cans through the central North Carolina pine forests. It's backbreaking work that seems on the surface like hazing to eliminate the weak. In some part it is, but in fact the task challenges you to work together as a team in tough conditions.

Meanwhile, Chris, the mechanic, had gathered up the repair parts—heavy jack, leaf springs, hoses, lines, and tools—and had already started repairing the damaged trucks. I found him covered in hydraulic fluid and oil underneath truck number 3's hood.

"How long we looking at, Chris?" I asked.

He spit and wiped his mouth, smearing the spilled fluid across his cheek.

"With all the vehicles on both teams, maybe a day, Captain. I can't really tell," he said.

Bad news, but given that ISAF might delay the operation, Jared didn't seem overly concerned with the repair time when I informed him. He wanted to take a day to recon the valley, rest, and wait for word on Team 36, Bruce's team, which was coming from Kandahar on a shorter route with the ANA's weapons company. The Afghan unit had about twenty men with heavy machine guns, recoilless rifles, and 82-mm mortars that provided tremendous firepower.

After we left, Bruce had waited in Kandahar for the second half of his team to arrive, and most of the guys spent about twenty-four hours on the ground before setting off. It took them about three hours to link up with us at the edge of the Red Desert, a fact that seemed to piss off Hodge in particular, given the bone-jarring days of stuck vehicles, heat rash, and aching muscles we had all suffered.

After four hours of unloading supplies, we finally got to the water, which we made sure was distributed equally between the American and Afghan trucks. The Afghans had learned about water conservation the hard way after spending a day without it, and as we hauled cases of water to their trucks, I hoped they'd listen to us next time. But their jugs were already full of river water. If any one of us had done the same without purification tablets, we would have been in the hospital within twenty-four hours.

The sun was still low on the horizon when we finished packing the supplies away. I laid my freshly washed shirt and socks on my truck and crashed in my seat. I woke three hours later baking in the sun. My shirt and socks felt like soft cardboard. Since the ridge offered us some protection, most of us left our shirts off. Tattoos and scars decorated my teammates' bodies. Skulls, tribal designs, the names of loved ones were scrawled on our biceps, backs, chests, and legs side by side with grotesque, stretched scars from past fights or injuries.

My back and legs ached and my body felt like it had been hit by a truck. *I'm getting too old for this,* I thought. As I stretched and worked the kinks out, I glanced over to Jared's truck. He and Mike, another air controller who traveled with Team 26, were crouched over a large spotting scope, Jared scribbling notes on a pad. He saw me stretching and waved me over to take a look. I wiped the crusted sleep from my eyes with my *shemagh,* the traditional scarf of the Pashtuns. Through the hazy waves of heat, I could see a group of tan compounds with mud-packed walls. A large antenna protruded from the roof of a hut in the village market. Standing outside, ten men catered to two better-dressed older men. My eye drifted back to the small antenna array.

"Well, lookie, lookie what I see. Now why would a small merchant shop in the middle of the desert need a satellite communication system?" I asked.

Jared laughed. "I'm glad you asked, because I want you to go down there and find out."

Bill stood on the other side of the truck, grinning like a hyena. He had lobbied Jared for the mission before my arrival. Now he got his wish.

Bill and I put together a hasty plan as we walked back to the truck.

"Let's do a simple movement-to-contact drill with our four trucks. Once we get into the village, we'll do a secure and lockdown on the main compound after setting blocking positions. I'll post one truck and some ANA at the exfil route," Bill said. "You lock down the blocking positions and do the command and control."

"Sounds good," I said. "You take assault one and hit the main building. Assault two will lock down the rear escape route and the roofs with Smitty."

I grabbed the map from my truck and opened it on the hood. Taking out my laser range finder, I attached my GPS to it and shot an azimuth to the antenna. Plotting the point on the map, I plugged it all into my computer and got a satellite picture of the target. The picture was three years old and some things had changed, but overall it was okay. I figured that we could probably drive to the target, but it would take some navigating.

Several dry irrigation ditches led up to the village, but the terrain remained unforgiving. I went back to the scope and searched for the best way in. I didn't want to get halfway down a ditch, tip off the bad guys, and watch them run out the back door. I turned to an empty page in my notebook, now full of notes about the village, and started to sketch. I focused on entranceways, high points, and possible ambush positions. I had been a scout sniper in my younger days and had done this kind of thing hundreds of times. My sketching skills were better then, but I had enough to brief the team and get the job done.

The team gathered around the map. The compound was two miles away. We decided to move several hundred meters down the riverbed before coming out at full speed about a mile from the village. They would give its inhabitants only about two minutes' warning before we arrived. From there we would surround the market and begin our search. Team 26 would be the quick reaction force ready to bail us out if we got into trouble.

Back at my truck, Dave cleaned the .50-cal heavy machine gun on the turret. Brian was already making the communication checks with 26, Jared, and headquarters in Kandahar. I put on my body armor and set my GPS on my wrist and on the computer in my truck, and then I cleaned the M240 machine gun attached to my door, checking all its optics and those on my rifle. After calling to Bill to let me know when the rest of the team was ready, I took out my pocket Bible and started to read Psalm 91 to clear my mind. It helped me focus on the mission. "A thousand may fall at your side, ten thousand at your right hand, but it will not come near you. You will only observe with your eyes and see the punishment of the wicked."

As the truck grumbled to life I remembered thinking that someday all this would end. Then what would I do? Where do warriors go when they aren't needed anymore? Staff and a desk, I guessed.

A huge dust cloud followed us all the way down the riverbed. All four trucks were side by side when we finally emerged and raced straight toward the market. I could see Afghan villagers running away or back toward the compounds. Over the radio Jared said he saw several men run out of the village, and that Taliban radio chatter spiked as soon as we cleared the riverbed, with fighters outside the village telling those near the market that they'd cover their escape. I gripped the machine gun and waited to see if they'd fight or flee.

"Four motorcycles just took off to the north," Jared said over the radio.

"Damn, there goes the commander," I said into my Peltor headset. We couldn't cut off the escape routes as planned—we were almost into the village and focused on going straight to the target compound instead of chasing them. Anything or anyone of value was probably gone, but hopefully they left something behind in their haste. Brian slammed on the brakes as we reached an intersection of dirt roads on the village outskirts, smashing me into the windshield and jamming Dave's big turret machine gun into his chest. He'd seen too many trucks race to a target, only to hit a mine. If it took us a few seconds longer to get there alive, I was willing to be patient. Brian raced around the intersection, made a sharp right-hand turn, and sped down a small pathway to the shop, stopping just past the front door. I jumped out and covered the building while Dave covered our rear with the big gun. Bill and the search team, interpreters in tow, fell immediately into line at the back of his truck and approached the shop. It was beautiful to watch. The formation was nearly in step, weapons covering every position as they flowed smoothly inside. Several minutes of screaming and yelling, but no gunfire followed. Finally Bill peeked out the doorway and came sauntering out.

"Captain, we have the building locked down and the perimeter is secure," he said. "We haven't begun the search but the roof is clear. We will be bringing out the occupants in a minute."

I asked if there were any PUCs (personnel under confinement). I despised that term. It was a politically correct, pussyfooted way of saying prisoners. Just saying it pissed me off. As the occupants filed out, it was obvious who they were. About six of the ten had dark olive-drab clothing and black turbans. These were the lowest-hanging fruit on the Taliban tree and usually the recipients of our fury in battle, the Talibs who are left behind to cover the escape of those more privileged who run off via motorbikes or Hilux trucks.

Bill lined them up on their knees in front of the building. Some of them were just boys.

An old man with thick glasses, a gray turban, and a cane came out and looked me square in the eye. I greeted him and asked him as a *mesher,* or senior, to please sit. He smiled. I knew he was not a combatant or an enemy. There was no sustained eye contact, scowling, head hanging, cursing. Instead, he looked at me and my long gray-and-white beard, which he slowly reached out and touched, his hand shaky.

"You. I have seen you before," he said.

I helped him slowly sit down on a bench near the market's door. His smile grew to chuckling, his chuckles to laughter. I was not in the mood for humor and told the interpreter to ask him what the joke was.

The old man, who turned out to be the shop owner, pointed an arthritic finger at me and continued to laugh as he said, "I know who you are, gray one. You are of the long beards. *Amerkaianu Mushakas Kawatuna.*" American Special Forces.

He then pointed his crooked finger at the men lined up in front of the store.

"These Talib boys will not run like wild animals while you are here." He laughed in a low, vindictive tone. "You have much work to do here, gray one. Many Talibs have returned with their Arab friends."

In my full kit with weapons and assault pack, I weighed nearly three hundred pounds, but right then, you could have knocked me over with a feather. I nodded respectfully and took out my notepad. Bill stuck his head around the corner of the doorway of the store and said that he, Riley, Smitty, and the others were going to start their search. I nodded and returned to my notebook. I wanted to capture every word. What the old man told me about the current situation, the enemy, and the attitude of the local population surpassed two weeks' worth of intelligence work.

The heat of the day was sucking the life out of everyone, and it was obvious that the Talibs were getting thirsty. I went to my truck and pulled a bottle of water out and handed it to the old man. An ANA soldier squatted by him and wiped his brow. Afghans have a great admiration for their elders. They appreciated the fact that I showed him respect.

The PUCs had been separated from one another so they could not communicate, and the ANA were more than happy to begin questioning. The teenage boys were the first to get the ANA's full attention. They were the youngest, least trained, and would usually be the first to provide useful information. When the ANA found someone they were sure was a Taliban member, he was pulled off to the side and given a GSR, or gunshot residue and explosives test. Whenever a gun is fired, the shooter gets sprayed with an invisible blast of chemical residues that are by-products of the incomplete combustion of gunpowder, primer, and lubricants. The kit can identify very small amounts of these chemical markers on a person's hands, arms, or clothing. Out of the six Talibs, the one who scowled the most had residue all over his hands.

"Hey, Captain, we need you in here," Bill called from the store.

Jackpot, I thought to myself. My guys would only call for me if there was something of interest. Riley and Smitty had been first inside. The interior was cluttered with pills, injectable antibiotics, and bandages. The other side was stocked with clothes, candy, and trinkets. Riley had been poking around the back wall near the antenna base. He casually swept the ground with his foot. Unlike the usual earthen floors in the country, baked hard from decades of heat and blistering sun, this one was soft. Someone had disturbed it. Digging down about six inches, Riley had uncovered a notebook wrapped in a plastic bag, which Smitty handed to me as I stepped inside. It was a small green tablet, about three inches long, text reading from right to left. The only markings were names and numbers. Jackpot.

There was no sign of the phone that belonged to the satellite array. I was absolutely sure that the others had taken it with them when they made their hasty exit. The antenna on the roof ran to a hidden cable and charger. Riley took great pleasure in snapping the antenna from its base and tossing it off the roof.

Intravenous needles, IV bags, clotting agents, pressure dressings, morphine, tourniquets, needles, and sewing thread were packed in boxes and stacked neatly in the back of the shop. When I came out and asked the old man who the medical supplies belonged to, he told me Hafiz Majid's men. Hafiz Majid was one of the top-five Taliban commanders in all of Afghanistan. If those supplies belonged to his men, he couldn't be far away. I wondered if he had been one of those who fled, but I doubted it. Senior Taliban commanders did not travel without Al Qaeda bodyguards, and their visits were no secret, heralded by much fanfare. They generally wanted the entire area to know they were there in the face of the infidels' invasion.

We spent the next several hours questioning the Talibs. The ANA squad leader stood smiling at me.

"We take them, Captain?" the Afghan soldier asked.

I knew what he meant. If I had said yes, the whole bunch would have been taken on a one-way trip into the desert and never returned. It sickened me to have to deny the ANA request because I knew we would be fighting these Talibs later, but something had to separate us from them.

"No," I said flatly.

The Afghans understood, but they always asked anyway, hoping I might say yes.

I walked over to the Talib who scowled the most and drew my knife to cut his plastic flex cuffs. I commanded him not to move. Then I took his right arm and with a Sharpie marker drew an American flag on his wrist.

Grinning, I said clearly for the others to hear, *"Nanawateh tisme-*

del." I had just given him safe passage according to one of the most primary Pashtunwali benefits. Like it or not, he now owed me a favor.

He was obligated to obey.

"I have a message for your boss. Show him this," I told him through a terp, indicating the flag. "Tell him we are looking for him."

He jerked his hand away and glared. I gave him a little wink and stepped up into my truck. We made the turn out of the compound fully prepared for an ambush. I saw the ANA squad leader wave to the Talib who had just walked away with his life.

As we headed back to Jared's position, I got a call on the radio that there were some serious arguments among the Taliban as to why we were not ambushed on the way out of the compound. Apparently there was a very, very irate Taliban soldier who wanted to engage us but was told by his commander he was obligated not to.

At the top of the ridge, Jared waited anxiously with his interpreter for the captured notebook. I handed it off to him as we drove by. Now the administrative pain would begin. I was hoping someone on the ridge had kept our timeline for the after-action report. I began a brain dump of everything I could remember, while Bill and the team began cleaning gear and weapons.

A shadow fell over the door of my truck. It was Jared, grinning from ear to ear. "Do you know what this is?" he asked, holding up the notebook Riley and Smitty had found.

"Yep," I replied. "It's a list of Taliban commanders and phone numbers. This wasn't left there by accident. It was hidden."

I studied the list carefully and recognized at least four of the names immediately as men I had been hunting during my last rotation. This time we might not have to chase them all over Afghanistan.

Chapter 11

THE VOICE OF AN
ANGEL AND DEATH

The difficult we do immediately;
the impossible takes a little longer.

—AIR FORCE MOTTO

A t daybreak, our fully loaded trucks rolled down from our perch over the Dori River and headed into the valley. Our teams' mission from this point was to continue to move west and gather as much detailed intelligence as possible, while keeping the enemy watching. The idea was to draw their attention to us and away from the northern areas where the ISAF main force would be launching an attack. Before we departed that morning, we rehearsed within our team and with the others what to do if one of the trucks got stuck in the slimy, silky mud of the riverbed. We would be skirting the riverbed, but if we had to drop down into it in a pinch, we needed to be sure what to do. This close to the Panjwayi, we might not be able to recover a vehicle, especially in a firefight.

It was a nice morning ride until we approached what looked like a giant earth-covered finger pointing straight into the riverbed. The ridge made a perfect ambush site. It was very narrow at the base and at its bottom there was room for only one vehicle at a time to squeak past. It provided good cover, had numerous draws running through it, and provided an easy escape route to the open desert. Dave nudged me with his right foot. Glancing over my left shoulder, I could see him sunk down into the turret. Suddenly, three muffled rifle cracks snapped over the rumble of our truck engines. Hodge called over the radio to report that a man on a motorcycle was fleeing around the ridge toward the network of villages.

"Told you," Dave said behind me.

Hodge's truck scratched and clawed up the bank, throwing dust and dirt into the air. The other trucks followed in quick procession like fat armored dune buggies. Clearing the ridgeline, they sped across the open desert in pursuit of the Taliban spotter. My team crested the hill and set up on the ridge finger to cover them with our machine guns and grenade launchers.

I smiled, imagining what was taking place. Inside the security of a mud-walled compound in the village across from us, a shocked Taliban commander was being abruptly roused from his peaceful sleep by an excited guard. He and his entourage would have luxuriated for months in the area, preying on the local population for food and living quarters while terrorizing the villages with their ideology of fanaticism. Now, as his scout came screaming into the village with his tail between his legs, he would look over his compound walls and see five American gun trucks and dozens of Afghan soldiers all on line, headed straight for him. Taliban radio calls confirmed my intuition.

The labyrinth of the valley swallowed up the motorcyclist before the team could catch up to him, so Hodge and Jared called to say that they were returning. But the false sense of security the Taliban had enjoyed for months was over. The rumors that the long beards were back in the area had just become reality.

As I scanned the village and surrounding area, it seemed familiar. I just couldn't put my finger on why. Staring at the snaking river, I realized that I'd been in this valley in 2002 as a first lieutenant in the 82nd Airborne Division. We had protected an explosive ordnance detachment (EOD) sent to destroy tons of leftover Soviet munitions.

The Soviets left massive amounts of ordnance, explosives, and bombs at Kandahar Airfield during their hasty departure from Afghanistan. The Taliban loaded the bombs onto trucks and dumped them in a series of large wadis near the Dori River. When I say bombs, I mean some of the worst kinds, in all sizes, types, and shapes. Fuel bombs, like napalm, anti-personnel cluster bombs, and massive thousand- and two-thousand-pounders.

So the EOD came out and blew it all up. The fireball lasted twenty-five seconds and slowly morphed into a mushroom cloud that hung in the sky as the shock wave rolled through the valley, sending Afghans running for cover. At that time, it was the largest controlled explosion in Army history—so big that NORAD, the missile defense command in Colorado, detected it.

Now, the Taliban radios all over the valley came online. The commanders didn't know what to make of us. We had just achieved part of our mission. We had their attention. They hadn't seen an American patrol in years, one commander said. ISAF weren't aggressive; they kept to the main roads and rarely took the fight to the Taliban. American patrols meant trouble.

Jared decided to keep them guessing. We headed west, deeper into the district toward the villages at first, and then cut south back toward the river in a zigzag maneuver. By now the hazy waves of heat poured over the desert floor like water, blurring the images in the distance.

"Who wants to live here?" Brian asked when we stopped.

"It is all they have," I said, taking my helmet off.

Days of crashing through the open desert and bouncing off the bottom of sand dunes had taken their toll. Our backs were tight and sore, our legs and stomachs cramped. I gently rubbed my swollen, sand-crusted eyes under my sunglasses. I could barely see through the binoculars and my head throbbed. Once, in a restaurant while on leave, I was quizzed by a college student who wanted to know what it was like in Afghanistan. "The only way to describe the average hundred-and-twenty-degree heat would be to stick a salon-sized hair dryer in your face at full blast and leave it there for days," I told her. "While doing this, try to stay hydrated by drinking warm bathwater while stepping into and out of the bathtub holding a radio, trying not to get killed."

My headache was quickly becoming a raging migraine. I didn't want to show weakness. A lot of times when we work with conventional units, they stay in full kit, even when it's not required, until they keel over with heatstroke. I learned quickly that there is a time and place for everything. If you don't need to be in full kit, take it off. Afghanistan is one place where uniformity will not just make you combat ineffective, it will kill you.

Operate smarter, not harder. That's why you were selected, remember? I said to myself.

Bill called me over the radio. He didn't like this area.

"Sir, there is no way to establish a security perimeter at this location. We are going to recon a spot on the high ground and maybe set up there," he said.

With the desert at our back and the entire river valley laid out in front of us, the ledge Bill found turned out to be perfect. I scanned the riverbank and the honeycomb of mud compounds and villages sprawled before me. I didn't see any trucks. No farmers tending to the fields, which were thick, green, and ready for harvest. Something didn't add up. This valley should be alive with activity.

Suddenly, Victor, my normally cocky terp, ran up to me, frantic.

"*Turan* Rusty, you must hear this," Victor said, nearly out of breath. "The Talibs are watching us, many, many of them."

I tried to get him to calm down and explain what he had heard.

Usually the term "many" in Afghan math meant twenty to thirty, more or less. Afghan math was simple: Take the number they give you and cut it in half twice, and then it is only about 10 percent of that. Afghan numbers are always exaggerated.

I listened as one commander after another checked in. I counted fourteen total, and all sounded confident and calm. Some even laughed or had music playing in the background. Chills ran down my spine. How could so many fighters get this close to Kandahar city undetected? I tried to write down their code names but couldn't keep up. We would find out later that the village directly in front of us was the Taliban's headquarters in the southern part of the district.

"The Talibs say they beat Americans in Pashmul. Taliban commanders now say they do it again," Victor said.

The Taliban commanders were talking about Shef's team, and his warning to not come here without a battalion of troops echoed in my mind. When we left Kandahar Airfield, our intelligence shop estimated that three to four hundred fighters were in the valley. There were sixteen Taliban commanders in the notebook we found. If each enemy commander had fifty or more fighters, the intelligence was wrong. Way wrong. Good ole American math told me there were more than eight hundred enemy fighters before me, and that did not include those on the north side of the river. The north side of the river was twice as big and most likely held twice as many fighters. That put the total at more than two thousand.

The number rattled me. I immediately thought of the fights at Anaconda and Tora Bora. The difference between those and ours was that those battles were fought in the mountains. This was smack dab in the middle of a city. I focused on our advantages. Returning over and over to the same regions in Afghanistan gave Special Forces a very distinct advantage. We knew the people, the local leadership, the terrain, the enemy. I knew I had hunted at least four of the men I was hearing on the radio, who had been named in the captured notebook. And, maybe more importantly, they knew us. Their rapid retreat from the compound earlier proved that. Hopefully we'd live up to our reputation.

Jared was shocked when I told him what I'd heard.

"Are you sure?" he said.

"As sure as three combat rotations in the same place can make me."

"Okay, I got it. ISAF will never believe this, but I'm going to send this up now," Jared said.

"Make sure our TOC gets the information out to the ISAF ground commanders."

Now we were accomplishing one of the most important pieces of our mission—intelligence gathering. And what we were collecting was not secondhand or hearsay from an informant. It was real-world, real-time information on the enemy. Intelligence rarely gets more accurate.

After sending up the report, Jared passed word along the ridge that we likely faced an attack. The Taliban knew they couldn't fight in the heat of the day. Instead they would wait until evening when it got cool.

We broke out our sniper rifles, made sure all of the machine guns and grenade launchers had full ammo loads, and dug in. As the last rays of sunshine faded, painting the whole sky orange, I split open a thick green pouch of spaghetti and started to eat. A few spoonfuls in, Victor was back, even more agitated than before.

"Captain Rusty, the Talibs are going to attack! They were speaking with each other, talking in strange languages, then stopped talking. Everyone stopped talking."

"What do you mean they are talking in strange languages and stopped talking?"

"They were saying prayers, like, Be glad to be martyr for Allah, *Allah akbar, allah Akbar!* This is very bad."

"Yes, partner, it sure is," I said, heading toward Bill.

Typically, the prayers come out when it's time to fight or celebrate. In the videos of suicide bombers, that is what you are hearing them say or scream: *Allah akbar.* God is great.

As twilight turned to a thick blanket of darkness, the radios stayed silent. There was nothing we could do but wait. Scanning the valley with my binoculars, I just wanted them to come. Combat was hard, but nothing fried my nerves like waiting. It was far easier to just fight the enemy instead of the battles in my head. You couldn't prepare for everything, but you try, and it grates on your mind.

Casey, Jared's turret gunner, first saw vehicles moving. It started with a group of four pickup trucks speeding north along the main road. Several seconds later, another convoy started moving, then another and another. We stopped counting at fifty-seven vehicles, all rolling at the same time. Some may have been decoys because they would stop, shut off their lights, and then proceed again. They were moving important people around the battlefield and positioning their forces.

Jared called for an AC-130 gunship for support but was told one wouldn't be available for at least an hour. The only thing they could send immediately was a 1980s-era B-1 bomber built to fight the Soviet war machine. Its dart-like shape and long wings now patrolled over Afghanistan and Iraq delivering precision-guided bombs. From the ground, it looked like a fighter. I missed the massive hulking frame of the B-52. Bombers are great for hitting bigger targets like buildings, but at twenty thousand feet it was hard to hit moving pickup trucks.

The B-1 bomber arrived shortly and circled high overhead for several minutes as the Air Force controllers tried to talk it onto a target. By the time the B-1 identified a column of trucks, it was short of fuel, as it peeled off to top off from fuel tankers flying a racetrack pattern nearby. We had thirty minutes remaining before the AC-130 gunship would arrive.

Reports started coming in that Taliban fighters had moved into the riverbed on our left and right flanks. Bill and Jeff started setting up ANA soldiers in a defensive position, using lasers to identify sectors of fire under night-vision goggles. As the Taliban moved, we countered. Like the early rounds of a boxing match, neither fighter got within reach of the other.

I stayed focused by keeping up with the Taliban movements on the map and trying to anticipate the next one. But with no air cover and an enemy setting up for what looked like a complex attack, much like the one that had hit Shef, I started to get nervous. As soon as I heard the buzz of the AC-130's turboprops, I exhaled.

The stout Spectre gunship flew over us, bristling with guns. We couldn't see its 105-mm artillery piece, the world's largest airborne gun, and the 40-mm cannons poking out of its belly, but they were there. Radar pods and infrared cameras situated around the guns allowed the crew to shoot with pinpoint accuracy night or day. Jared and Mike stood nearby, and I heard Mike get on the radio and start painting the picture. He described our position and tried to focus the gun crew onto several of the convoys and Taliban positions.

"Roger, Talon 30, Reaper 21," a silky female voice answered back.

Jared nudged me in the ribs. Reaper 21 had one of the sexiest voices I've ever heard. She sounded like Shania Twain to me, and for the rest of the night my mind saw the attractive country star behind the controls, although the way we smelled and looked, I doubted she'd be remotely interested. I turned toward Mike and saw Dave, Brian, Smitty, Bill, and Riley all gathered around the truck.

"Ooh, yeah," someone said.

I wished we could let the Taliban know that their ass whipping was coming from an attractive American woman pilot.

When the Taliban heard the engines, the airwaves exploded with commands.

"The death plane," one Taliban commander said in a raspy voice. They started ordering their fighters to get to their attack positions and hide. The commanders seemed eager to attack and continued to bark orders to their troops for several minutes.

"Put down the watermelons," the raspy commander said, using their code word for mines.

Reaper 21 saw a group of several trucks move toward the river and banked the AC-130 toward them. When she got there, only a compound was visible—no movement. The raspy Taliban commander had also stopped transmitting.

Nothing.

Mike had Reaper 21 fly away for a few minutes, hoping to trick the Talibs into an attack. The buzz of the props faded, leaving nothing but silence and tension. We waited patiently.

Still nothing.

When Reaper 21 returned, Mike worked her up and down the irrigation ditches looking for groups of fighters.

Nothing.

"It must be hard to get good help these days," I said to Jared. We both had a good laugh.

Finally, Reaper 21 radioed back and said the gunners saw a group of eight men moving through the thick brush on the south side of our position. Mike ordered the bird to watch them closely. If they saw a weapon, shoot.

I could visualize the gunners in the cramped plane huddled over their black-and-white screens, searching for a weapon. No luck, but just because they couldn't see the weapons, it didn't mean that they weren't there.

Not far away, we spotted two trucks just off the road. The Spectre picked up two heat signatures, but those men scrambled onto the trucks and took off. Still no visible weapons and the truck didn't pose a threat. Radio calls weren't enough to sanction an attack.

I wanted to fire. I've seen the Taliban hide behind women and children, and it made it easy to despise them. Their ideology does not value their own people, except as sacrifices for their cause. It is sickening and inhumane. Every day I saw my soldiers and others accept enormous risk to prevent civilian causalities, even to the point of letting our enemies escape.

As the vehicles sped off, Mike focused the Spectre north of our position along the riverbed. Again, another group of about ten Taliban were trudging away. This group was moving much slower. David fired a white star cluster in their direction, and they took off in a dead sprint.

For the next several hours, we waited for an attack that never came. We'd won without firing a shot, but watching the Taliban operate told us they could coordinate a large attack with multiple groups of fighters, something that I'd never witnessed before in my three rotations to Afghanistan.

Finally, Reaper 21 flew on to other targets. Mike said good-bye for all of us. We all hated to hear her go. Her soothing female voice was a connection to what we all held dear. Even though we were far, far away from any ground support, we still had the full might of the United States of America at the end of our radio.

After chasing ghosts all night, I'd finally dozed off around five a.m. I woke to the swish of Dave cleaning the dust and grime from the .50-caliber machine gun with a stiff brush. It had been another night in my seat next to the driver, handsets lying on my chest and the weight of my vest slowly crushing my sternum. I cracked my eyes open and stared at the laminated pictures of Rachel Hunter and Dana Delany taped over my seat.

It was eight a.m. and my guys had let me sleep two extra hours, a treat not lost on me. The day was already hot and on its way into triple digits. The Afghans had put tarps up to shade their positions, which seemed unnecessary since we didn't plan on staying. Bill was standing near his truck, and I asked him why the Afghans were dug in.

"Bill, what's with the tarps? When are we taking off?"

"Ask the major," he said, clearly not wanting to get in the middle.

Over at their truck, Jared and Mike had the scope out, scanning the maze of villages in the valley. Jared had a *shemagh* headdress, the traditional scarf of the Afghans, wrapped around his head and his uniform pants on. Like the rest of us, he preferred to shed some clothing rather than invite more misery.

"What did you find today for me to visit?" I asked Jared.

"Nothing. Nothing is moving," he said.

Considering last night's aborted attack, there must be something of interest out there. I took my turn at the scope; no movement in any direction. Not a donkey cart or Hilux truck on the road. No farmers tending the lush green fields that surrounded the mud compounds.

I called Victor and the other interpreters, who had been dozing in the hot sun, over to Jared's truck. "What are you hearing?" I asked them.

"We hear nothing, *Turan,* everything is quiet."

ISAF was running behind schedule, and Jared had decided to stay another night. We could literally be in our blocking position in a hard day's ride. The Army had trained me to do a lot, but the best thing was to teach me to appreciate the simple things: water, clean clothes, and comfortable shoes. Today was a good day, and I bowed my head to give my gratitude.

Bill walked the perimeter to make sure the Afghans knew we planned to leave around five the next morning. We had an elaborate exit plan, and it required everybody's attention. The Taliban knew our location, but we didn't want them to follow us to our blocking position.

Before dawn the next day, on cue, every driver started his truck in concert with the others, generating one undifferentiated roar that made it harder to count the total number of vehicles. The Afghan soldiers hunkered down under blankets in the truck beds. Special Forces soldiers drove using night vision. We crept slowly down the hill and into the riverbed. No one spoke either in the trucks or on the radio.

I watched small fires we had set and left behind burn brightly in the side mirror. Flares ignited large bundles of scrub brush, wood, and boxes left behind. From across the river, it would appear there were still soldiers on the ridge, and the Taliban might choose to hit the easier target instead of a heavily armed convoy. I have no idea if the ploy worked, but we didn't get ambushed.

The jet blue sky was turning orange behind us and we made good time in the rocky river bottom. As we got closer to the mountains, we saw a massive caravan of jingle trucks, dusty cars, mules, buses, vans, and carts streaming out of the valley—a mass exodus of civilians from Panjwayi. It looked apocalyptic. Those without transport walked. It looked like a dark line of ants, each carrying his worldly possessions on his back or in his car toward Kandahar.

The day before, we had learned that Asadullah Khalid, the governor of Kandahar Province, had told the citizens of Panjwayi in a series of radio messages that a massive NATO operation was coming and that all civilians should leave the area. The spectacle was staggering. These people had lived under the Taliban for months and they wanted out bad, so bad they were willing to leave crops in the field and their houses and farms unattended.

Hodge led the convoy to the far right of the refugee caravans so as not to become engulfed in their moving quagmire. Once up into the mountain passes, I watched our vehicles peel off into their respective blocking positions. It was good to see things running as scheduled again.

Hodge's team set up on the northern side of our sector, on a long peanut-shaped mountain called Kheybari Ghar. My team split into two groups and occupied two narrow passes between the mountains to the south. Bruce's team occupied a saddle between the mountains. We set up observation points and before sunset positioned the machine guns to cover the passes. That officially completed our final task for this phase of the operation. All we had to do now was keep the Taliban bottled in and send intelligence reports.

"I'm glad this nonsense is over," Brian said.

"Get ready for some long, boring days," I said, hoping and praying that the bad feeling buzzing in my head was just paranoia.

Chapter 12

——

"SHOOT INTO THE BUSHES, DADDY!"

If men make war in
slavish obedience to rules, they will fail.

—ULYSSES S. GRANT

M y day started with a tug on my foot. It was Jude, waking me up for my guard shift. I hadn't seen much of him on the road during his stint driving Jared's truck. It was good to have him back in the fold.

"Nothing going on out there, Captain," he said.

"I've gotta have a cup of coffee today or I'm gonna break something," I said.

He shrugged and handed me the night-vision goggles. Before I could get out of the truck, he had disappeared into his sleeping bag for a few hours of sleep. I opened the door and pulled a bag of ground coffee and filters from a metal box.

It was just after four a.m., with the sun just below the horizon. While the coffee was brewing, I walked over to check on the ANA. Taz sat with his legs tucked under him, the American-made AK-47 magazine carrier I bought him on the last rotation strapped across his chest, the small squad radio at his ear. He gave me a thumbs-up and grinned.

"*Dodee wharlee, Turan?*" he asked. Do you want food, Captain?

"*Walee na zma, malgaree,*" I said. Why not, my friend.

Coughing and a growl issued from a sleeping bag behind me.

"Roostie." Shinsha jammed a cigarette in his mouth before completely sitting up. He slapped my leg, nearly knocking it out from under me.

"*Sahar pakair, Komandan,*" I said in Pashto. Good morning, Commander.

We could still see torches flickering down in the valley as the long lines of civilians continued to flee Panjwayi. Taz and Shinsha were clearly disturbed by the refugees and the prospect of their country being torn apart, again.

Operation Medusa was set to kick off in just a few hours, and talk soon turned to the Canadian attack. Shinsha was sure he knew how the battle would turn out.

"This is same as with the Russies," he said. "They attack and the Taliban will make defense and absorb attackers until they are too weak to go on."

"This time, though, you're rooting for the attackers," I teased him.

By the time the sunrise sent streaks of brilliant gold light into the deep blue skies above the desert, I was nearly full of tea and bread. *I hope today is better than yesterday,* I thought.

A Canadian special operations unit had infiltrated onto Masum Ghar, five kilometers north of our position, under the noses of Taliban fighters during the night. We heard them on the radio for the first time that morning. Masum Ghar was the northernmost terrain feature, with commanding views of the Canadian objectives. The Canadian plan called for several days of bombing, targeted in part by the Canadian special operations team, followed by a ground attack across the Arghandab River.

The first dull gray A-10 streaked high across the desert overhead, engines wide open. It climbed straight up for several thousand feet, banked hard left, went wings level, then dove like an arrow, belching fire. Like preying birds, bomber after bomber swooped in, pounding Taliban positions.

I stood on the hood of Ole Girl following the aerial assault with my binoculars, my adrenaline spiking. I felt like a Spartan captain watching the Persian navy smash into the Greek coastline.

"Ahhhhhh," I bellowed, bringing Brian out of his sleeping bag, pistol in hand.

"Where, where, where?" he yelled.

"Be cool. The Canucks are crushing some nuts across the river," I said, grinning.

The bombardment was the "softening," or targeting of the objectives in the valley to destroy enemy communications, command positions, defenses, and logistical sites. I had never seen this much firepower from either side in all my tours in Afghanistan. Streams of anti-aircraft fire arched into the sky, trying to clip the fighters. The lofting wave of bullets coming out of the valley was as transfixing as the arsenal going in. This was not a collection of hillbillies. These were hardcore fighters.

Then word came that a general somewhere in the chain of command had moved up the attack without conducting a reconnaissance, or recce, of the target. Instead of following the plan, this general had received "intelligence" that the Taliban were breaking and made the change of plans to attack early. You never conduct a deliberate attack without conducting reconnaissance. It didn't shock me, though. I am never amazed that certain generals, however far away they are, know more about the battlefield than those standing on it.

Jared and I studied the maps and the new timeline. Brian and Dave monitored the radios and called out friendly and enemy positions to the group in order to keep everyone informed. The aerial bombardment had just begun when we heard an unusual noise. I looked at Jared.

"What the hell is that?" I said.

South of Masum Ghar, one of the men attached to the Canadian recce company commanded by Major Andy Lussier pointed to the sky. Andy saw it immediately: a four-engine British Nimrod on fire and trailing thick black smoke. Seconds later, the plane disappeared in a massive fireball. Not waiting for orders, Andy and his men started for the crash site. The Canadians knew the unspoken code as well as we did. Andy could not, would not let the Taliban get there first.

The explosion reverberated deep in the ground. We felt it at our position, grabbed weapons, and scrambled to the top of the small ridge behind our vehicles. "Lord," Dave mumbled, looking at the distant fiery debris. We said a prayer for those on board and their families.

As we watched, the radio announced what we already knew. "All Task Force 31 units, this is a net call. We have a coalition aircraft down. Aircraft is a British Nimrod. Can anyone identify?"

Andy's team was having difficulty finding its way through the villages and around the irrigation ditches that crisscrossed the district. Finally, an American Apache helicopter guided the Canadians to the gruesome crash site. Parts of the aircraft were strewn everywhere across the scorched earth, but the plane had impacted with such force that there was little to recover. All fourteen British crew members died.

That night on duty, I listened to the coalition satellite radio transmission to help pass the time. Settling into the turret, I had the radio in my ear when I heard a transmission about the Taliban leader Mullah Omar and Mullah Dadullah Lang, commander of southern Afghanistan. Both men, according to the transmission, might be in Panjwayi. If they were down there, we would dearly want to be in on their demise. After my shift I found Smitty and we spent the next few hours drilling down on our hard intelligence and educated assumptions about what we could expect to face in the valley. If there were senior-level Taliban commanders and foreign fighters in there, the resistance would be particularly stiff, Smitty insisted.

For the moment, there was little we could do but remain on station, ready to support the Canadians.

The next morning, our radios crackled to life. The main Canadian ground attack had started. Over the next few hours, as we listened intently, the situation deteriorated rapidly. Very soon, Charles Company was fighting for its life near Objective Rugby.

Rugby was a small white schoolhouse in the middle of Panjwayi. The array of irrigation ditches, bisecting tree lines, and dense marijuana fields, their plants taller than a man, made the schoolhouse the natural center of the Taliban's defense. We could see the fight from nearly a mile away. It was vicious.

Charles Company of the Royal Canadian Regiment had come under lethal fire and taken heavy casualties almost immediately after crossing the river. General Fraser's intelligence about a weak, broken Taliban was wrong. In minutes, several Canadian vehicles were destroyed and four soldiers dead.

We tracked the battle on our maps from our blocking position. The concept was to keep the enemy compressed in the meat grinder. "Battle tracking" was the only way to keep up with what was going on and pass the time. It also kept us abreast of where everyone was located on the battlefield. Midway through, my interpreter, Victor, raced to me, his eyes filled with tears. He held out his radio and I tried to make sense of what I heard. Taliban soldiers screaming. Gunfire, so dominant that I guessed the fighter was holding the radio against his weapon. He said the fighters were forcing the remaining civilians who hadn't escaped into the open courtyards and streets at gunpoint as shields against air strikes. Fighters circled above but didn't attack. Stalemate.

Establishing the Blocking Positions (August 31–September 1, 2006)

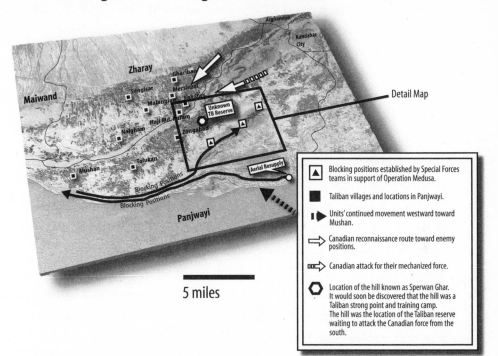

Detail Map

Arghandab
Kandahar City

Zharay
Gharibar
Sangisar
Mersinzai
Malangian
Siah Choy
Maiwand
Haji Md. Karam
Unknown TB Reserve
Nalgham
Zangabad
Talukan
Mushan
Aerial Resupply
Blocking Positions
Blocking Positions
Panjwayi

5 miles

▲ Blocking positions established by Special Forces teams in support of Operation Medusa.

■ Taliban villages and locations in Panjwayi.

▶ Units' continued movement westward toward Mushan.

⇨ Canadian reconnaissance route toward enemy positions.

▯▯▯⇨ Canadian attack for their mechanized force.

⬡ Location of the hill known as Sperwan Ghar. It would soon be discovered that the hill was a Taliban strong point and training camp. The hill was the location of the Taliban reserve waiting to attack the Canadian force from the south.

Ambush at Sperwan Ghar (September 3, 2006)

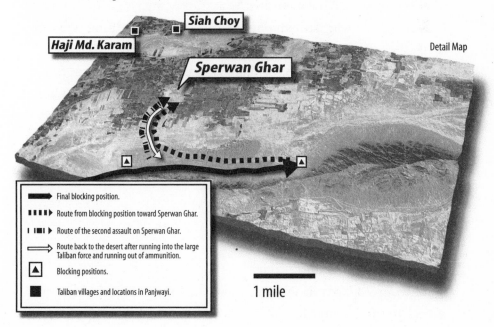

Siah Choy
Haji Md. Karam
Sperwan Ghar

Detail Map

▬▶ Final blocking position.

▪▪▪▶ Route from blocking position toward Sperwan Ghar.

▐ ▮▮▐ ▶ Route of the second assault on Sperwan Ghar.

⇨ Route back to the desert after running into the large Taliban force and running out of ammunition.

▲ Blocking positions.

■ Taliban villages and locations in Panjwayi.

1 mile

Mere spectators, we could only watch and listen to our comrades fight for their lives. After a few hours absorbing the panicked radio calls, I gazed out over Panjwayi. Dozens of thick black smoke plumes climbed into the blue sky as buildings and Canadian vehicles burned. Secondary explosions shook the ground. Each time the fighting spiked, Smitty raised his big bushy eyebrows at me as if to say, "I told you so." The fierce resistance he had predicted earlier was playing out now in real time.

Slowly the sun slipped below the mountains, and I thought of the Canadian soldiers, pinned down and buttoned up in their vehicles in the hellish heat, surrounded by scores of enemies, with little air cover.

We listened as the Canadian infantry moved forward again. This time, Andy's unit would fake an attack to the north to draw fire and Charles Company would push across the river. Artillery and 25-mm cannons signaled the push. The Taliban answered with recoilless-rifle and machine-gun fire, and we periodically heard the metallic thump of RPGs against the Canadian trucks' armor plating. Even with superior equipment, the Canadians weren't gaining ground. The terrain was as much the enemy as the enemy.

Andy's feint was dashed when we heard over the radio that an A-10 called in to engage an enemy position had strafed the Canadian forces by mistake, killing one soldier and wounding more than forty. The whole attack stopped as the Canadian forces reorganized and evacuated their wounded.

Jared, Shinsha, and I stood over the map. The attack had to be re-organized, but quickly. "It wasn't necessarily a bad decision—unless, of course, they wait too long," I said to Jared.

Several critical hours passed.

"This is bad," I said.

Jared agreed. Shinsha inhaled heavily on his umpteenth cigarette, as engaged as if it were his unit in the fighting. "If they wait too long, the Talibs will move into positions closer to the Canadians than before," he said urgently. "It will be much more difficult to use the airplanes. The fighting will get very, very bad."

The whole intent of my training was to teach us always to remain two or three steps ahead and to think like an insurgent. I pulled out my notepad and started to work out the scenarios. If I was trapped what would I do? Where would I go? How could we get in there and help?

Then I saw it. Sperwan Ghar. It wasn't really a mountain—it was more of a tall hill surrounded by villages. It hadn't captured our attention during planning, but now, with the battle unfolding before us, it was clear that not only was this key terrain, but based on their radio calls, the Taliban thought so too. I knew that once on top, we could call down hellish air strikes in support of the Canadian forces pushing west. I picked my words carefully as I pointed it out to Jared on the map.

"Sir, this terrain feature could be the key to success or failure for this entire operation," I said.

For the next several minutes, I laid it out. Charlie Company had attacked Objective Rugby and had been repelled. The enemy's numbers and strength were far, far greater than anyone had expected, and they were wholly committed to the fight. The Canadians had had to stop to evacuate their wounded, and their ability to use air cover was limited.

We had just lost the initiative.

"Look at the defense they put up against a mechanized task force," I pressed. "This is bigger than anyone ever planned. This hill holds too much potential to either side not to own it."

I presented three alternatives. The first split our force between the blocking positions and the hill. The second moved our force to the top of Sperwan Ghar and used the advantages of the high ground to control the whole southern part of the valley. The last option was to stay put and take our chances.

Slowly, Sperwan Ghar became an obsession. The more I discussed it, the more certain—adamant—I was that we had to take it.

"If the enemy takes this hill, and holds it, the Canadian forces will be open to direct observation and will have their flank and rear unsecure when they push farther south," I argued. "No doubt about it. Whoever is out there advising the Taliban is experienced, probably foreign—Pakistani, or worse, Chechen."

Jared studied the map one more time and agreed to call Bolduc and brief him—on one condition: "You can go if you convince another team to go with you," he said.

Jared headed over to his truck and pulled out his satellite phone. Twenty minutes later, he gave me the thumbs-up. Good. I set off to recruit the other team.

I went to Bruce first, figuring he would take the longest to make a decision. He was new and tended to debate more before approaching his team. I understood. No one wanted to come to their team with a stupid idea and look bad. I gave him the same pitch I gave Jared and he agreed to take it back to his men.

My second target was Hodge. He and I thought alike, and before I got halfway through the pitch, he and his team sergeant, Jeff, were on board. I suspected they would have done anything to get us into the action.

"Hodge's boys agreed to go," I stated, walking toward Jared.

"Well, I'm glad to hear it, because Bolduc thinks it's a really good idea in light of the current circumstances and we're all going," Jared said. "He'll call once the movement is approved by ISAF. Get me a plan pronto. We move on Sperwan as soon as I get the call."

I glanced over at Hodge; he looked at me and laughed. "Oh, no, brother. This is your idea, you do the planning. We're just along to make sure you're alive to pay for the case of beer this is going to cost you," he said.

Bill drove over in his truck, his shit-eating grin making it clear he had already gotten the word from Dave or Brian.

"S'up, Captain?" he said. "You know I'm not going to let you make the plan without me."

"This might be a little detailed for you, Bill," I said, straight-faced.

Bill knew tactics better than I did. After a little more requisite ribbing, we spent the next several hours poring over maps, satellite pictures, and checklists. On the satellite imagery, Sperwan Ghar was not that impressive. The ashy gray mound stood nearly sixty feet tall and looked like the world's largest dirt pile. A large berm, nearly twenty feet tall, surrounded it. It looked like it had a large circular pool at its top—probably an abandoned water storage facility. A circular road wound from its bottom around to the top. A U-shaped building at the base looked fairly new; another, smaller building stood a short distance away. Only two roads led to the hill, one from the south, where we would be coming from, and one from the north. From the aerial photo, the site resembled a spoon, with the hill and the buildings in the bowl, accessed by way of the handle. The location was entirely surrounded by compounds, grape huts, and walls.

The plan seemed easy enough, and now all teams would be involved. Two teams would move into the bowl of the spoon and one would be in reserve at the handle. My team would be in the lead, with Jared as the ground force commander (GFC). His truck would follow me, as the command and control unit, as we probed forward. Bruce's team would trail us as the last element moving toward Sperwan Ghar and maneuver to the left or right depending on enemy fire. Hodge's team would provide fire support and reinforcements at the entrance in case we got trapped inside. If things got out of hand, Hodge would knock the wedge in between the enemy and us so we could get out. Shinsha's Afghans split into their platoons and were distributed among the teams.

When the attack started, my team would clear the route to the mountain and set up on the first large berm, covering Bruce's team as they cleared the buildings at the base of the hill. Hodge's team would set up a defensive perimeter. Once on the hill, we'd set about leveling the Taliban positions that were delivering lethal fire on the Canadian task force across the river.

We briefed the plan to the other teams and the Afghans, checked our equipment, and waited for Bolduc to give us his final approval. After more than ten days in the field, I finally found myself with nothing to do and realized that I hadn't talked to my family since I arrived. A phone call home would settle my nerves.

The black satellite phone was hot when I pressed it to my ear. The distant, scratchy ringtones were finally interrupted by my wife's familiar voice. After a short hello and family update, she put my child on the phone.

"Daddy, whatcha doin'?"

"Oh, just getting after the bad guys," I said.

"Be careful. Daddy, I had a dream. In my dream the bad guys were shooting at you from the bushes. They wanted to hurt you."

"Well, what do you want me to do, honey?" I asked, pouring all the support and love I could muster into my voice.

"Shoot into the bushes, Daddy. That's where they are hiding. Shoot into the bushes. Shoot everywhere."

Chapter 13

———

BLACK ON AMMO

*Nothing is as exhilarating in life
as to be shot at with no result.*

—WINSTON CHURCHILL

.

F rom a distance, the westward end of the Panjwayi Valley looked
like Eden. The endless sea of sand slowly gave way to the lush
vegetation that embraced the mud huts and compounds strewn
throughout the fields and irrigation ditches. The jagged mountains
surrounding the valley seemed to protect it from the outside world.

But as my eyes scanned east toward the river I saw the mirage melt
away. Scars and wreckage from the battle stretched for miles. I could
see gunfire tracers and flashes from rockets exploding. Buildings and
vehicles smoldered in all directions. The Canadian task force clogged
the radio with messages about how they continued to "consolidate
and reorganize" under enemy fire. Victory was slipping away.

We had no choice but to occupy Sperwan Ghar. Without control
of that ground, the Canadians could not advance and would be
stopped. Losing this decisive battle would be catastrophic for the
people of Kandahar, the coalition, and all of southern Afghanistan.

The wind felt hotter than usual as everyone loaded up. I checked
the radios inside the gun truck and scanned the laminated notepads

and quick reference sheets stuck to every available empty space below the windshield. Tucked neatly around my seat were ammunition
bandoleers, smoke grenades, medical equipment, water, and signal
flares. Ready, I grabbed my hand mike and called Kandahar.

"Eagle 10, this is Talon 31. We're moving."

The convoy of gun trucks tucked into a perfect V-shaped formation. The route took us down from our perch on the ridgeline and past some green pine trees that masked our approach to
Regay, a small village in the valley between us and Sperwan Ghar.
We'd been watching the villagers from up and down the valley
flee for days, but the scene when we entered the village was still
shocking.

The villagers hurried past us, packed on broken carts, tractors,
donkeys, camels—anything that could move. Regay was the final
stopping point for the caravans of refugees seeking water before
their journey to safety in Kandahar city. Hundreds crowded around
the well. Each villager gripped a bright yellow or lime green water
jug. No one made eye contact with us. They knew who we were and
who was waiting for us.

Some of our ANA soldiers in a Ford Ranger were flagged down by
a man leaving Regay in a faded white Toyota Corolla sedan. He never
stopped but pointed to the hill, said, "Mines," and drove off. The
warning was radioed up to us. "This just gets better and better,"
Brian said.

The open desert faded into Ole Girl's side mirror and the tactical
nightmare of villages and compounds opened up like the mouth of
an immense beast. I glanced down at the map. After Regay, we were
headed straight for Sperwan Ghar.

As Hodge's team passed Regay, we switched the formation from a
broad V to a straight line or "Ranger file" of trucks to maneuver
through the never-ending labyrinth of broken buildings, irrigation
ditches, marijuana, cornfields, and grape vineyards. Centuries-old
ashpsh khana, or grape-drying huts, which stood three or four stories

tall, dotted the fields, perfect redoubts for snipers. I kept one eye on the huts and the other on the dust-covered display of the digital map. We were close to the point of no return, an imaginary decision point on that map.

My nerves spiked as we raced down the dirt track toward the first compound. There was too much vegetation and too much cover. It was harvesttime, a bad time to start any operation. The enemy could hide anywhere. Shooters could be ten feet inside any one of the fields and we'd never know it, until they started firing. Brian, as driver and senior communications sergeant, always rode "dirty," meaning he had his shotgun out the open window, ready in case an enemy fighter popped up. In this case, it would likely come from behind the compound walls or out of the fields.

The radio finally squawked to life. Jared, our ground force commander, wanted a countdown to the marker. "Talon 30, this is Talon 31, two hundred meters, wait one," I responded.

Just as I said it, I caught a glimpse of movement—a figure, half crouching, half standing, on top of the thick walls of a large grape-drying hut. Snatching my binoculars, I focused in on him. I knew in my gut that he shouldn't be there. The jet black turban and dark brown clothing stood out in stark contrast to the biscuit-colored dry mud walls. The hair on the back of my neck rose. RPG! I prayed that I wouldn't see the flash of a rocket-propelled grenade headed toward my truck.

"Contact front. Enemy at eleven o'clock, two hundred meters on top of the grape hut. Kill that motherfucker," I called to Dave, my gunner on the .50-caliber machine gun mounted on the top of the truck. The World War II model machine gun—known as an M2, or "Ma Duce"—with modern optics is as lethal today as it was sixty years ago.

The words had barely gotten out when Dave confirmed the target. "Got it," he said coolly, sighting in on the Taliban position. He cut loose with a long burst, riddling the grape hut. A four-foot flame belched out of the M2 barrel, marking its tremendous firepower. Dave continued to shoot as we got closer.

My heart was pounding and sweat dripped into my eyes—I knew we were driving into an ambush. I pulled my headset down from the visor and called the report in to Jared. "Talon 30, this is Talon 31. Enemy contact eleven o'clock. They are in the grape huts."

It didn't matter if the enemy scout on the grape hut reported our position now. The machine-gun blast definitively announced our presence. I wished I had a dip or even a piece of gum to calm my nerves. But that thought disappeared with the vapor trail from the first RPG.

I saw the first rounds of the battle smack off my windshield as a hail of rocket-propelled grenades and machine-gun bullets sliced into our trucks. After that, there was no shortage of fire or targets to shoot at. From the top of the hill and surrounding compounds, they could see us coming. The Taliban knew what we knew: that Sperwan Ghar was prime real estate and they owned it.

"All 31 elements, watch your sectors and stay tight," I radioed to the convoy. "Gunners, stay low in the cupola."

Enemy snipers target the machine gunners; if our big guns went down, the vehicles would be defenseless. My mind focused again on the scout. How many were with him? What weapons did they have? We definitely needed more firepower. We had M4 rifles, M240 machine guns, .50-caliber heavy machine guns, a sniper rifle, and the Goose, a Carl Gustav 84-mm recoilless rifle, but this was the kind of situation where a mini machine gun is priceless, and I wished I had at least three.

"Eagle 10, this is Talon 30. We are troops in contact. We have twenty to forty enemy one hundred meters northeast of our position and are receiving intense RPG, PKM, and small-arms fire from numerous compounds," I heard Jared radio to our headquarters at Kandahar Airfield. "Request immediate close air support."

Within seconds the radio responded clear and loud. "Talon 30, this is Eagle 10, roger, we copy troops in contact. Stand by." The wait lasted only a few moments, but it seemed like forever. Back at the tactical operations center dozens of men on radios and telephones would be scrambling to find us the help we needed. They would have to coordinate with the Canadians, who controlled all the aircraft for this operation.

"Talon 30, this is Eagle 10. We have emergency aircraft inbound to your target area. ETA twenty mikes [minutes]."

Twenty minutes from now this fight might be over, I thought. Neither Taliban fighters nor their ammunition were in short supply. Shouldering the smaller M240 machine gun mounted to the door on my side of the truck, I started firing at the muzzle flashes and fighters moving near the compounds surrounding the base of the hill.

The firing was heavy from the right side, and the Taliban fighters seemed to continue to maneuver from right to left. But now our heavy weapons began "talking" the way their operators had been trained. This meant that one machine gun would fire a short burst into an enemy position and would rotate with another machine gun doing the same thing, all rotating firing at the target until it was destroyed. This technique allowed us to destroy the enemy using maximum firepower and minimal ammo.

In response, the Taliban fighters unloaded airburst RPG rounds all over us—rigging the rockets to explode so that shrapnel rained down on us. The volleys were meant to take out the gunners and wound troops in the back of the trucks.

"We have fire coming from our six o'clock. I say again, we have fire coming from our six o'clock," my team sergeant, Bill, said over the radio as I shook off the effects of the RPG blasts.

"Move truck 3 and 4 to my left and into an L shape," I barked back to him.

The whole fight was a giant chess match. By putting our trucks in an L shape, we had managed to keep the Taliban at bay on the left and rear and make room for the rest of the convoy to move forward.

Brian called "Set"—the command that the truck was going to move—and quickly turned the vehicle to face the compound. Now we had the engine block between us and the enemy. I had no sooner reloaded my next can of ammunition than Dave called for a reload for his .50-cal. He laid a fresh belt of ammunition in the gun just as an RPG exploded on the truck's front bumper, throwing up a massive wave of dust and debris. My teeth hurt and I had the strong metallic taste of explosives in my mouth.

Damn, we need more firepower. "Where is the CAS?" I screamed to Ron, my Air Force JTAC, one of the most important members of the team. It was his job to call in air strikes and get us the close air support we needed. I could hear the rounds cracking around me as I took a quick look into the back of the truck. Ron was firing at fighters behind us. That was good and bad. He wasn't injured, but he also wasn't calling in air strikes on the Taliban fighters surrounding us.

This time Dave, Brian, and I all saw the source and unleashed our fire into the tree line beside a compound directly in front of us. Almost as quickly as we started firing, it was returned from the compound—a mosque. We were being attacked from a mosque. According to the Geneva Convention, if the enemy engages you from a holy site, using it as a military position, it can be engaged.

Dave went to work on the enemy machine-gun positions firing from inside the mosque. I called for him to give me covering fire and I got out of the truck with an AT4 and a LAWS. The AT4 is a disposable light anti-tank round. The LAWS is the Light Anti-Armor Weapons System for destroying small trucks and fighting positions. Both were made to destroy armor, but they'd also work on buildings.

I fired the LAWS first at the building directly in front of us to get my bearing and range. I might as well have thrown a tennis ball for all the good it did. I heard the loud *thwack* of rounds pass around me and I ducked back into the truck before I could fire the AT4. When the firing broke, I hopped back out, sticking closer to my truck, and took aim at the compound in front of us. The firing procedure was second nature: Front and rear sights up. Three hundred meters distance, set. Pull safety pin. Check back blast. Safety off and fire. *BOOM*. Solid impact. Dust and debris flew from the main entranceway and every window. Just as I slid back into the truck, Bill appeared in my doorway.

"How you doing up here, fellas?" Bill asked in his slow Texas drawl, despite the maelstrom of fire around him. I've had the pleasure of serving with several Texans, and they were all born fighters. It must be something in the water down there.

"I need a round count, things are too crazy on the radio," he said. As team sergeant, Bill kept the guns running with plenty of ammunition. He went to take stock of our stores, and returned shortly. "Got bad news, Captain. We are amber on .50-cal," he said. Amber meant we'd already shot half of our ammunition.

I told him to get some bigger guns going, but he was already a step ahead. Sean, an ETT, was breaking out the Goose. The 84-mm recoilless rifle, dubbed the Goose in honor of its original manufacturer, Carl Gustav Stads Gevärsfaktori, could shoot a high-velocity, high-explosive round the size of a football into the buildings. "We're going to try the AT4 first," he said.

It sounded good, but I told Bill to use the radio next time he wanted to talk with me. He was too valuable to be running around without cover. "I need you alive and not leaking," I told him.

He disappeared just as I heard the sweet *whomp, whomp* of helicopter blades. The AH-64 Apaches had arrived.

"Okay, motherfuckers, now it's really on!" screamed Dave at the top of his lungs.

I turned to Ron and he showed two fingers. Two aircraft. Jet fighters were also arriving on station, and Ron began to coordinate and identify targets.

Since the main effort for Operation Medusa was the Canadian task force across the river, we had to get permission from them to use the Apaches. At the time, the Canadians were not under attack, and they eventually released the helicopters to our control. The Canadian task force had also wanted to keep the jets we had requested, American A-10 ground attack fighters, in reserve, but they relented and released them as well. While Ron sorted through the A-10 mess, Jared identified targets for the Apaches droning above us, which were part of the ISAF Dutch contingent. At his direction, the gunships made runs on the heavily defended buildings in our path to drive out the occupants. But the Dutch pilots were nervous about shooting too close to us. They didn't want to be blamed for friendly fire.

"If you do not engage the targets we tell you, then we cannot use you," Jared finally snapped, exasperated. "The enemy is within two hundred meters of our location and we need the fire now."

The first two 2.75-inch rockets from the Apaches slammed high into the grape house in front of us, collapsing its entire front. The sharp cracks of the explosions marked a good hit. As the dust cleared from the rocket blasts, Afghan Army soldiers to my right cut down the four or five Taliban fighters who came stumbling out of the building dazed and confused.

As I reached down to grab another box of ammunition, a red glow flashed across the hood of my truck. The RPG exploded just outside Brian's window, showering the truck with shrapnel. Stunned momentarily, we were snapped back into focus by Jared's voice on the radio. He was still trying to muster fire superiority to push up toward the hill. Then the TOC in Kandahar came back: "Talon 30, this is Eagle 10. Here is your situation: the enemy count is not dozens, but hundreds, maybe even a thousand. Do you copy, over?"

I shot a glance at Brian. "You have got to be shitting me."

The slapping sound of rounds hitting vehicles got my attention and I again focused on engaging targets with my machine gun. Nearby, the Apache gunships strafed Taliban fighters hiding around the hill. I could hear the giant zipper of the 30-mm cannons tearing up the compounds and irrigation ditches beyond us. Usually Taliban fighters hid when the Apaches showed up, but this time they held their ground and dug in. After a final pass, the Apaches banked, and the low thump of rotor blades faded in the distance as they headed back to Kandahar to refuel and rearm.

If these fighters weren't afraid of the helicopters, then they'd only get bolder now that the birds were gone. I could hear Ron over the radio trying to get more helos. Ammunition in my truck was going fast, and based on the level of fire, I suspected the situation was the same in the other trucks.

As I turned back to my machine gun, Riley, my senior medic, arrived at my door. He had two AT4s, the light anti-tank rockets.

"Where do you want them?" he asked.

I directed him to one of the most active compounds. On his signal, Brian, Dave, and I fired every weapon we had to give him cover as he crept along the backside of my truck. Taliban machine gunners saw him, and their short bursts came within feet of him as he stepped out of cover to fire. He fired off the first rocket while trying to dodge the incoming fire marked by dusty flicks of dirt. It missed the doorway and exploded into the thick mud wall. Riley dove back to the truck for the second AT4. Racing back to the same spot, in the open, he shouldered the rocket and fired. Another cloud of dust flew in all directions around him. The 84-mm round impacted exactly where the Taliban machine gunners had been seconds before. Nearly a dozen more explosions followed, all around our trucks. I turned to ask Brian where we got all the AT4 rockets, thinking others were firing at the enemy too. Then I saw the fright in Brian's eyes.

"That's RPGs!" Brian screamed. Incoming enemy rockets.

It was like standing in a Fourth of July fireworks display complete with razor-sharp shrapnel. In the turret of his vehicle, Zack winced as an airburst RPG exploded beside him, sending shrapnel slicing into his arm. He ducked into the protection of the armored shield mounted around the MK19 grenade launcher and made a quick self-assessment. Seeing his arm still attached and being able to move his hand, he resumed firing at Taliban positions. The MK19 grenade launcher fires tennis-ball-sized grenades for hundreds of meters.

The call came over the radio. "Zack's hit!" Riley darted to his own vehicle, grabbed his aid bag, and sprinted over to Zack, climbing up to the mount, completely exposed to the Taliban, to treat the gash in Zack's arm while he continued firing. It wasn't life-threatening. Riley bandaged the wound, calmly climbed down, and ran to the other three trucks in turn, checking everyone's status.

Moments after Riley left, a grenade jammed in the smoking-hot barrel of Zack's MK19. The grenades had kept the Taliban fighters at bay, but Zack could see them moving through an irrigation ditch and tree line on our flank. Not an ideal time to reduce firepower. Zack climbed out of the protective turret and around to its front, where he hunched over the gun, rear end to the enemy, jammed a steel clearing rod into its barrel, wrenched out the grenade, and repaired the damage. Miraculously intact, he was soon back to hammering the flanking fighters.

Ron hollered to me from the bed of my truck. More bad news: we had lost the A-10 aircraft, which had to go refuel. "Shit, we can't get a break," I answered, then gave the heads-up over my handset: "As soon as we lose the aircraft, the savages are going to hit us hard. We need to be ready."

Hodge and his team were spread out in a broad line, watching our rear in the narrow opening leading to the hill. When the ambush was sprung, my team had moved forward, and now the thick smoke from explosions and fires masked us from Hodge.

"Pop a smoke grenade to mark your position," Hodge said over the radio.

"Negative," I responded. The smoke would also give the RPG gunners a target to shoot at.

Hodge figured he could at least try to neutralize the enemy moving to reinforce their positions and increase the pressure on us. As he maneuvered, trying to glimpse us, an RPG barely missed his truck. The back blast caught the team's attention. About twenty Taliban fighters were hiding in a deep irrigation ditch. They'd pop up, shoot, and then crawl back down and reload. Hodge's truck jerked to a halt and opened fire.

Hodge's second truck belonged to Jeff, the team sergeant; it was also armed with an automatic grenade launcher and quickly pulled up alongside Hodge's truck. The gunner sank behind the boxy green launcher, flipped the safety off, and started pumping out dozens of grenades directly on top of the fighters in the irrigation ditch, strafing from left to right.

The rest of Hodge's team pulled abreast and poured fire down the length of the trench, trapping the Taliban fighters. Bodies burst into pieces as the rounds tore into the group; an RPG shot straight up into the air.

Two fighters made a dash for it. Wearing baggy shirts and pants, AK-47 magazine pouches strapped across their chests, they darted into the open and were promptly cut down by two Afghan soldiers with a PKM machine gun.

The grenade launcher worked up and down the ditch repeatedly. No one was coming out of that trench ever again.

I called Jared and asked him to send Bruce's team up to me. We literally needed to circle the wagons inside the bowl in order to maximize our firepower. Jared said they were dismounted from their trucks in the compound's entrance, rooting out Taliban fighters, and couldn't move. Some dire necessity had to have prompted that—you never send troops out on foot unless they can be covered by machine guns. I prayed that no one got isolated and pinned down.

I found out later what had happened: when the ambush was sprung on us, fighters in the compounds to the left and right side of Bruce's team also opened up, smashing them in a hellish crossfire. The thick walls of the compound offered great protection—so good, in fact, that the team's .50-caliber machine guns and 40-mm grenade launchers couldn't penetrate them.

Bruce had decided to send in a small fire team to clear out the fighters. Ben, an engineer sergeant, and J.D., a medic, led a squad of six Afghan soldiers from the cover of the trucks to the lead compound, where they pressed themselves against the compound's thick tan walls and heaved grenades over to a spot near an entranceway. Their red and green tracers tumbled and spun, crisscrossing the interior as they flooded inside.

Ben and his men found four Taliban fighters in the back of the compound trying to flee through a small door. Three made it out. The fourth fighter broke for the door at a sprint, firing his AK from the hip. He hit the door and bounced back, surprised when it didn't open, and collapsed in a heap when the Afghan soldiers with Ben fired.

The ANA squad leader shot Ben a toothy grin and a thumbs-up. Ben, known for his dry sense of humor, grinned back. The soldiers pushed on to other compounds and the scene repeated itself two more times. Each time, the bond between the Afghans and Americans solidified.

The third compound was really a large, three-story grape house running right beside a deep, dry irrigation ditch covered with vegetation. The Afghan soldiers threw another grenade into the ditch, then dashed across to secure the outside of the building. Peeking inside, they spotted several dozen large ammunition boxes and RPG rockets. Just as the combined team of soldiers was about to enter, an Afghan soldier outside started screaming. Hanging above the door was a Russian 107-mm rocket. A wire at head level would have set the booby trap off.

Between bursts, I listened to Ben's radio report back to Bruce. I'd had enough of getting shot at while we waited on Bruce's team to finish clearing the compounds. I sprinted across the open field to Jared's truck. "Where the fuck is 36?" Our conversation and the explanation played out in shouts over the hammering of .50-cal machine guns and explosions all around us.

"The ambush cut off our element. Bruce's team couldn't get to our location—his guys went to push the enemy back so we can get all the vehicles together," Jared told me. "Predator says we have hundreds of fighters here."

"Well, we need those guys back here now!" I shouted. "If they get stuck in there, we'll have hell to pay getting them out. Can you get them back here so we can get out of this mess?"

The meeting was cut short when Casey, the gunner in Jared's truck, shouted, "Ammo!" Jared and I scrambled over the back of the truck together to move ammunition boxes to him so he could keep the gun firing. The machine guns and grenade launchers were keeping us alive.

Bill came running to the truck. "Captain, I have bad news," he shouted. "We have two boxes per gun and four rockets left. We are about to go black on ammo."

Black on ammunition meant we were about to run out. I reached down and hit the talk button on my radio.

"Bruce, have your guys break contact and get your men out of there NOW! We are about out of ammunition. If they stay in there any longer, we cannot support you."

Bruce called Ben and told him to get back to the vehicles. The teams were short on ammo, but Ben had to get out, and he couldn't leave the enemy a cache as lethal as the one they had found. Taking a knee, he fished out a green bag with two blocks of C-4 explosives from his assault pack. The tiny packages were primed and ready to go.

Ben called Bruce on the radio. "Sir, we have cleared to the third compound due west of your location. We have a large booby-trapped cache at this grid. Cache includes a large amount of ammunition and RPGs. Demo countdown begins in two minutes on my mark. MARK."

Ben ordered the Afghan squad leader to start moving his men back to the first compound. As each one passed, Ben tapped him on the shoulder to ensure everyone was accounted for. Two minutes was not a lot of time. Ben and the Afghans had to move fast.

Ben set his stopwatch and the timer. He glanced at the detonation cord, time fuse, and blasting caps to ensure they were properly set, then he carefully slid his fingers into the green blasting caps and gave a jerk. The small plastic containers popped and spewed streams of thick gray smoke. Ben calmly slid the C-4 into an opening next to a large stack of rockets and backed away.

The calm part was over. "Burning, burning, burning!" Ben said through the radio static as he sprinted from the grape hut. The demo was armed.

"Talon 36, this is 36 Bravo, thirty seconds to detonation."

As soon as Bill and I heard Ben on the radio, we sprinted back to our trucks. Bill warned the last two trucks and I warned the first two.

"Button up, demo in thirty seconds!"

Brian slammed his door shut. Dave quickly dropped down into the turret. Ron crawled under Dave's feet. I got in the passenger's side and hunkered down as far as I could. We were only about a football field away. Two blocks of explosives setting off a cache would be . . . *Whoom!* The flash hit first, then the sound, and a heat wave swept over us, rocking the trucks. Everything not tied down went airborne. Huge chunks of mud wall, clay bricks, rockets, and mortars rained down from the sky.

"All trucks give me a status," I barked into the radio.

"Truck two up." "Truck three up." "Truck four up."

The blast covered everything in a thin layer of dust. I looked up at Dave squatting in the turret. He burst out laughing. Soon, Brian and Ron joined in.

"What the hell are you laughing at?" I demanded.

"You look like a two-hundred-and-twenty-pound sugar cookie, Captain," Dave got out between laughs.

It wasn't a leap to realize that I looked ridiculous, half stuffed into the space between the floorboards and my seat, covered in dust, and barking into a radio. I had to laugh. "What else can happen today?" I said sarcastically.

"The day ain't over yet," Ron said.

"Coming out," Ben said into the radio. He had no more than spoken when the first of the Afghans appeared, exiting the hole in the outer compound's wall. Our rear gunners covered them as they and Ben sprinted toward the trucks.

Hodge's team still couldn't see us. J.D., the medic on Bruce's team, knew we were stuck in the kill zone and took off with an Afghan soldier to flag them down. Running back along the road and skirting a marijuana field, he finally found Hodge's group.

They were under fire too. The safety glass on two of Hodge's trucks had been popped from bullet impacts and was laced with a webbing of cracks. There was no cover other than the trucks, and Hodge knew his team couldn't stay in that position for long. But they were stuck. If they abandoned their rear covering position, the rest of the teams might never make it back out. Our entire situation was deteriorating rapidly.

It was time to make a no-bullshit assessment. We were receiving accurate fire from all directions. We were also low on ammunition. We couldn't push forward to seize the hill. If we stayed, we'd eventually be outnumbered, facing hundreds of Taliban fighters—with no machine guns. I got on the radio and called Jared.

"Thirty this is 31. Recommend we break contact so we can consolidate, reorganize, and call in an emergency resupply."

Jared called 36, Bruce's team, to make sure they were ready. Their fight had turned when the Taliban started firing armor-piercing rounds, which easily cut through our thinly armored trucks.

"Do it," Jared shot back.

"All 31 elements BREAK CONTACT, I SAY AGAIN, BREAK CONTACT! Peel out in movement order. Provide covering fire," I ordered.

Brian called, "Set," and everyone held on. Our truck jolted backward, accompanied by an avalanche of brass shell casings cascading from the roof and hood. The other trucks on my team followed suit, and we stayed in one another's tire tracks to avoid land mines

and IEDs. As we blew back out through the entranceway, the suffo-
cating sensation of being in the kill zone evaporated. I watched the
collage of colors on the digital map fade flat as we moved several
kilometers into the desert.

Round one went to the Taliban.

Chapter 14

SEVEN TWO-THOUSAND-POUNDERS

War is the remedy that our enemies have chosen,
and I say let us give them all they want.

—GENERAL WILLIAM T. SHERMAN

Jared's truck skidded to a halt near mine, enveloped in a thick, choking dust cloud. I grabbed my map and headed straight for him. He was out of his truck, a radio handset in his fist, and motioning for me to hurry by the time I got there.

"Rusty, we finally have a Predator and a B-1 bomber overhead. Listen to this," he said.

The comfort of having a B-1, its contrails weaving high above us, cannot be overstated. Pressing Jared's mike to my ear, I could hear the Predator operator clearly from thousands of miles away. He was probably sitting in an air-conditioned control room outside Las Vegas as he zeroed his camera in on several trucks armed with machine guns and swarming with Taliban fighters. They were moving in and out of an L-shaped series of compounds near the hill. Other fighters were unloading boxes of ammunition nearby, the operator said.

"Talon 30. This is just in one compound. Do you copy?" the Predator operator said. "There are seven total compounds with this type of enemy activity directly ahead of you."

We could clearly see Sperwan Ghar in the distance. We were only about a mile away from the hill. The enemy hornets' nest was another half mile from there.

Wow, I thought as I looked down at my vest. Three magazines left. Not enough to last much longer. I called Ron to make sure he was setting up a link to the video feed. Mike, standing alongside Jared, was talking to the B-1, Jared to the Predator. "This is Talon 30. We need to know the number of personnel and type of vehicles."

His response was sobering. "We stopped counting at one hundred enemy personnel with weapons. There are at least eight Hilux vehicles at the first compound," the Predator controller reported.

Just then, Ron got the video feed. We watched dozens of dark figures as they scurried back and forth on the small screen. Jared leaned in, focusing intently. We all knew what he was looking for—civilians. After several seconds, he hit the talk button on his vest.

"Mike, do you have control with the bomber? If so, level that target. I mean level it."

I marked the enemy position on my map. No matter how many bombs we dropped, I knew someone always survived. This had to be a devastating blow or they'd be on us in no more than a few hours. I grabbed Jared. "Sir, we need this strike to be crippling for the enemy. Let's enhance this by hitting them with a mortar barrage right after the bombs impact."

Hodge nodded in agreement. "Yep, that'll do 'er!"

"We can fire from top to bottom on the target for about two minutes after the bombs impact. That will take care of the enemy who survive the strike and come out of the remaining buildings."

Jared approved it without hesitation. We scrambled to set up the tubes and ammunition. Hodge's team planted the first tube, and the Afghans and other teams followed suit. Before long, we had a half dozen tubes aligned between the trucks. While the weapons sergeants plotted firing resolutions, the rest of us continued to rush boxes of ammunition up to the mortars.

Jared yelled for a status. We responded that we were set. He turned to Mike, who had spent the last few minutes planning the strike and talking the bomber onto the targets.

"The pilot is confirming the grids and inputting his data. He needs another minute to ensure everything is correct. This is a big drop. Ordnance will be one bomb for each building," Mike said.

Jared turned back to the video feed, checking one last time for civilians. Finally, Mike gave the thumbs-up.

"The aircraft is cleared HOT. Everybody find cover! I am not kidding!" he shouted, hustling behind the trucks.

It looked like a fraternity stunt as we all stuffed ourselves into the trucks.

"Bombs away!" I heard Mike yell.

The B-1 bomber was a black spot in the sky. As it got closer, I could see its arrowhead shape dive down, flatten its trajectory, then rise sharply as a series of gray dots fell from its belly. The seven two-thousand-pound bombs streaked to earth and disappeared in flashes, followed by a deep rumble, as though the earth itself were erupting. Then a massive discharge of earth and debris shot hundreds of feet into the air.

"Are we good?" I hollered over to Bill, who, like me, was hunkered down in his truck.

"Everyone is okay," he said.

I reached down and hit the two-minute timer on my watch. I wanted to give Taliban survivors a chance to come out of cover before we started lobbing mortars. Before the smoke had blown away, I asked Ron if he could see the target. Huddled over the Predator feed, he said two buildings had survived and several dozen Taliban fighters were stumbling around the wreckage. More would emerge.

At thirty seconds, Hodge had the Americans and Afghans, mortar rounds in hand, posted beside their mortars.

"All tubes stand by. On my command . . . Hang . . . FIRE!" Hodge yelled.

The consistent *tump, tump, tump* of rounds sang out, accompanied by large plumes of fire from the tubes. Like a conductor, Hodge synchronized the mortar barrage, making sure the rounds kept a steady beat. Still dazed from the air strike, the fighters fumbling through the rubble probably never heard the whistling arch of the ten-pound missiles as they slowly fell to earth. Ron watched the Predator feed as the rounds hit the remaining two compounds and the rubble from the other five. Enemy fighters crumpled as barrage after barrage landed.

Round two belonged to the Green Berets.

Everyone was running on fumes as we loaded the remaining boxes of ammunition on the trucks and gave the guns a quick oil bath. I walked to Bill's truck, and we checked on the rest of the team and our Afghan soldiers. I needed to see for myself that my men were all right. We stopped to see Zack. The metal was still there in his left arm, but it hadn't hit a major artery. We asked Riley for an assessment.

"It's not bad, Captain, but he needs to get that metal out and get treated for infection," Riley said.

I looked at Bill and he nodded.

"This is bullshit! It's just a scratch," Zack said.

I knew the only way I could get him on the medevac helicopter was to promise to return him to the team as quickly as possible. Whether he liked it or not, he had to get his wound looked at in a sterile environment.

"Bill, can they get him treated and back out here on a resupply bird?"

Bill nodded.

"Don't worry, Zack you'll be back out here tomorrow," Riley added, although none of us honestly knew that for sure.

I took a moment to look over Ole Girl. The truck told the whole story. Brass casings covered the floorboards and filled every nook and cranny, overlaid by dozens of empty rifle magazines, ammo cans, and water bottles. Bullets had shattered the windshield and headlights. RPG blasts had sheared off the front and rear antennas. Deep shrapnel grooves scarred the armored chicken plate surrounding Dave's machine gun on the turret. Blackened telephone-book-sized pieces of Kevlar on the hood and sides of the truck were shredded; bullet holes the size of a pinkie finger pockmarked the rest. All of the trucks looked the same. I pulled out a black Sharpie marker and darkened in the "MISSED ME BITCH" message that I had written on Ole Girl's hood two years earlier, this time with more arrows pointing to more holes. Pocketing the marker, I gazed over at the hill again. Today was the first time in my entire career that I had broken contact with the enemy.

One disaster averted, we started working on an emergency resupply. I had two grenades, sixty-eight rounds for my M4 rifle, and a single red smoke grenade for signaling. Brian, Dave, and Ron had less. We all desperately needed ammo, water, spare parts, and replacement equipment.

Bill canvassed each truck, including the Afghans, to get an update on how much ammunition and equipment we needed. Riley, Steve, and Greg inventoried the medical gear. Dave and Zack checked weapons and night-vision equipment. Brian and Jude inspected the radios. Dave split the remaining ammunition, rockets, and demolitions across all the trucks in case of attack.

Shinsha's driver had already broken out the chai when I arrived to check on the Afghans. They were in a celebratory mood. The driver stuck out his hand and greeted me through the cloud of his own cigarette smoke.

"Roostie, *der sha, der sha;* very good, very good," Shinsha laughed, pulling me into a vise-like hug. "The Taliban were expecting much better today my friend. Now they are angry and calling for their commanders and soldiers on the radio. They will never hear them speak again. It is good, yes?" It appeared the air strike and mortar barrage had killed not only foot soldiers, but several commanders as well.

We had two wounded Afghan soldiers who needed attention. I radioed for Greg, Riley, and Steve, who hustled over and began treatment. One Afghan soldier had had a bullet pass through his arm and another had shrapnel in his leg. Neither wound was life-threatening.

The ammunition resupply helicopters were inbound, so we took the Afghans out to wait with Zack at the landing zone. Soon, the reassuring echo of large rotor blades could be heard in the distance. Help was on the way. Bruce threw a purple-colored smoke grenade to mark our position and the Chinook maneuvered to land. Nearby, an Apache attack helicopter circled like a hawk.

The hulking green cargo helicopter, with its two massive rotors, looked menacing up close. It crept into the perimeter, just twenty feet off the ground, its wheels barely clearing the top of a gun truck. The twin Lycoming engines let loose a high-pitched whine as the wheels touched down softly. Wind and sand whirled like a tornado around us. It felt like having your body rubbed with coarse sandpaper. As the dust settled, the ramp at the rear of the bird dropped. The crew chief looked like Darth Vader in his flight suit and helmet with black faceguard. The engines revved and the helicopter slowly rolled forward. The cargo, now unhooked, slid down rollers on the deck toward the ramp.

I walked over to Zack and shook his hand. Bill did the same.

"See you soon," I said.

Zack nodded and walked up the ramp. He was pissed. The two Afghans, wide-eyed, followed. Bill and I loaded them up into the red-and-silver jump seats and helped them buckle into the vibrating, rumbling beast. Both stared intently at the formidable crew chief and then turned to Bill, who flashed them a reassuring smile and patted their shoulders. Both smiled wearily and sat back, still unsure what was going to happen.

We jogged back to our trucks as the whine grew louder. The helicopter bounced slightly, then pitched nose forward and rumbled into the air. Making a hard turn left, the bird gained speed and disappeared over the mountains. I always felt a sense of relief after a medevac, knowing the wounded were headed toward safety. I pulled my sweaty vest off. Leaning against the rear tire of my truck, I poked holes into the top of the cap on the water bottle with my knife and squeezed its contents onto my face. My head throbbed.

Another day at the office.

I noticed a clean hole above the wheel well and poked my finger into it, wondering why the bullet hadn't gone through and hit Ron in the legs. It was probably tucked neatly away in someone's backpack or stuck in a Kevlar panel. A miracle, one of many today. I looked out over the valley and knew this would be our Fallujah—except we didn't have battalions of Marines, tanks, armored vehicles, artillery, or air support at our disposal.

But the stakes were the same. If we didn't succeed, Kandahar city would soon be overwhelmed with enemy fighters, and the momentum of the war would shift. Kandahar was the ultimate prize, the heart and soul of southern Afghanistan and the Taliban movement. This was their birthplace, their home. To defeat them here, now, would be crushing. Conceding a single foot was a defeat for either side.

I fished a plastic bag from my sleeve pocket and pulled out a cross and small cloth American flag.

Unfolding it, I tried to smooth out the wrinkles.

The flag and cross belonged to my good friend Captain Charlie Robinson. He was killed in 2005 by an IED in southern Afghanistan and had them in his pocket when he died. At his memorial ceremony, the flag was bunched in his wife's hands. When she gave it to me, she stared me straight in the eye and made me promise that at every available opportunity, I would make the enemy pay a high price for their actions and her husband's sacrifice. It is a promise I still fulfill.

But that day, I clutched the cross and said my thanks to the Lord for sparing me and my men.

As I folded the flag and replaced it in my pocket, Dave popped his head out of Ole Girl's door.

"Hey, Captain, think we can get a pizza delivery out here?"

"I don't think Domino's was on our resupply request, Dave."

The rest of the day, we unloaded supplies. Two more Chinooks floated in, and at sundown we cleaned out the vehicles and reloaded them with ammunition. No one wanted to talk about the next day. We all knew we were going back up that hill.

Except for a few scattered gunshots, the night was quiet. Around midnight, Jared summoned all the detachment commanders to his vehicle. We crowded around the hood while the major cut on a small green light to highlight the map.

"Gentlemen, I think you knew this was coming. Tomorrow we go back in to take the hill. The movement time is yet to be determined because we have several more resupply aircraft coming in the morning. We will execute the same plan, with one change: Bruce, your team will be in reserve this time. Hodge, your team will be the assault element and follow me. Rusty, your team will stay in the lead and establish the supporting fire for Hodge. I will be second in the order of movement and follow your team in."

No big surprise. At least now we could notify our teams and start getting ready. Everyone was gearing up for round three. The Canadians north of us were also preparing an attack, and Taliban commanders spent the night calling the surrounding provinces, especially Helmand Province to the west, and Pakistan for fighters and supplies. They were determined to salvage their plans to overthrow Kandahar city by winter.

I headed back to my truck knowing in my gut that the next day would be much worse. I found Bill sleeping next to the radio and decided to let him and the rest of the team get some rest. They'd earned it. I'd fill them in on the mission at dawn.

After Hodge relieved me on the guard shift, I caught a few hours of sleep. I woke to the distinctive smacking sounds made by a helicopter rotor and sat up just in time to see the long, lean Apache gunship cut directly in front of my truck. This one had American markings and was flying between Sperwan Ghar and the Chinook resupply helicopter that was settling onto our landing zone.

The Apache's multibarreled 30-millimeter cannon searched back and forth in synch with the gunner's eyes. Several dozen red tracers snaked their way into the sky as a Taliban machine gunner decided to shoot at the helicopter. I heard the pilot call out, and the Apache dipped out of the way before firing back. This motivated the Chinook crew, and the pallets seemed to come out much quicker than usual. Not far behind, a bearded man in full kit walked off the ramp, grabbed a bag, and headed toward our trucks.

Zack.

The bandage was visible from a distance, but he didn't favor the wound. I hollered for Bill.

"Guess who's back?"

"I bet it's our boy Zack," Bill said.

Zack was holding a small sack full of Copenhagen and Gatorade powder. Pure gold.

"Well, look at what I found here, boys," Zack said, enjoying the fact that his little jaunt to Kandahar benefited the team.

"Good to have you back, partner," I said, smiling and shaking his hand. "Have much trouble getting out of the hospital?"

"Nothing Lieutenant Colonel Bolduc couldn't handle on his end."

Bill and everyone else were right behind me to welcome him back, but the homecoming was cut short when Jared radioed that the last resupply helicopter would arrive in two hours. Then we'd move on Sperwan Ghar.

We spent the next several hours restocking the trucks and finished just after lunch. The last resupply bird was still a no-show, and the math was turning against us. If it didn't come in soon, we'd have to attack in the evening. I talked with Hodge and Bruce about postponing the attack, given the Afghans' lack of night-vision equipment.

Jared didn't want to hear it. He felt pressure to take the hill and help the Canadians. We all did, but we weren't willing to execute just because of a timeline. We all agreed, though, to defer the decision until the resupply helicopter actually arrived.

Time moved in slow motion. Teams inspected and reinspected both their own and the Afghans' equipment. Almost everyone spent time checking their watches. The helicopter finally crested the mountains about two p.m.

Two hours later, Hodge, Bruce, and I went back to Jared. We all agreed it was too late to attack—there wasn't enough daylight. Jared saw us coming.

"Don't even start, you three! We will assault as soon as the resupply is complete," he barked.

"Sir, I need you to listen to me," I said. "If we assault that fortified enemy position with an indigenous force as the sun goes down, it will turn into a nightmare. There is a distinct probability of fratricide. The ANA do not have night-vision equipment and don't operate at night. They will shoot whatever moves in front of them. It is already difficult to command and control them, much less control their sectors of fire or rates of fire," I explained.

As Jared weighed my argument, Hodge and Bruce voiced the exact same assessment. He didn't want to hear it from them either.

"Listen, the battalion commander wants us to seize that hill, and you are gonna fucking assault that hill. Do you understand?"

"Sir, I do, and we will, but not tonight if we can help it," I pressed.

"We must set the conditions for success. We do not have close air support. It does not make tactical sense to go up there now. I have done this dozens of times at night with the ANA before. It's a tactically unsound decision. Not to mention that the Taliban are using armor-piercing rounds and a good set of foreign advisors, based on the previous ambush. We can attack in the early morning when we have all day to use close air support. We are not the U.S. Marines. We don't conduct head-on assaults without setting the conditions for success. That means CAS. We're too small a unit. At least call and ask if the assault is an operational necessity. If it is, we go. If not, then ask for an extension till early tomorrow. We cannot lead these men on an assault, knowing we will bury some of them, if it is not an absolute necessity."

"All right, you made your point. I'll call the commander and explain the situation. BUT, if he says go, then we go, no arguments." Jared slammed his helmet onto the hood of the GMV, grabbed his satellite phone, and walked off into the desert to call Lieutenant Colonel Bolduc.

Cooler heads did prevail. I was lucky that Jared knew the difference between insubordination and candor. To his credit, he discussed our assessment with Lieutenant Colonel Bolduc, who wasn't afraid to let his ground commanders make the final judgment. Jared came back a few minutes later.

"We will assault at five a.m. Get ready."

Chapter 15

PUT YOUR MOUTHPIECE IN

Everybody in Afghanistan ought to know
we're coming in and hell's coming with us.

—FORMER NATIONAL SECURITY ADVISOR
ROBERT MCFARLANE (*Face the Nation,* October 28, 2001)

G rowling, barking, and hissing jolted us awake the next morning. A pack of wild dogs was fighting close by, just on the outer
edge of the perimeter between my truck and Smitty's.

Brian rolled off the hood of the truck with the first growl, his rifle
at the ready. We slept on the hoods of our trucks to avoid camel spiders and vipers. It looked like the dogs were fighting over a large
stick. But when Brian and I got closer, we realized that the stick was
an arm, probably from one of the Taliban soldiers killed in the fighting the day before.

The pack was a mix of Afghan wolfhounds and mastiffs brought
over by the Russians and bred for fighting and protection. They tow-
ered over most rottweilers and had the temperament of pit bulls
with roid rage. I didn't want them coming any closer. I'd seen them
maul ANA soldiers in the past and wasn't going to take any chances
now.

"Shoot that SOB before he comes over here," I told Brian, locking eyes with the leader, a massive gray animal with dirty, matted fur and a wild look in its eyes.

Without saying a word, he shouldered his rifle and fired. The bullet clearly passed through the dog, which shot its attention to us, but it didn't seem to notice the bullet. Brian raised the rifle again and fired. The second round slammed into its chest. The dog staggered back, howling, and dropped dead, scattering the rest of the pack. But they wouldn't stay away long. The fresh kill would be difficult to resist, and I knew they'd be back after a while to tear it apart too.

As the sun peeked over the mountains, I started packing up my sleeping bag and gear. My mood turned foul when I realized the dogs had cost me nearly an hour's sleep. We made our preparations using night vision and made sure the Afghans knew the plan. Finally, Jared radioed the countdown to start the engines. As before, all eleven trucks started at once, like the beginning of a NASCAR race.

Dave racked the charging handle on his Browning twice to ensure the new .50-cal round was seated cleanly in the chamber. Brian fiddled with his kit, leaned his rifle out the window, and stuffed bottles of water beside his seat. I cradled my machine gun and reached back to make sure my rifle, boxes of fresh magazines, new rockets, and water bottles were in place. It was just a formality, but touching them eased my mind. I popped in a piece of cinnamon gum and tapped the can of Copenhagen in my pocket. *Dagga tse dagga da;* it is what it is.

We were ready.

"Talon 31 elements, give me an 'UP' when you are ready to go." All three trucks responded in kind over the radio, and I called Jared to let him know we were ready.

"Eagle 10, this is Talon 30, request permission to kick off," Jared called back to the TOC.

In my mind I could see Bolduc sitting in front of the monitors in Kandahar waiting for the show to start. Predator drones buzzed overhead, giving him a bird's-eye view of the action. Modern commanders can now watch a battle unfold live from complete safety,

Assault on Sperwan Ghar   (September 5, 2006)
Enemy Counterattacks   (September 5–10, 2006)

Detail map below depicts the numerous fields, irrigation ditches, and compounds surrounding the hill known as Sperwan Ghar.

① Initial assault position.

② SFC Stube and SFC Mishura hit an IED.
This is where SSGT Voss's rescue of SFC Stube took place during the attack on Sperwan Ghar.

③ Schoolhouse that ODA 26 and CPT Hodges's team had to assault.

④ Sperwan Ghar.
This was the primary location of the Taliban concentration and was the focal point of the assault. Whoever owned Sperwan Ghar owned the southern half of the valley.

⑤ Compound and stronghold of a high-ranking Taliban commander, Hafiz Majid. As we assaulted Sperwan Ghar, horrendous fire poured into our flank from this location, which also had a direct line of fire to SSGT Voss as he tried to rescue SFC Stube.

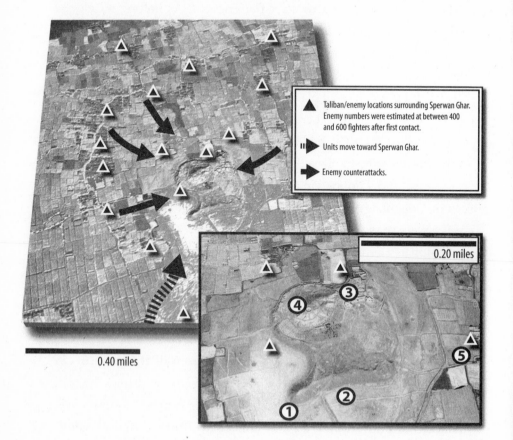

▲ Taliban/enemy locations surrounding Sperwan Ghar. Enemy numbers were estimated at between 400 and 600 fighters after first contact.

❚❚▶ Units move toward Sperwan Ghar.

▶ Enemy counterattacks.

0.20 miles

0.40 miles

but we knew Bolduc wanted to be out here with us, not watching the action on a monitor. But on this day, the Predator was as close as he could get.

"Talon 30, this is Eagle 10, permission granted."

I grabbed the black radio hand mike clipped to the sun visor above my head.

"Put your mouthpiece in for this one, boys, cause it is gonna hurt."

Brian just nodded his head. Nothing more needed to be said. I squeezed the handset again. "All Talon 30 elements, truck 1 is moving."

Sunlight streaked through the valley. The light was a blessing for the ANA, who didn't have night vision, and a curse for us all, because now the Taliban could see us coming. We slowly passed the mounds of empty shell casings that marked where Dave's team had pried us out of the ambush two days ago. The grape hut where we spotted the Taliban scout on the first assault came into view. Hopefully, the Taliban would be still asleep or praying when we got to the hill.

No such luck. The speaker systems in the local mosques that usually announced morning prayers began a call to arms.

"Contact front!" Dave shouted. He dropped down in the turret as bullets cracked around the truck.

"Talon 30, this is Talon 31, contact front. Troops in contact!"

Bill wasn't in the mood to screw around. Calling for us to stop, he snatched the Goose recoilless rifle from his truck, darted out, and took a knee. From behind our truck I heard someone yell, "Back blast area clear!" and then "Oh, shit!" from the back of the truck, as the high-explosive rocket streaked past my door at nearly a thousand feet per second and slammed into the mud compound.

"GO! GO! GO!" Bill yelled before the dust settled. Now we had the initiative, at least mentally. If the Taliban wanted to fight it out today, by God, they'd get all they wanted.

We shot through the dozen or so shallow irrigation ditches crisscrossing the open field and drove quickly toward the berm at the base of the hill. The fire was sporadic and we managed to make it past the point where we had been stopped two days earlier. Had we really just caught the Taliban off guard? Maybe they thought we weren't coming back. Sometimes lightning does strike twice in the same spot. Either way, it was a good sign.

We stayed off the main road leading over the berm to the hill. If there were any mines or IEDs, they would probably be on the road. When we came to the base of the berm I jumped out and took cover behind a twenty-foot-tall earthen mound. I motioned for my Afghan machine-gun teams and shouted commands in Pashto. This was one of those times my seven months in language school came in handy. An Afghan soldier carrying a Russian PKM machine gun cursed as enemy fire kicked up dirt all around us. The rate of fire increased steadily. The Taliban were awake now.

We had to clear a new berm, not visible on the two-year-old imagery on my computer, before we could get a clear field of fire. I crawled to the top and saw a set of compounds and a building to my right. Towering over us was Sperwan Ghar.

The ashy gray hill stood nearly sixty feet tall, looming over the small U-shaped building we'd seen on the map. There were six smaller structures at the base of the hill, all collapsed, as well as several old rusted Soviet trucks and a water tank. I caught a glimpse of movement in the windows of the main building.

I crawled back about a yard from the crest and gave the final assault call. Nearly two dozen Special Forces soldiers and ANA soldiers sprinted off their vehicles toward the safety of the berm. An ANA soldier plopped down beside me, set up his machine gun, and started firing while Bill collected the remainder of the ANA machine gunners and moved them into a line with my position on the berm.

"You—fire north to first building! You—take ammunition to machine gunner. You—protect right side machine gunner from Taliban," I screamed in Pashto. No doubt the grammar and pronunciation weren't perfect, but no one gave a shit at that point.

The return fire picked up and soon a maelstrom of fire rained down on us. Tracer fire zipped so close I could reach up and touch it. Rounds exploded in the dirt near my head. I rolled on my back to try to see where it was coming from. Rounds hit from the right, front, and rear of the berm. I raced back to my truck and grabbed my M240. Leaning over in the seat, I shouted at Brian to move up. "Drive up the side of the berm and just crest the top so Dave can fire! No matter what, stay off the road."

Brian ground the gears into place and crept up the berm until Dave opened up with his .50 cal, swinging the massive machine gun from side to side to keep the fighters' heads down. The rounds punched through the walls of the buildings. There would be no back room for the enemy to hide in. Jumping out of my truck, I dashed along the base of the berm toward some Afghan soldiers huddled behind it. Grabbing a PKM machine gun from an ANA soldier, I crawled with it up the hill and stopped exactly where I wanted it, fixing the bipod legs in position. I fired a ten-round burst, showing the Afghan gunner behind me where to shoot, motioning for him to fire in an arc. He flashed a quick smile, nodded, and went to work.

I wanted to get back to my truck and my gun. I ran along the backside of the berm, dirty, salty sweat pouring down my face. There was no covert way to get there. Rounds kicked up the dirt around me. Bullets cracked, passing way too close to me, to everyone. I needed to get down soon, before one of these assholes got lucky.

As I dove into my truck, Hodge staged the assault force behind the line of machine guns.

"Hodge, it's Rusty. There's a slight depression on the far side of the berm that you can use for cover," I radioed. Procedural call signs and normal radio procedures take too long in the midst of a firefight. You say what needs to be said.

The assault force could set up in the defilade while we fired into the enemy positions, but they would still have to charge straight over the berm, into the teeth of the fire, and then clear a school built on a little plateau partway to the summit of the hill, which we couldn't leave occupied by the enemy. "This school was donated to the people of Afghanistan by UNICEF" was clearly painted over the doorway.

"Now, go! Go! Go!" Hodge screamed.

His commands were quickly lost in the roar of machine-gun fire coming from both sides. It looked like a microcosm of the storming of Omaha Beach. The twenty Special Forces and ANA soldiers bolted over the hill at a full sprint, enveloped in the cloud of dust they threw up. From where I was poised behind my gun, the assault seemed to unfold in slow motion. I could see the rounds cut through the dust cloud, impacting in wisps nearby.

Two ANA soldiers tripped and fell in a dusty tumble. One managed to get to his feet and keep running. The second did not. Another ANA soldier hopped the last few feet to the depression on one leg, his screams barely audible as blood spouted liberally. It was a femoral wound. An ANA medic crawled to his aid as a small group of soldiers sprinted for the side of the white schoolhouse.

They threw themselves against the wall, weapons targeted on the open doors and windows. We continued to fill the rooms with fire. Before they could seize the hill, they had to push the Taliban fighters out of the school, one room at a time. We had no idea how many rooms or fighters they faced.

"Rusty, stop firing or shift your guns left toward the hill," Hodge called over the radio.

"Shifting left!" Dave and Brian adjusted immediately. Bill, who was now positioned with the ANA machine gunners to my right, began turning their fire to the enemy fighting positions on the hill itself.

No fighters remained in the school—any that had been there must have taken off after seeing the assault force, choosing to flee and fight another day.

On his signal, Hodge's team burst out of a side exit and began their scratching, sliding assault up Sperwan Ghar. I could not help but be impressed as I watched Hodge, at forty-one, ascending the hill with his NCOs and ANA soldiers.

"Talon 30. Talon 31. Where is our air support?" I radioed Jared.

"I don't know," Jared responded, a beat before we both heard the TOC come over the radio with the word that we'd have fighters and Apaches to us soon. Fanning out, Hodge's team worked their way up the side of the hill, hunched over with their weapons at the ready, clearing small caves and avoiding the spiraling road, wary of mines. Sure enough, halfway up the hill, there was a muffled explosion and an ANA soldier crumpled, shrieking in pain, his ankle a mass of bloody flesh. A medic on Hodge's team made a beeline for him, despite the threat of more mines. Steve, my team's medic, hopped into an ANA truck and took off toward their position.

"Mines!" Hodge screamed over the radio. The assault stalled. Mines tended to have that effect. The assault team wedged themselves into small washouts in the side of the incline and tried to fire back at the Taliban positions above. Others probed for mines. I called Bill on the radio.

"Link up with 26 and push over the hill now!"

Bill motioned to Taz and his squad to follow and took off at a sprint. I knew if anyone could pry the enemy off the hill it was Bill and Taz. Bill led Taz and his squad up the hill as Hodge's men covered them. Soon, everyone was out of the washouts. Hodge's team literally dragged the Afghans toward the top, firing at defenders above. As they neared the crest of the hill, I saw several hurl hand grenades over the lip. Crashing explosions were followed by automatic rifle fire, then more crashing explosions. I felt absolutely helpless.

One small ANA soldier scurried up the hill like a mountain goat. It was Taz. He crested the hill and fired his AK from the shoulder like a lifetime professional. He knelt at the top, near a Special Forces soldier who was struggling to find a footing under the immense weight of his equipment. Taz fired intermittently, controlling his expenditure of ammunition, until the Special Forces soldier steadied himself. Side by side they walked forward toward the bunkers, covering each other.

A few minutes later, the call came over the radio. It was Hodge.

"We own the hill, but I don't know for how long. There is a hell of a lot of movement down there. Do you copy?"

We had Sperwan Ghar. Now we just had to hold it.

Chapter 16

_____

FRIENDS FOR LIFE

American soldiers in battle don't fight for what some presidents say on TV, they don't fight for mom, apple pie, the American flag. They fight for one another.

—COLONEL HAL MOORE (7th Cavalry, Vietnam)

The steady crack of bullets overhead, followed by the constant drumming of machine guns returning fire, made thinking impossible. Occasionally, the uniform tapestry of noise was torn by the whoosh of an RPG or the blast of a recoilless rifle punching a hole in a grape hut.

Between bursts, I tried to assess our situation. We had assaulted the defended enemy position twice and held. We now controlled some significant tactical real estate that the Taliban wanted back.

Hodge's team occupied the Taliban's previous fighting positions on top of the hill, but the enemy was hammering us from the nearly fifty compounds at its base and from the irrigation ditches, walls, fields, and grape huts that surrounded them.

Bill and Steve stabilized the wounded Afghan soldier with a tourniquet and pressure dressing. They put his detached foot into a black plastic bag, hoping surgeons in Kandahar could reattach it if we could get a medevac helicopter in time. They moved him to the casualty collection point (CCP) near the berm.

I was watching the small Afghan truck pull away with the wounded when Brian noticed movement in the schoolhouse. We needed to know how many Afghans Hodge had left in the school for security, but my call to him was interrupted.

"Captain, Captain, Taliban moving back of school," Ali called over in Pashto, as I glimpsed a few figures in dark shirts and scarves dart around the back of the school.

"I left six Afghans," Hodge radioed back, but he reversed himself half a minute later: "Rusty, the six Afghans are up here with me. No one is in the school."

Shit. Taliban fighters were back in the school. We could see them darting between the windows and climbing up the hill near a graveyard at the back of the building, probing to see if we were still there. If the Taliban held there, they would split our small force.

Hodge, Bill, and the rest were on top of Sperwan Ghar fighting for their lives. Jared, Casey, and Jude were at the casualty collection point defending the growing number of wounded and the medics trying to treat them. The job of clearing the school again fell to us. The Predator that had arrived on station was calling to alert us to the threat moving behind the assault force as I ordered my machine-gun teams to pick up their guns and ammunition and prepare to move.

"All Talon 30 elements: Talon 31 Alpha [commander] is moving to clear the school," Brian said.

Since we were the support fire team, we had only machine guns—not the best room-clearing weapon, but we'd have to make do. Same plan as before—no sense in getting cute. Plus, the hasty plan would be second nature to everyone. Muscle memory over thinking.

"Dave, Brian," I barked before I left, "mow those motherfuckers down when they come out the side of the school. I don't want to deal with these assholes again! Hodge, you have enemy in the school. We are gonna clear it. DO NOT shoot down there!"

Turning to my squad of six Afghans, I put in a fresh magazine and checked the chamber. "You all come with me. Are you ready?" I said in Pashto. They greeted me with a chorus of *"Wa sahib"*—Yes, sir. Taking a deep breath, I screamed *"Hamla!"*—Attack!—and we headed over the berm at a full sprint.

Bright red tracers poured from the guns on my truck into the school while multicolored Taliban tracers streaked in front of us. Taliban in a group of compounds only one hundred meters away spotted us and let loose with their machine guns, frantically trying to zero in on us.

"ZA! ZA! ZA!"—GO! GO! GO!—was all I could muster as we cleared the last twenty yards. We made it to the entrance on the far right of the schoolhouse as bullets chipped away the concrete walls around us. I quickly had two Afghan machine gunners set up their weapons. One hammered the compounds that had just fired at us. The other protected our rear in case any Taliban were feeling unusually brave.

I grabbed a grenade, showed it to the four Afghans behind me, flicked off the thumb safety, and pulled the pin. The Afghan soldier next to me turned and fired into the doorway, clearing my path. I stepped out, peered down a long hallway flanked by about four rooms on each side, and threw the grenade as hard and as far down the passage as I could. Rolling back behind the wall, I pulled the Afghan out of the doorway as the building vibrated, dust and razor-sharp shrapnel flying in all directions.

I heard gunfire from my truck on the berm and knew that the enemy must be trying to move away from us. I pointed to the Afghan soldier and motioned for him to fire down the hallway again. Basketball-sized flames shot out of the barrel of his PKM machine gun as he fired from the hip down the hallway, accompanied by the clanking of brass casings hitting the concrete floor.

I could feel splintered shards of concrete hitting my neck and equipment; the gunfire from the compounds was getting too close for comfort. I considered my options. We could stay outside and get shot or go inside and get shot. I chose inside. I'd place our skills in a room against theirs any day.

With a quick glance at the long belt of ammunition feeding into the PKM, I grabbed the gunner's uniform top and pushed him forward. "Fire down the hallway, I'll shoot into the rooms," I commanded. "Everyone else behind me."

Five of us moved inside, leaving one machine gun covering our men. The PKM gunner was first, I was second. The third and fourth men carried AKs, and the last was my other PKM gunner. Yellow and red sparks from our bullets bounced around the hallway. The deafening roar of the machine gun took its toll. As we maneuvered down the hallway the ANA shook their heads, screaming *"Tse?"*—What?— to my verbal commands, and I realized they were now all deaf. Before long, I was close to deaf myself, despite my Peltor headset.

Shadows moved in the light of a doorway and I readied another grenade. I showed it to the Afghans and pointed out the doorway to the machine gunner. He fired a short burst and then, *thunk*, nothing— a dead man's bang. The bolt goes forward into the chamber with no bullet in it. Out of ammunition.

I grabbed his shoulder and jerked him behind me, hurled the grenade into the room, took two steps back, shouldered my rifle, and fired into the entranceway until the grenade exploded. Dust and smoke billowed into the hallway, virtually blinding us. I heard Dave and Brian on the radio and caught something about fire and smoke coming out of the school. I called out our location and told Dave to cease fire. He saw the explosion and could see no one else on his side of the school.

"Brian, get my truck down here at the breach point and suppress the enemy from there."

I grabbed the machine gunner in the rear of the group and moved him to the front, keeping contact with him as we continued our slow creep forward. I could hear the crunch of glass and rubble beneath our feet and the occasional zing of a bullet passing through a window. We turned a corner and moved through a large, open, empty foyer.

As we entered the second dust-filled hallway, light streamed into the building. I heard Ole Girl's engine and Dave yelling commands as my truck came flying past the school. Seconds later, the steady rhythm of Dave's machine gun opened up.

I told the Afghan to stop firing and peered into the last rooms, confident that the Taliban fighters were gone. Inside, there were at least four smoldering fires and dozens of blankets, digging tools, food, chairs, and boxes. I called over the radio that the school was clear and then screamed, "Five friendlies coming out!" We waited a beat before emerging. I didn't want to come this far only to be shot by one of my own. I stuck my arm out first and slowly peered out, helmet first.

An Afghan soldier was on the berm waving back at me. I turned to my Afghan soldiers and smiled.

"Deersha kar kawi." Good job. One smiled back and the rest just nodded in agreement. I ordered Smitty to move his truck up between the school and the hill and saw the truck moving over the berm toward me. Now we were getting some real firepower up here. I called Jared next.

"Any word on that CAS?"

"Not yet, I'm working it," he said.

"Roger, I am going to move the rest of my team and the Afghans to the school and reinforce from there. Bill, did you copy that?"

Bill and his Afghans came half sliding, half running down the washout of the hill. As he reached the bottom, I told him to secure the far side of the hill, including the school, while I cleared the buildings between the berm and the hill. "These jokers are gonna want to take this hill back. Get the Afghans set in a defense and make 'em pay dearly for it if they try."

Bill moved off and I hollered for Smitty. I told him no one had cleared the buildings between the berm and the hill yet.

"You okay, Captain?" he asked. "You look smoked."

"Do I look that bad?"

"Well, honestly, it's hard to tell, because you never really looked that good," he cracked as we clambered over the small walls on the back of the school and skirted the side of the hill.

I was much more confident clearing rooms this time. Smitty was a natural. I watched him move toward the first building with a singular balance that allowed him to almost flow with his rifle at the ready. He approached the doorway of the squat one-story building and I moved to provide security. He took a knee and tossed a grenade inside. *BOOM.* As dust and debris billowed, we burst into the room, covering our sectors just as we had dozens of times in training. In a matter of minutes, we cleared three more buildings. Bill came on the radio as we were coming out of the last building, calling for more firepower. All of our positions—on the entire perimeter and on the hill—were under murderous fire. Both of my trucks were firing away into enemy positions near the hill. Smitty called back and said we were on our way.

Smitty and an RPG arrived at his truck at the same moment. The rocket slammed into the hill just above his head, knocking him into the door. Zack and Chris responded with as much fire as their guns could muster, reducing the wall where the rocket had been fired from to rubble.

With the buildings clear, I called up Sean's truck to help reinforce Bill's position between the hill and the school. Greg heard my call and gave Jude a thumbs-up as he and Sean started up the hill.

Jude was hunkered down next to Jared's truck as they continued to receive fire. Casey, in the turret, tried to keep the Taliban fighters' heads down as they fired rocket-propelled grenades set to air burst directly over his head, showering the truck with molten metal. Jared, on the other side of the truck, continued to plead for air cover.

Greg and Sean approached the berm, careful to drive precisely in the tracks of the other vehicles.

The flash was immense. "Oh GOD" was all I could say.

The bomb exploded under the right rear wheel well, setting off the gas tank and forty gallons of diesel fuel in jerricans in the back. Flames rose thirty feet high. The frame of the truck shot into the air, sending equipment and ammunition everywhere. Greg, in the turret, was blown skyward, twisting in midair and landing horribly mangled across the front bumper, flames and exploding rockets, bullets, and fuel all around him.

The shock wave from the blast sent Jared flying ass over end onto his back and knocked the air out of Casey's lungs, slamming him down from the turret. As the flames climbed high, Jude, shielded from the blast by Jared's truck, watched as a huge cloud of dust slowly enveloped everything around him. He could barely see the vehicle, but caught a glimpse of Greg through the flames and thick black smoke streaming out of the GMV.

A huge fireball rocketed out of the smoke cloud, bringing with it a long, heavy mortar tube and a boot. The tube landed with a *thunk* next to Jared. "I'm dead," he thought. Seeing the boot, he scrambled for a tourniquet and checked to make sure he had both legs. They were both there.

Shaking off the shock of the blast, Jared sat up in time to see Jude race across a small open field, under direct enemy machine-gun fire and into the flames around the truck, where Greg lay slumped, motionless. Fighting through the black smoke and fire, Jude grabbed Greg and hauled him to the ground.

I was calling for Jared, but he was down, and I was sure the IED had hit his truck too. Screaming for Brian and Dave to hold the school, I sprinted a hundred or so meters across the field, through heavy small-arms fire, the whole time trying to raise Jared on the radio.

No answer.

Riley had just finished bandaging a wounded Afghan soldier when he saw the fireball and the figure flying into the air. Grabbing his aid bag, he ran toward the burning truck, where he could see Jude pulling someone from the wreckage.

I dove headfirst into the depression we'd used for cover during the assault and damn near broke my neck. I frantically radioed for the closest vehicle to provide some suppressive fire. It took me a minute to get to the burning vehicle because I had to maneuver from ditch to ditch. A nearby gun truck finally covered me for the last several meters.

Spent, I clawed my way over the final berm. Coughing and gagging from the dust, I was face to face with absolute carnage. Equipment, rockets for the Carl Gustav, water bottles, and truck parts were scattered around the melting hulk. I saw Jude at what used to be the front bumper dragging Greg's inert body out of the flames.

Greg's uniform was on fire. Jude tried to smother the flames, burning his own wrists and gloved hands, but he didn't stop.

The flames around the truck were horrific, with rounds cooking off at a feverish pace. More than twenty thousand 7.62 rounds, ten thousand 5.56 rounds, numerous rockets, mortars, recoilless rifle rounds, and grenades burned and exploded uncontrollably. The truck quickly became a raging inferno. Realizing they had to get out of there, Jude started to drag Greg toward a ditch.

I tumbled and fell down the berm to get to Jude and Greg. I grabbed what was left of Greg's body armor and pulled with all my might with Jude toward a shallow irrigation ditch at the edge of the marijuana field about ten meters away from the truck. As we neared it, we realized that it was only eighteen inches deep. With no other choice, we stuffed Greg into it.

"This is as good as it gets, Jude," I shouted.

Jude tried to pull out Greg's first aid kit, but everything on him was either burned or melted. He took out his personal first aid kit instead and started to treat Greg's wounds. As he fumbled with the kit, he looked up at me and nodded toward the marijuana field. "I've never smoked this stuff, Captain. Now I'm going to die in this shit," he said.

"Not today, hoss," was all I could think to say.

Ammunition continued to cook off, spraying us with hot shrapnel. I removed Greg's body armor and stuck it sideways next to him as protection while Jude began the head to toe examination, calling out the wounds as he found them. Bill came over the hill and knelt down beside us.

"Bill, find Riley and get him over here fast," I snapped. "Grab any other medics and bring a trauma bag from one of the other trucks. Then begin linking all the defensive positions together."

Bill took off like a shot. We started first aid. A pound-and-a-half piece of jagged shrapnel had punched a huge hole in Greg's hip and shredded his intestines and stomach. We worked feverishly to keep the organs sterile and stuffed inside his abdominal wall.

At first we couldn't find his leg. We figured it was gone, but we finally realized that what was left of it was folded underneath him. What amazed me was that Greg was not yet in shock and was alert enough to tell us how to treat him. His background as a former medical instructor at the top-flight Special Operations Medical Training Center was in full evidence as he told Jude and I where he was bleeding—or "leaking"—and how to stop it. While Jude packed the large open wound and I tried to secure his neck, Greg continued to spit up blood.

Squatting in the ditch, I could see that the nylon pouches on Jude's body armor were slick, partially melted from the flames, and his beard was smoking. His hands were obviously swelling and very sensitive after patting out the burning equipment on Greg's body. But he never quit working on Greg.

Sean, the ETT, was missing; I hadn't seen him since the explosion. "Where is Sean?" I screamed to Jude over the explosions.

Jude shrugged. "I didn't see him in the vehicle."

Taking that as a sign he might still be alive, I went to look for him. I would leave no one out here. I scrambled on all fours out of the ditch, past the front of the truck, and into the smoke on the high side of the vehicle, waving my arm around in front of me, trying to clear the air. The noxious black cloud made my eyes and nose burn, and as soon as I got my first lungful, I threw up.

The smoke smothered me as I focused on searching for Sean. Then, just up the hill on the north side of the vehicle, I saw a dark figure slumped on the side of the berm. It was Sean. The explosion had blown him through the driver's door into the hill. He had tried to crawl back to the truck to help Greg but never made it. He moved when I grabbed his arm, but his respirations were shallow, probably from breathing in all that toxic smoke.

"Let's go partner! I gotcha," I said.

I grabbed the drag handle on his equipment and pulled him out of the noxious cloud, then half carried, half dragged him toward the ditch. He became somewhat responsive in the fresher air and staggered the rest of the way. I placed him head to head with Greg, so we could watch both of them and protect one another. The Taliban fighters were now taking deliberate shots at us, and their rounds sliced through the nearby marijuana plants, which tumbled into our position as they were cut down. My back to the fire, I was sure they'd shoot me in the ass.

Sean was not on this planet. He kept trying to crawl out of the ditch to look for Greg, and I had to hold him down while we assessed his injuries. I ran my hands under his helmet and opened his body armor, rolled him to his side and searched his back. I combed his entire body from head to foot, but found no major trauma—only small cuts and bleeding from his nose and ears.

"You are one blessed SOB," I told him.

Riley had been with a wounded Afghan when he saw the explosion and headed for it, but it had taken time for him and J.D. to cross over from their position. As soon as he got to us, Riley grabbed me and screamed into my face, "Which one is worse?"

I pointed to Greg, and Riley knelt next to him, ripping open his aid bag. Greg was totally black from head to toe, and Riley didn't know who he was treating until Greg started talking.

"I think I can move Sean to the CCP," I shouted.

"Wait a minute," Riley said.

Jude gave Riley an update on Greg's injuries. Riley had never seen injuries like Greg's. Even in the Special Forces medics course he never imagined he'd see someone so damaged. He started cutting off Greg's charred uniform. Each time he pulled away a piece, he found a new injury. Fractured ankle. Broken tibia. Shrapnel wounds in his knee. Third-degree burns from his waist down.

When Riley got to Greg's right buttock, he found a hole the size of his fist going straight into Greg's abdomen, where a huge piece of shrapnel had blown through and lodged deep, exposing the intestines. It was the same devastating wound we had tried to treat.

"How is he?" I screamed over the steady rattle of machine-gun fire.

If Riley shook his head up and down, he thought Greg would make it. But he and Jude both shook their heads no, and my heart sank. Greg's wounds were way beyond what we could treat.

"His heart rate is low as well as his blood pressure. He needs blood and level-three attention fast," Riley said. "He's in the golden hour."

This meant that we basically had one hour to get Greg to a medical facility before it was too late. Riley continued to treat him, but the irrigation ditch was too dangerous. The Taliban were now focusing their undivided attention on our position. Dirt and debris continued to rain down on us and into Greg's wounds. I had to get Sean to the casualty collection point. I didn't want him to be there if Greg died.

Bill sent two Afghan soldiers down to cover us. Another small explosion sent more truck parts and recoilless-rifle rounds shooting past us. Riley, J.D., and Jude instinctively hunched over Greg as I hovered over Sean, trying to protect them from further injury. We had to move.

Jude ran back to Jared's truck and grabbed a stretcher, got back and unfolded it, only to realize it had been broken in the initial blast. He raced back to get another. I told Sean I was going to move him to a safer spot and managed to lift him to his feet. I slid my arm underneath the back of his shirt and grabbed his collar. Slinging his arm over my neck, I grabbed the front of his belt until he could get his legs moving.

Diving into the marijuana field on the other side of the berm, we staggered our way through the thick stalks, which snapped back to slap us as we shoved past them. I could hear Casey's .50 cal firing, and we moved toward the sound. We finally made it through the field before both of us collapsed.

"Do you remember what your name is?" I asked.

"Yeah, Sean," he said.

"Do you know what day it is?" I asked.

"I don't know," Sean said, and I smiled.

"Well, can you get to your feet? Because I can't carry your big ass over this berm," I said.

He shook his head yes. We made it about ten yards from the top of the berm, when he suddenly collapsed on top of me. I grabbed both his arms and with him on my back half dragged, half carried him toward Jared's vehicle. My legs wobbled like a newborn's and my back gave out after a few steps. We went down in an exhausted heap. Jared ran over when he saw us fall, looking himself like someone had cleaned his clock in a bar fight. I asked if he was okay. He said yes and took Sean.

I lumbered back to Jude's position, where Riley was still working on Greg. The enemy fire was increasing. Riley needed everyone to move before someone got shot. I told him the casualty collection point was near Jared's truck and then moved to link up with Bill, stopping to make sure nobody had left any sensitive items like night-vision goggles in the ditch. Behind me, I watched an Afghan soldier pick up Greg, throw him over his shoulder, and carry him to safety.

The vehicle continued to burn. I looked at the small ditch where we all had just been. The dry wheat-like grass was mashed flat and covered in blood. Used first aid supplies, needle cases, tubing, bits of clothing, and plastic wrappers littered the ground. Then I noticed the bloodstains all over my gloves, sleeves, and pouches.

When I got back to the casualty collection point, Jared grabbed my arm. "We have medevac birds inbound in thirty minutes. CAS will come in with them. Get me a target list pronto!"

Armored gun trucks were circled like wagons around the wounded in the center of the CCP. Men lay sprawled on litters with medics hovering around them. Jude was busy convincing the medics that his burns were not that bad and he could still fire a weapon.

My thoughts circled back to Greg. He had been in a Special Forces unit before and knew the mission could be deadly, but he hadn't just volunteered, he'd insisted on coming. I second-guessed my decision to let him join us and didn't know how I'd explain it to his one-year-old son.

At the CCP, Greg was convinced he was going to die. Every time he took a breath, his body wrenched in unimaginable pain. Riley pumped him full of antibiotics and painkillers, hoping to ease his fears. Riley tried to keep him talking: Fishing. Hunting. About the old days in training. Anything to keep his mind off the pain.

"You okay, man?" he asked as he snapped on a tourniquet and wrenched it down. Greg screamed. Grabbing Greg's penis, Riley moved it out of the way so he could apply another tourniquet higher on his leg.

"Hey, Riley," Greg said between tortured breaths. "If I die, last thing you're going to remember about me is that you touched my dick."

"Fuck you, homo," Riley said, wrestling to secure the tourniquet to staunch the bleeding from Greg's mangled right leg.

As the medevac helicopter approached, Greg refused to fly until he talked with Jared and Jude. They ran over and knelt by his side. He told Jared he was proud to serve with our unit and that it wasn't his fault. He'd volunteered to go on the mission. Greg's message to Jude was simple.

"You are a friend of mine for life, if you like it or not," Greg told him.

Jude smiled. "I feel the same way."

Chapter 17

———

"THESE JOKERS
JUST DON'T GIVE UP!"

Will yourself to stand ready and courageous on the battlefield.
In this way, all that is difficult or dangerous will be yours.

—THE WAY OF THE SAMURAI

T he image of my broken men weighed heavily on my mind as I
scrambled back through the marijuana field. This attack, this
hill was, after all, my idea. I looked down at my hands and body armor, smeared with blood. Most commanders are not on the ground
with their men when they get hurt or die. In this business, you are,
and you know the names of their wives and kids.

When I met up with Bill, he said we needed to request another
emergency resupply of ammunition.

"I know, Bill, just get me the numbers of supplies we need," I responded. "It looks like we finally may have close air support coming
in, and I need you to get me targets from your side of the perimeter.
We also need to go tell the rest of the team about Greg and Sean."

Most already knew they were wounded, just not how badly. Bill
and I staggered back up the two-story berm. Exhausted and soaked
with sweat, we sank down and rolled over on our backs, gasping for

air. I'd never been more tired, even during Ranger school and the Special Forces Qualification Course.

"Hey Captain, we're probably going to get shot up here," Bill joked.

"After what we just lived through, I doubt it, Bill," I managed, gulping in air. "I honestly never thought we would live this long."

I reached into one of my ammunition pockets with my torn, bloody glove and pulled out a small hand-crafted silver snuff tin. It was a gift from Shinsha. I offered Bill some Copenhagen. Both of us took a second to hang a dip and sip from our warm CamelBaks. The team needed us both focused, and the momentary break allowed us to collect ourselves.

The break was short-lived. *Thwack, thwack.* Two rounds hit the dirt beside us, breaking up our little corporate meeting.

"Shit," I said, rolling over and tumbling down the berm to the shelter of the depression. This was the third time today I'd found myself in this hole.

"Don't these fuckers ever give up?" Bill said.

"I reckon not," I replied before we took off for the safety of the vehicles.

Back at the truck, I heard the familiar chugging of rotor blades. I could barely hear Jared call me on the radio through the sweat accumulated in my earphones. I pulled the ear cups off and spilled it out.

"Rusty, you and Ron control the rotary-wing aircraft and Mike and I will control the fixed-wing," I heard him transmit.

The medevac was inbound and called soon after.

"Talon 31, this is Viper 08, I am coming in from the southeast on a one-hundred-fifty-five-degree azimuth. I am five kilometers out from your location with medevac in tow. Call sign is Dustoff 03. Request approach azimuth for medevac and current ground situation."

Ron had the map in front of him and he gave me a hard look. "Not now, Captain," he said firmly. "I have to plot the enemy compounds." I knew what he was saying, and I didn't mind taking directions from him. What he was working on was the most important issue—air support.

I also couldn't lie to the pilot, but I fervently didn't want to tell him the truth either. I didn't want him to call off the medevac because he was afraid of getting shot down. But at this point that was a very real concern. I decided to lay it all out.

"Viper 08, this is Talon 31. Please pass to Dustoff 03. Current ground situation is not good. I am three units on one terrain feature surrounded by enemy as close as fifty meters and as far as one kilometer. We are in a large teardrop-shaped open area with a hilltop that looks like a volcano. We own the high ground and the U-shaped building fifty meters northeast. Expect ground fire on approach and exfil. I have eight casualties who need immediate medical evacuation. Some are Americans. I can talk on the Viper 08 to known enemy locations but expect more ground fire than you can suppress. Talon 30 will control Dustoff 03 and I will control Viper 08. Do you copy?"

The long pause concerned me. The pilots were weighing their options. I was starting to second-guess my decision to lay it out when the radio crackled to life.

"Talon 31, this is Viper 08. I am coming in to the northeast for a marking pass and will suppress while Dustoff 03 comes in."

Relief.

"Hot damn, now we're in business!" I shouted.

This time the Apache attack helicopter didn't make circles, but flew swiftly over our position as we held out a large orange panel. As soon as the Taliban saw the Apache, they opened fire. The Apache peeled off; we stowed the panel and fired back.

"Talon 31, I see you. Where do you want it?"

Behind the schoolhouse wall, Ron plotted the targets on his map with a compass, GPS, and pencil while I talked to the Apache. We needed to hammer the remaining fighters long enough for the Chinook to get the wounded out.

"Viper 08, next pass, come hot. Concentrate your fire on the east-west-running irrigation ditch due north of my marking about one hundred meters. There you should see two grape houses and a compound joining the irrigation ditch. Hit all three of them as hard as you can on the first pass and then we will guide you in on the next pass."

The Chinook circling in the distance was now tucked in behind the attack helo.

"Roger, get your heads down," the pilot said.

It seemed funny that the pilot wanted us to duck.

I heard Jared call in something about red-colored smoke to the medevac pilot, then the familiar *whoosh, whoosh, whoosh* of rockets and the grumbling *bup, bup, bup* of cannon fire erupted overhead. The rockets smashed into the ditch as the Apache shot skyward, preparing for a second pass. In the attack helicopter's wake, the Chinook banked hard to the left and seemed to drop out of the air near the red smoke column. The pilots didn't want to expose the helicopter's belly to Taliban fire.

Jared and about six guys from Team 36 carried the wounded, IV bags in their teeth, to the waiting helicopter.

Taliban rockets and machine guns immediately zeroed in on the helicopter. I heard the *tunk* of bullets piercing the hull. An RPG flew past the helicopter's tailgate near Jared's truck and exploded into the berm wall. The American pilot never wavered. He stayed in place as the medics rushed the wounded into the helicopter's belly.

Our guns hammered every position we could identify. I told Viper 08 to watch our tracer fire and come in closer.

"Closer?" he asked hesitantly.

"Roger, danger close," I responded. "Danger close" was not a term ever taken lightly. It was only used as a last resort and meant that the soldiers calling in the air strike will possibly be hit with the ordnance they are calling for. The slightest deviation in the targeting of the rockets, aircraft, or rounds meant you had just wounded or killed yourself. It was perfect or you were dead.

Dave banged away at the building and tree line with his .50-cal machine gun, marking the spot for the pilot. The Apache swooped in just above us. Rockets and 30-mm cannon fire leveled the tree line and smashed the building.

"Very nice," Brian said, flashing a freckled grin.

It was then that the small, clear voice of a child reminded me to "shoot into the bushes, Daddy, shoot into the bushes." The moment gave me goose bumps.

"Earlier we couldn't convince the other birds to fire that close," Dave added.

Behind us, the Chinook's rotors whined as it prepared to take off. As they gained power, a huge dust cloud mushroomed out in all directions, cutting visibility. A blessing for the helicopter.

"Everyone on the perimeter, find a target and open fire," Jared radioed to the teams.

I heard Dustoff 03 call Viper 08: "I'm coming out."

The helicopter leapt into the air. "Now! Now! EVERYONE open fire!" I barked into the radio.

We flicked the kill switch on. My three remaining trucks, Bruce and Hodge's team, ETTs, interpreters, and the ANA soldiers opened fire on the compounds and grape huts. Everyone who could fire a weapon started shooting.

As the helicopter rose through the dust cloud and banked hard toward the open desert, I said a silent prayer for those inside we probably would never see again. With the Chinook out of harm's way, I called for another pass from the Apache.

"Viper 08, this time I need for you to come in and make a run on the three buildings only. Do you copy?" I said.

I was not happy with his reply.

"Talon 31, sorry, got to go. Escort for Dustoff 03. You guys be safe. Viper 08 out."

Just then, a round shot straight between Ron and me. I winced visibly and scooted to the back of my truck. My nerves were shot. I ducked down under the rear tire as a volley of RPG and recoilless-rifle fire crashed into the schoolhouse. Someone screamed "Incoming!" as explosions from mortars shook the ground and enemy machine-gun fire peppered the vehicles. I was rattled. Collecting myself, I shouldered my rifle and fired. Brian and Dave were, as always, cool as cucumbers.

The windows in the three compounds directly across from my support vehicle flickered wildly. An ANA platoon leader screamed, *"Der dushman!"* Many enemies!

Flashes from bullet impacts wreathed our positions. The truck engine whined, almost as if in agony, as Brian roared back about ten meters toward a concrete latrine, desperately seeking some cover. I expected any minute to see Ole Girl burst into flames around us.

We faced well over two hundred enemy, and their numbers were growing. We'd already fired rockets into the compound, but hadn't slowed them down. More Taliban simply occupied the building.

Bill moved the Carl Gustav recoilless rifle from his truck and fired a half dozen rockets at the large compound. The 84-mm high-explosive rounds blew large chunks from the thick walls but didn't penetrate. "Captain, I just can't punch that thing!" he yelled.

All three compounds kept up a steady stream of machine-gun fire. Brian called out that fighters were moving to the left. I crawled up the side of the truck and into my seat.

"Show me," I said.

Dave let out a long burst from the .50 cal. The rounds riddled a three-sided wall and irrigation ditch a football field away. It was a counterattack. I called Jared immediately.

"Sir, we have a no-shit counterattack of sixty to eighty enemy coming from the northeast, maybe more. Distance is about one hundred to two hundred meters."

Jared came back moments later with a shocking order: "Pack up and be prepared to move."

"Move where?" I asked.

"Fall back to the desert."

I refused to accept it. I knew that if we gave up the high ground, the enemy would be on top of us in no time, intermingled with our forces, causing unspeakable carnage. We would be mauled. All of my experience as a soldier screamed that we had to make a stand.

"Move? Where the fuck are we gonna go? Back to the fucking desert? I will not fall back off this hill. We have paid for it in blood. This fucking hill is ours and I refuse to give it back to those fucking savages. They can have it if they can take it! Let them get a mouthful of attacking OUR defenses."

Hodge and Bruce agreed. We stay.

Up to this point, I had tried to be controlled and methodical, but a primal rage consumed me. The feeling is indescribable. There are very few in our society, other than soldiers, who understand it. It is the physical combination of adrenaline, testosterone, exhaustion, and emotion. My rage surfaced, and it unleashed a previously harnessed power. Whatever it is that the brain produces during those moments, I liked it—no, I loved it. I knew we could hold. Instantly, I felt all my exhaustion leave me and my nerve restored. I paused to look around, ignoring the radio.

Jared knew I would not change my mind, and his orders confirmed it. "All right, everyone, dig your heels in. If you think we can hold it, we will make the school our Alamo. I am going to pull the lanyard. All 30 elements, move to the school and hill. Hold your positions and stay low. The sky is about to fall."

There was no choice but to keep the enemy at bay and try to grind them to a pulp.

We owned the high ground this time, and the RPGs and recoilless rifles simply could not shoot uphill without hitting the berm or shooting over our heads. Ali's men spotted a group of fighters trying to set up on a nearby roof—an RPG is most effective on a flat trajectory—but Ali's machine gunners caught them in the open and left them up there.

On the top of the hill, Hodge's team didn't have enough firepower. Jared sent Bruce's team to reinforce them. Engineers had come in with the resupply aircraft and they, along with our team engineers, began the dangerous and painstaking work of probing for mines under fire. They uncovered another IED in the road and several antipersonnel mines on the top of the hill.

We were holding on, but just barely, when the Taliban hit the school with a recoilless rifle and set one room ablaze. Taliban radio intercepts flooded the airwaves with requests for reinforcements at the "commander's palace." The Taliban communicated predominantly in code. Fresh fighters had come from across the river and had no idea where to go. Typically, they would wander around, calling the commander every few minutes until they found their linkup. The advantage to us of this type of bumbling was that they had no real sense of tactical movement and could be outmaneuvered and killed. The disadvantage was that they could show up anywhere, anytime, and surprise you. They did both.

At first the radio call made no sense, until I started to scan the compounds.

"Brian, Dave," I asked, "do any of those compounds look like a palace or a place that belongs to a senior Taliban commander to you? Anything especially ornate or out of place?"

Ron quickly pointed out the cluster of compounds we had been ambushed from on the first day. They had high walls, large grape houses, and ample, once-manicured fields now decimated by gun runs from the Apaches. It had to be the place.

Suddenly, the whine of jet engines filled the air. "Here they come," Jared said excitedly. Mike, standing on Jared's truck, now orchestrated nearly a dozen inbound aircraft. We'd finally gotten the air support we needed, and the fighters and bombers swarmed around us like hornets waiting for their chance to strike. A refueling tanker had also been brought in to keep the fighters on station. The modern angels of the battlefield would finally level the playing field.

Ron, sitting in the back of my truck, turned on his computer to get a video downlink so we could confirm the target and description. Otherwise, the ordnance could end up on top of us. The snowy gray-and-white screen flickered, but no picture resolved. Ron called the aircraft to confirm the code again, but it was no use. There would be no video feed today.

"I got it under control, Captain. I'll do this talk on and we'll start putting this stuff right up their ass," Ron said, throwing the computer back into the truck.

Mike started passing aircraft over to Ron, and I ran over to him with my map and GPS to confirm the targets. Ron held up four fingers, indicating that four aircraft were available.

"Level that one damn building if you do nothing else!" I said.

"Captain, the pilot says we are two hundred meters away. It is officially 'danger close' for a bomb that big," Ron told me between radio calls. "The pilot wants your initials."

I knew exactly what that meant. If the bomb blast killed any friendly forces, the pilot did not want to be held responsible. I understood but didn't have much choice.

"Romeo Bravo," I said.

Moments later, I heard the shrieking sound of jets dropping altitude and looked up to see two A-10 Warthogs swoop in, wings loaded with missiles, bombs, and rockets.

"Okay, I have a solution and verbal target confirmation," Ron said. "That building will be the first to go. One thousand-pound bomb in thirty seconds."

Wasting no time, I put out a net call over the radio to notify everyone and closed the door on my truck, as if that would do any good if the bomb was off target. But a sense of security is all. I noticed an Afghan soldier looking over the edge of his foxhole, ignorant of the danger, and yelled at the top of my lungs for him to get down. WHOOM! The entire building vanished in an upward cloud of smoke and dust. The rolling energy from the blast streaked across the short field, roiling the tall marijuana plants, racing up the hill like an invisible tidal wave.

"Two more coming, stay down!" Ron yelled.

Two more thousand-pounders crashed into the buildings, sending more waves. Everything hit on target, and an eerie silence followed the blasts.

"Gun runs!"

The short steady burping of cannons from the A-10s shattered the silence. Trees snapped and burst in slow motion, rolling through the air as exploding shells ripped them to splinters. The irrigation ditches that once provided cover became death traps. Shells landed on the Taliban fighters huddled there, each round bursting a bucket full of hot steel in all directions.

"That should take some piss out of them," Ron said, feeding adjustments to the pilots between runs to maximize the carnage.

Whoever was advising the Taliban understood the gravity of the situation. They made the only plausible decision and tried to close the gap between us, hoping to make it impossible to bomb their position without hitting us. Too bad for them, we had planned for that. We had discussed this type of situation in the team room prior to deployments. We had all decided we would rather die in a botched rescue attempt by another American than have our heads cut off on the Internet for our families to see. I had already made up my mind that if I was going to die today, I would rather do so fighting than retreating and getting shot in the back.

The airwaves flooded with wounded Taliban leaders and foot soldiers calling for help. A Taliban commander came on the radio screaming and wailing for his brethren.

"Send the tractors, we have many dead and injured. We cannot get closer!" another Taliban leader reported.

Ron continued to level the grape huts as I called Hodge and Bruce on the hill to let them know about the enemy calls for assistance.

"I know, I see them coming," Hodge said, counting at least seven dust trails from tractors moving along a series of roads and irrigation ditches northeast of Sperwan Ghar.

The A-10s made one more gun run on the grape huts and then climbed to the tanker for more fuel. Two Apaches arrived, and Hodge's team sent them after the tractors. Flying fast, the Apaches gained altitude and doubled back for the kill. But by then, all of the tractors had disappeared into the high marijuana fields.

Like dragonflies, the Apaches hovered and circled the area, looking for the tractors. Finally, the lead gunship dipped down and fired a short burst into an irrigation ditch, then flared hard right and scooted away. The burst spooked more than thirty Taliban fighters, who started shooting into the air. The second Apache, closing in on the ditch, fired nearly a dozen rockets into the tangle of trees above it. The helicopters made three more runs before peeling off to look for more fighters. Jared gave them the green light to attack any Taliban fighters within four hundred meters of the hill.

For the next several minutes, the Apaches teased fighters into shooting at them to give away their positions. It would start with a burst of gunfire, the tracers climbing into the sky, followed by some deft flying and colorful language as the lead pilots moved to safety and the trail Apache followed up with a gun run, ending the threat.

We had so many aircraft in the area that anyone who had any experience controlling them was on the radio. Mike divided the hill down the center with an imaginary line. He worked the aircraft to the south of the line and Ron worked the aircraft to the north. For nearly two and a half hours more than twenty attack aircraft—fighters, helicopters, and Predator drones—chased the Taliban fighters through the irrigation ditches, leveled their compounds, and smashed the almost impenetrable grape huts.

I scribbled notes anywhere there was space. The entire inside of my truck was a notepad. The dashboard, hood, my sleeves, the window—all contained precious information as I tracked targets, aircraft, and Taliban movements.

Taz interrupted me with a hiss, the Afghan version of "Psst, dude, over here." He pointed to his AK-47 magazine and held up two fingers. His men had two magazines, or sixty rounds left. I pulled out my knife.

"Taso chaku bulla kawalishi." Use your knife next.

Taz just smiled and bobbed his head enthusiastically. He disappeared behind the school. We were in it together, and I was confident the Taliban weren't getting past Taz and his men. If they did, I would know Taz and his men were dead.

The air support afforded us a brief respite from the fire. Jared's truck pulled to a dusty stop behind mine. Everyone grabbed bags and boxes from the trucks and set up a command post in a small corner room of the schoolhouse. Empty ammunition crates became chairs and tables. We packed empty ammo cans full of dirt into windows to guard against RPGs and shrapnel. Battlefield details in white chalk decorated the gray spackled walls.

The gun trucks cross-loaded all the remaining ammunition, replaced Taliban defensive positions on top of the hill with U.S. or ANA machine guns, and cleared the school of unexploded ordnance. The school was now our Alamo.

Inside, we scoured the rooms for intelligence. I walked into one room near the foyer and was immediately uneasy. The walls were jet black; names were scrawled across them. Taliban voodoo. The Taliban often mark their presence by pouring diesel fuel into a bucket of sand and igniting it in a designated meeting or council room. The smoke turns everything in the room black, which provides them with an evil and almost invincible aura for the benefit of the local people, who believe the power of the Taliban alone is responsible for the transformation.

Sandal prints peppered the ceiling, symbolizing that whoever saw them was under the foot of the Taliban. The names on the black walls were those of the Taliban leaders. In theory, the locals, who would eventually discover the scene, would also witness the Taliban's power.

One of the names caught my eye. I called Jared and told him he needed to see this.

"What the fuck is this?" Jared said, stunned, as he joined me.

I pointed to one name that I recognized from the notebook we had recovered from the village on the outskirts of the Red Desert. Jared fished the book out of a pouch on his body armor and flipped through it. An interpreter ran down the list. All sixteen names in the notebook matched the names on the wall. We had the true names of the major Taliban leadership in Panjwayi and southern Afghanistan.

Jared flipped open his satellite phone and walked outside to get a clear signal. This needed to get to Bolduc and our intelligence people as soon as possible. The next time those assholes tried to communicate, we would be ready and on them.

By the time the sun set, we'd fought for thirteen straight hours. Two Chinooks arrived with our resupply of ammunition and weapons. During the battle we had broken or destroyed more than a dozen machine guns.

The helicopters barely landed. The crew chiefs knew the situation and quickly kicked the bundles out of the back. An additional explosive ordnance disposal team also arrived to clear the trails and footpaths of mines. We'd found nearly a dozen mines, planted all over the hill.

After the helicopters left, the two A-10s that earlier had dropped the life-saving bombs to halt the counterattack returned. They'd flown to Bagram Airfield north of Kabul, to rearm and refuel.

Swooping down, they quickly unloaded all of their bombs and rockets into Mike and Ron's targets. Their final gun run with their 30-mm cannons crumbled the walls of a nearby compound.

"Talon 31, this is Tusk 16. It looks like you guys will be okay. From up here, the enemy seems to be moving back. We have numerous dust trails from vehicles moving away in all directions. Unfortunately we have to go off station. You guys keep your heads down and hold on tonight. We WILL be back tomorrow morning before sunup. I guarantee it."

Pulling up, they started to climb into the darkening sky. The lead A-10 made a steep left turn and came straight toward Sperwan Ghar. He couldn't have been more than a hundred feet off the deck. I could see him clearly inside the cockpit as he rolled the plane slightly onto its right side, looking down at us over his shoulder as he gave us a thumbs-up. As the plane cleared the hill, he leveled out, rocked his wings back and forth, and shot straight up into the sky doing a slow, steady barrel roll.

To this day, that scene is burned into my memory. I knew at that moment that I was truly part of the most magnificent fighting force on the face of the earth. I knew for certain that if I needed it, help would come. It was a sense of relief and confidence that words can't convey.

I was sure we'd need such help. With the Canadians bogged down to the north, the Taliban would turn their ferocity on Sperwan Ghar.

I expected a very long night.

Chapter 18

————

HOLDING ON AT ALL COSTS

*History does not entrust the care of freedom
to the weak or timid.*

—DWIGHT D. EISENHOWER

The explosion jolted Brian and me from a deep sleep atop the hood of Ole Girl, throwing us to the dusty ground. Another explosion rocked the earth as soon as I hit the dirt. Brian and I scuttled quickly on hands and knees toward the rear of the truck, the thorns and prickly ground bushes digging deep.

"You hit?" I asked Brian.

"No, you?" he said.

"No, I'm good," I said catching my breath. My hands and knees were on fire and I had nearly soiled a good pair of pants. Then I heard the snickering. Still half asleep, I crawled around to the far side of the truck, where I found Ron and Dave smiling, enjoying themselves, crouched against the wall of the schoolhouse.

The AC-130 gunship had arrived soon after I fell asleep. It announced its presence by slamming several 105-mm artillery rounds into a compound a hundred meters from the hill. Dave and Ron controlled the gunship and knew in advance the explosions were coming.

"You move pretty quickly for an old man," Dave said.

"Up yours, Dave!"

The barrage sent a shower of yellow-orange sparks in all directions. Smoke from small fires drifted in and out of the moonlight, creating dark gray clouds that hung over the decimated buildings. The AC-130 crew had worked all night firing at the massing Taliban fighters, its cameras scanning the ground for enemy soldiers. Invisible to the naked eye, they circled overhead. We dubbed them our "night angels," and in fact their guns sounded like trumpeting as they hammered the fighters trying to reorganize and attack.

"Target! Load! Gun is set! Ready! Fire!" *Boom!*

From the top of Sperwan Ghar, we could see numerous fires. The Taliban were still bringing fresh troops across the river. Nearly two hundred enemy fighters walked or rode in trucks, lights off, across the dry riverbed toward Sperwan Ghar. The fires lit the way. Others probed, trying to assess our defenses. They absolutely had to attack at dawn. It was a fight for initiative.

Still exhausted, Brian and I simply crawled under the truck's bumper and went back to sleep. We would get three hours before we took over guard duties for the night. The comforting echo of the gunship's attacks let us rest easy. When I felt the familiar tug at my foot a few hours later, I sat up and hit my head on the bumper.

"Damn it," I said, rubbing my now throbbing forehead. Ron stood there, absolutely exhausted from having stayed up all night calling in strikes.

"How did it go last night?" I asked.

"Busy, very busy," he said. His hard work had killed at least 110 fighters.

Several large rockets slammed into Sperwan Ghar with the arrival of the sun, just after the first call to prayer from the local mosque. I thought it sickening that the mullahs who presided over prayers were the same Taliban who used the mosque speaker systems to broadcast messages to fighters. I estimated about one hundred fighters on my side of the perimeter. We could see them moving through the orchards, across irrigation ditches, and between the thick mud walls of the compounds. The faint cry *"Allah akbar"* echoed around the hill.

Bill moved team members into position to cover the enemy advance. Gunfire raked the back side of the hill, where Hodge and his team were located. The familiar zing of passing bullets again became commonplace.

"Tango, Tango, Tangos from the north," an SF soldier's voice came over the radio, notifying us of targets and their location. The call was cut short by the deafening sound of machine-gun fire from the roof.

About a dozen fighters tried to advance, but Afghan soldiers moved to reinforce the machine-gun position and stopped them. I scanned the area through my binoculars and saw a group of fighters, including a teenage boy, huddled in the intersection, dead or dying. Birds and two large dogs descended on the bodies.

Better them than my men, I said to myself.

It made me sick. The Taliban fighters were being led to slaughter by zealots who cared only for their cause. Those who preached Sharia law the loudest were unwilling to die for their distorted and perverse ideology. They forced many a young boy to ferry ammunition or fight. It was a matter of choosing between ignorance and understanding. My men would not die for an act of foolishness.

The attack quickly shifted to Hodge and the south side of the hill. Ali Hussein called over the radio in short excited bursts and reported more fighters headed for the narrow, shaded passageway.

"Okay, Ali," I said, trying to sound reassuring, "when the enemy arrives, just shoot them."

He got the joke and then ordered three Afghan soldiers, including Taz, over the embankment to counter. Pumping his arm ferociously, Taz led the soldiers into the enemy-infested grape fields.

They disappeared over the small embankment and reappeared along a compound wall leading to a small building deep in the fields.

I reported their movements over the radio, making sure our shooters knew that friendly forces were outside the wire.

Taz's crew carefully climbed the mud stairway leading to the top of the compound wall. The wall ran directly along the irrigation ditch where we had gunned down the dozen fighters. Taz pointed toward the wall and I knew there were Taliban on the other side. He held up three fingers, a countdown, and then all three men rose and fired. Two just sprayed their AK-47s like garden hoses, but not Taz. He kept his rifle tight into his shoulder and fired methodical bursts into the fighters, then snatched a grenade from his pouch and tossed it into the ditch. The other soldiers followed his lead and all three jumped from the ten-foot wall and ran at a dead sprint back toward our perimeter. Three crashing explosions sent dirt and tree limbs flying behind them.

Taz came dashing with his team through the school hallway to my truck, knowing from long experience that I would want a situation report. They had found twenty fighters on the wall and wounded or killed half of them. I hugged my good friend. I was proud of them, and I remember wishing that others could see what I saw, Afghans fighting for their freedom. As they sprinted back to their positions, a friendly voice came over the team radio net. It caught me off guard, and I stopped to make sure I wasn't hearing things.

It was another SF team, but not just any team. It was the boys from 333—Triple X. Joe, the team sergeant for Triple X, was on the net and his voice was music to my ears. This was another serious group of pipe hitters coming to the party. *Hot damn.*

Bolduc knew how high the stakes were for Sperwan Ghar and had moved 333 into the battle. We were finally getting more Special Forces soldiers on the ground. I pulled my microphone down from my face and told my team members, whose confidence visibly swelled. We were not alone.

Team 333 had arrived the night before and wedged itself between the jagged rocks on top of Masum Ghar, the ridgeline overlooking the Canadian task force to the north. Virtually invisible up there, they watched the battlefield through powerful Steiner binoculars and Leupold spotting scopes. We now had friendly forces watching over the Canadian task force, cutting off the enemy to our north, fresh resupplies coming in regularly, and ownership of key terrain. Matt, the team leader, called me for an update.

For the last several hours his team had patiently waited, plotted, and observed Taliban forces moving up and down the valley. Joe (known as "Kramer"), their warrant officer, and Matt's men marked targets in the valley below with what would turn out to be deadly accuracy. From their vantage point, they could see the entire Canadian side of the valley and the front half of ours.

Between us, we came up with a detailed sketch of defensive positions, destroyed vehicles, ditches, enemy fighters, and the locations they moved to. When Jared got on the radio, I gave him the overview. When the time was right and when the air power came, they would unleash hell.

The familiar high-pitched whistling of incoming rounds sliced through the air and I threw myself facedown on the concrete floor of the school. Several crashing *crumps* of explosions impacted behind the school near the latrine. RPGs and recoilless-rifle rounds exploded close to my trucks and the Afghan machine-gun positions. I hit my face on the rear sight of my rifle and busted my lip open.

The attack on Hodge's position had been a feint. The main crux of the assault hit my positions within minutes. As the fire became more intense, I called Hodge for reinforcements.

Ron called for me or Jared on the radio. He had something for us. We radioed back that he would have to wait, but then I heard him checking Navy fighters on station above the valley.

"NAVY? Where the hell did they come from?" Jared asked.

"Apparently an aircraft carrier, sir," Ron said.

Now everyone out here was a smart-ass. Ron had been hanging around Dave too long.

Mike called in that, based upon the number of call signs checking on station, we were no longer in short supply of aircraft. The fighters had to refuel after the long flight from the Indian Ocean and would be back in an hour. We had no idea where the other aircraft were coming from and truly didn't care. All we knew was that they were finally here.

While we waited, I imagined what was taking place in the United States. I knew the process. I could see the phones lighting up at the Pentagon, spurring decision makers to act.

REGION: SOUTHWEST ASIA

THEATER: AFGHANISTAN

SITUATION: U.S. Special Forces unit possibility of being overrun.

BACKGROUND: A U.S. SOF unit, supporting a large ISAF operation, is under heavy attack.

INFORMAL SUMMARY: A major ISAF operation, code name "MEDUSA," is under way. It has stalled due to unexpected numbers of enemy and our troops are in heavy contact in southern Afghanistan's Kandahar Province. An SF unit has pushed into enemy territory to reestablish the initiative and relieve the ISAF forces. In doing so, they have located a large number of Taliban and foreign fighters (^1000) CONFIRMED, and an enemy training camp. They are taking them head on. Every available asset is required.

DIRECTIVE: Make every asset available, even if it means it has to come from Iraq.

END MSG

We spent the lull reinforcing our fighting positions and distributing ammunition and fuel. Each truck had small caches that could be accessed easily. We couldn't afford to lose any more vehicles, equipment, or men. Since we started the assault, two Afghan vehicles had been shot to pieces, four U.S. GMVs disabled, and nearly a dozen soldiers wounded. All three team leaders approached Jared.

"Any chance higher headquarters might finally realize this is a major offensive? We'll need reinforcements soon," Hodge said.

"Honestly, no," Jared replied. "We have asked for anything and everything, Marines, Rangers, SEALs. Supposedly the CJTF-A [Combined Joint Task Force—Afghanistan] commander will make an 'assessment' soon. That's all I know, so don't say another word. Good call on holding this place."

We had gotten intelligence that more than twenty Taliban commanders were in the area. One was Mullah Dadullah Lang and maybe Mullah Omar, the supreme Taliban commander. Matt's team was too far away to confirm if either man was there. Jared told him to lay low and keep watching, hoping that the Taliban commanders would meet and we could hit them all at once.

Jared reported the possible meeting to Kandahar and Bolduc, but the commander wasn't there. He was headed to Sperwan Ghar with the commander of U.S. forces in Afghanistan, Major General Benjamin Freakley. The general wanted to see the battle for himself.

The general's helicopter dipped into the valley and landed in a cloud of dust that covered the entire hilltop. I heard Smitty humming Wagner's "Ride of the Valkyries" at the end of the hall as they got off the helicopter.

The general wanted a tour of the battlefield and to know what we needed. I always loved it when they asked that. Bolduc knew best how to deal with VIPs.

"Sir, let me be blunt. We need more resources," Bolduc said. "This is an offensive push by the Taliban to seize Kandahar city, the first we have seen since the invasion. I know—I was here soon after," he said.

"The Canadian task force has been hit hard to our north and cannot freely maneuver. They have one mechanized company out of the fight. When we assaulted and finally seized this position, we dis-

rupted the primary Taliban command and control site south of the
river and their hub of reinforcements. By doing this we destroyed or
scattered a significant portion of their forces, preventing them from
continuing to organize mass attacks. Our intelligence confirmed that
the foreign advisors and Taliban forces had planned on letting the TF
Aegis forces push south and rolling up their flanks. Now that we own
this piece of key terrain, the Canadians can push out while we cover
their flank and bring them some relief. The enemy will now have to
fight us on multiple fronts and face to face. My men can hold this
position for the next twenty-four to forty-eight hours but not without heavy air cover and reinforcements. We simply need more resources."

Bolduc worded it beautifully and set the wheels turning in the
general's head. But he had a major dilemma: it was highly unortho-
dox for a conventional commander to put his forces under the command of Special Forces. He eyed our group, bearded nasty men in
tattered uniforms with banged-up equipment. He had to wonder if
we would care for his men. But we train and lead indigenous forces
on combat operations behind enemy lines. The commonsense factor
said it was a perfect fit, but would he buy it? He grabbed Bolduc by
the shoulder.

"You'll have it," Major General Freakley said.

With the decision made, the general boarded his Black Hawk heli-
copter, only to get word that it couldn't depart. During the meeting,
Matt, perched high above on Masum Ghar, had stolen the general's
Apache escort.

"Hammer 22, this is Talon 33, we have enemy at the following
grid, possibly a Taliban commander. Can you assist, over?"

It was an opportunity the pilots couldn't pass up.

"Roger that!" the pilots said, turning to get into firing position. I
don't think the helicopters made a full pass with the general on the
ground before they pushed toward the target.

Matt carefully eyed the target, a series of compounds surrounded by a pomegranate orchard, with the range finder. The trees were so dense that it was impossible to see down into the compound. Matt watched a group of fighters duck down and rush into the orchard, weapons in hand, and fed their coordinates to the Apaches. The helicopters cut south, turned 180 degrees, and lined up on the orchard.

Everyone watched in anticipation as the lead helicopter fired eight rockets. Two fell short, but the remaining six landed directly inside the orchard, sending thick plumes of dust into the air. It looked like someone had kicked an ant nest.

"Yeah, baby," Matt said over the radio.

Six men, all in black, carried the leader out of the orchard, his flowing white robes now caked in dirt and blood. The second helicopter, trailing the first, fired rockets, then guns at the group. The Apache's cannon collapsed a section of the wall, which landed on several fighters seeking cover. One Taliban fighter kept his wits enough to fire an RPG. The pilot narrowly missed eating it as he banked out of the way. The rocket left a vapor trail no more than thirty feet in front of the helicopter's nose. Other fighters set up a PKM machine gun and fired in a cone, hoping to lead the helicopter into the rounds.

The fighters were pros—likely foreign fighters and mercenaries from Saudi Arabia, Pakistan, or Chechnya on whom the Taliban relied for tactical help. That probably meant the leader in white robes was very important. After the helicopters' second pass, the fighters quickly ducked back into the orchard.

The pilots, now fully engaged, frantically tried to get a bead on the machine gunners. Unable to see them, they swung out into the desert, and Matt patiently talked them in again, watching as the group carried their leader into a covered building. Matt got the best grid he could and called it in with a precise description of the building. The first Hellfire missile streaked forward and hit the building; the second struck the edge of the orchard and collapsed two adjacent structures.

Matt was gearing up for another pass when the order came to call it off.

"Talon 33, this is Hammer 22, we got to go. We have a pickup and escort south of you. Thanks for letting us play. Hammer 22 out," the pilot said.

The Apaches swung back around and fell into a loose formation with the brass's now-airborne Black Hawk. As the three helicopters disappeared into the distance, another seemed to be coming straight for us. I looked at Jared and he just shrugged his shoulders. It was a Russian Mi-17 cargo helicopter painted all white with no nationality markings.

"Who the hell is that?" Bill and I asked in unison.

Matt asked the same question from his perch. No one knew who it was or what they were doing. Whoever it was, they flew like nothing else in the world was going on around them. The helicopter hovered and sank into the orchard near the now-destroyed building. Several men in full combat equipment similar to ours rushed out of the aircraft and formed a very tight perimeter, while others moved to where the missile had impacted and loaded several body bags onto the helicopter. Then the helicopter rose from the orchard and disappeared over the mountains. To this day, we have no idea what happened to the helicopter or the occupants. It just disappeared.

We did, however, find out that it was not taken well that we had "borrowed" the general's escort aircraft and used most of their ammunition.

Chapter 19

——

TODAY IS NOT YOUR DAY

No arsenal or no weapon in the
arsenals of the world is as formidable as the
will and moral courage of free men and women.

—RONALD REAGAN

The first F-18s checked on station and dropped down into view. The roar of their engines was a welcome sign that help was arriving. I could hear Mike on the radio starting to identify targets and buildings that needed to be leveled.

Standing on top of Sperwan Ghar, I could see hundreds of compounds in the sea of green that offered the Taliban fighters good cover. We needed to build "white space," or security, to patrol in around the hill because the Taliban had started to maneuver in smaller groups, making it harder to see them before they opened fire. They were learning very hard lessons and adapting quickly. This is what all insurgents do in guerrilla warfare. It reminded me of a snake slithering from dark spot to dark spot before it strikes. So we set about making fewer dark spots. The aircraft could destroy the structures. We'd focus on the thick, head-high marijuana fields, appropriately named the "fields of wrath."

Dave and Brian took a patrol of a dozen ANA soldiers into the fields. I stayed on the hill and Bill coordinated with Hodge's team to set up machine guns to cover them. Despite being less than a football field away, we couldn't see them once they entered the field. After a few minutes, thick gray smoke hung over part of the field, and the sweet smell of burning marijuana soon washed over us. Bill, Smitty, Zack, Jude, and Riley joked that they wanted to do the next "patrol." The jokes soon turned to who was hoarding the snacks—Doritos, Funyuns, pizza—for when they returned with the munchies.

Grabbing my binoculars, I zeroed in on a small clearing, where I could see Brian and Dave pouring diesel fuel on the thick green stalks. The plants were like rubber and wouldn't catch fire. When the fuel didn't work, they tried flares, illumination mortar rounds, and incendiary grenades to little or no effect. The patrol had lit more than a dozen fires, but none did any real damage.

I started to get nervous and called them back. I knew that sooner rather than later the Taliban would see them in the field and attack. Just before they got back on their trucks, a few fighters started shooting. A small attack compared to the previous ones, it lasted less than a minute when we opened fire with the machine guns on Sperwan Ghar. Afterward, Victor grabbed me. *"Turan,* the Taliban commander wanted more troops but another commander to our south said no." I smiled and thanked him. The short message told me a lot. After less than a week of fighting, the enemy was now fragmenting, and we knew that more fighters were staging south of us. Hodge and Jared heard the same thing. Jared started to plan an operation for the following day. He wanted a team to go recon Zangabar Ghar, a small set of hills to our south. He was sure the enemy was using it as a landmark when they came across the river, and we had taken intense fire from there.

After Brian and Dave got back from the patrol, Bill insisted that we get the guns clean, redistribute ammunition, reinforce positions, eat some chow, and then try to rest.

"Listen up, you know the pattern," he told us. "We're going to get hit soon."

We all went to work on our guns. Dave cleaned his big Browning .50 cal first. Then I stripped the machine gun next to my door. I brushed out the dust and oiled every part. When I had finished, it sparkled and the action worked smoothly. I finished about the same time as Brian. Sitting around the truck we got a treat: silence. We'd not enjoyed silence for more than a week and none of us dared interrupt it.

The Taliban had spotters constantly watching us, but in the thick fields and deep irrigation ditches it was impossible to see them. Occasionally a Taliban spotter peered over the thick stone walls. An attentive ANA soldier noticed movement in a small courtyard not far from the hill. Calling Taz over, he pointed the spotter out and Taz alerted me. I figured that if we killed the spotters, we'd be able to blind them one by one and instill enough fear that they would decide it wasn't worth attempting.

I sent Dave and Riley to take up a sniper position on the hill with sight lines to the operative compound and wait. Brian took over duties on the Ma Duce. Dave set up the sniper rifle and peered through the Leupold scope. Scanning the courtyard, he could see several pomegranate trees and a gray T-shaped hand pump for a well. He settled in to wait. After a short time, his patience was rewarded when the spotter's head popped over the wall. Riley called in and said they had him; Dave confirmed the range.

"Wait one," I radioed back. "Watch him closely and tell me what he does."

Grabbing my machine gun, I fired a short burst into a nearby field.

"He just popped up and then hunkered down," Riley said.

A few seconds later Riley came back with what I needed to hear.

"Captain, he has a radio."

"Drop him," I said.

When Dave was ready, I fired another burst. The spotter popped up again and Dave fired. The round hit high. Chambering another, he fired again. This time it hit the spotter. The 7.62 match-grade ammunition entered through the neck and traveled in an arc, exiting his back. The body dropped in a heap behind the wall. He'd never report our movements again. Dave returned to the truck, smiling like a Cheshire cat, and we again relished the quiet.

He had no more than crawled into the turret when the whoosh of an RPG cut it short. I glimpsed two Taliban fighters carrying a launcher seconds before the rocket flew over Dave's head and exploded just behind my vehicle, right outside the window where the command post was located. The dirt-filled ammunition cans we had propped inside the empty window frames gave rudimentary protection at best, but they prevented small shrapnel from hitting anyone in the post.

Dave dropped into the turret. "Move, move, move!" he yelled as he thrust a round into the chamber of the .50-caliber machine gun.

Brian started the truck and threw it in reverse just as another rocket exploded in front of the berm where the truck had just been parked. Contact reports of attacks on the vehicles flooded the radio. The Taliban were trying to destroy our gun trucks. They knew that the trucks had the most firepower and were essential to our defense of the hill. The fire grew more intense.

I took a bead on where I had seen the movement—a small three-windowed mud building quaintly tucked in between two larger compounds. I took a breath, exhaled slowly, and kept my eye on the building. One of the windows had a small red curtain, and I had seen two men carrying either a mortar or a recoilless rifle past it. I knew the ammunition bearers would be next, carrying sacks of mortar or recoilless-rifle rounds.

The first figure ran past and I squeezed the trigger, sending up a spray of sticky oil; I'd forgotten to wipe off the excess after I'd finished cleaning the gun. Wiping my face, I pulled the machine gun into my shoulder. It rocked rhythmically as I made adjustments to the sights. Brian fired repeatedly at the same point. I aimed just past the opening where I knew they would either run into the bullets or try to hide once they knew there was fire coming at them.

Three hundred meters, three hundred fifty, three hundred seventy-five, there!

I fired a six- to nine-round burst each time, and it finally put me on my mark. The rounds penetrated the wall, and there was a commotion behind it. I must have caught them resting on that side. A figure came into view on his knees and fell forward, clutching his chest, then slung violently backward. I depressed the trigger fully and counted to ten. Nearly an entire can of ammunition went streaking through the gun. I was running low, maybe twenty rounds left. Finding a target wasn't easy, and now that I knew where they'd hidden, I wasn't going to let them escape. I fired another whole can into the wall. Soon, Dave started to pound the hut with the Ma Duce.

Out of ammunition, I yelled to Brian to cover me while I ran for more.

"Grab me some too," Dave shouted.

Letting the machine gun hang in the gun mount, I sprinted for the cache in a nearby ditch. An ANA machine-gun position to my right rattled as I ran. Sliding into the four-foot-deep channel, my knees rebelled. Pain shot through my joints, and I felt old.

The machine guns brought me out of my funk. I snatched four boxes of ammunition, climbed out of the ditch, and took a step when I was overwhelmed by intense heat and pressure. I lost all sense of control and balance.

An RPG or recoilless rifle had exploded somewhere near my left front, hurling me violently back into the ditch. I landed on my left shoulder, followed by the rest of my 230-pound frame and another 50 pounds of equipment. I couldn't feel my shoulder anymore. I clutched it with my right hand just to make sure it was still there.

My helmet, sunglasses, and headset were gone. The strap on my left shoulder holding my body armor was shredded and the plates hung cockeyed across my chest and back. I couldn't focus—everywhere I looked I saw stars. I gagged and coughed out the dust and smoke, struggling to get enough oxygen into my lungs. Dave's .50 caliber sounded muffled even though I was only a few feet away.

I commanded my left knee to bend so I could roll over, stealing a quick glance at it. I expected to see it shredded. I winced as it bent but knew that meant it was still connected. I tried to spit some of the grime out of my mouth but couldn't muster enough saliva to do it.

I struggled to focus. Then panic set in. I didn't want to die. "NO!" I said repeatedly to myself as I clawed at the wall of the ditch, trying to see over it.

Every movement felt like slow motion. I expected to see Ole Girl in flames just like Greg's truck. Peering over the edge, I saw Dave banging away in the turret. My eyes filled with tears, half from the pain and half with relief. I even chuckled as I laid my head in the powdery dust and again thanked my creator. Crawling back down into the ditch, I found my helmet. I couldn't hear a damn thing.

Seeing my team still fighting gave me strength. They now stood in the face of fierce fire with only rifles; the ammunition for their machine guns was long gone. I needed to get to my truck. Rolling over the lip of the ditch, I crawled out and started back toward my truck when a round from an enemy machine gunner hit me just above my kidney. Pain shot through my body. It felt like a ball-peen hammer on the end of a semi-truck traveling at one hundred miles an hour slamming into me. I was too deaf to hear my own screams.

I fell flat on my face, helpless.

"This is it," I thought. "Today, I die."

I realized that everything I loved was going to be taken away. I could see Brian, hand extended. He had crawled through the cab to my side of the truck. Still deaf, it took me a second to read his lips.

"Come on, you can make it. Come on!" he said, motioning for me to come with his gloved hand. What I could not see or hear were the wisps of dust kicked up by rounds hitting the earth around me.

I didn't want to die.

I wanted to go to him. I drew my knees to my waist and crawled as low as I could, focusing on his reddish freckles. I watched as Dave kept firing and prayed I could make it to the safety of my vehicle.

When I got to the side of the truck, I stuck out my sweat-soaked hand. Brian grabbed it and pulled me into the truck with what seemed like superhuman strength and turned me onto my back. I squirmed around, trying to stop the piercing pain and find some comfort. This truck was home, and for a split second, I felt safe.

Brian unzipped my first aid kit and shoved a packet of pain pills in my mouth, stretching his drinking tube over to give me water. Even with the gritty dirt, sweat, blood, and pills, it was the sweetest water I ever drank. I struggled to draw my legs inside the open door. I could see Brian talking into the radio. I was on my back, facing up and looking at Dave's waist and legs behind the turret opening in the roof. Several pieces of hot brass from Dave's gun tumbled from the chamber and hit me in the face. I tried to shoo the brass away like flies. I knew I was messed up and needed help. Sunlight blinded me, and I tried to cover my face when a figure appeared in my truck door.

Bill.

He ran his hands down the top of my skull and neck, under my arms, over my waist and the small of my back, and down to the base of my feet. He only stopped at my lower back, which was soaked, to assess the small shrapnel wounds in my butt. Finished, he showed me his hands. Very little to no blood. I still couldn't tell which hurt worse, my back, shoulder, butt, or left knee. Bill said my shoulder was dislocated and called Riley.

He then pulled me up, face to face, and looked me straight in the eye.

"Today is not your day, Captain. Everything is still attached. You're okay." And with that, he laid me down and returned to the fight. I knew right then and there that I really was okay.

Riley showed up next. He did his own quick evaluation and told me my shoulder was dislocated and the ligaments in my knee were probably torn. Without warning, he grabbed my left arm and started to move it. I screamed. Riley had learned the trick during training at Fort Bragg, and after a few tugs and twists he popped it back into the joint. The sensation of numbness retreated from my wrist and fingers. He didn't even flinch when several rounds pinged off the truck as he worked.

With my shoulder in place, he wrapped my knee to keep the swelling down and gave me a pain shot.

"You'll feel better in a few seconds," he said before running to another truck to tend to a wounded Afghan.

Wow, this does feel nice, I said to myself.

The bullet had hit the lower left corner of the ceramic plate on my body armor. But it shouldn't have. Had my vest not been damaged from the blast and the plate knocked out of place, the 7.62 bullet would have passed through my kidney, liver, intestines, and possibly my lung.

I sucked hard on the tan tube of my CamelBak, but nothing came out. The shrapnel that struck my body armor had traveled across the plate and shredded the plastic bladder. The wetness that I feared was blood soaking my back and butt was water. Fumbling on the floorboards, I found a bottle of water and poured it onto my face. I had cheated death, but now I knew I wasn't bulletproof—not a feeling you want to have in the middle of a firefight. I covered each nostril and shot snot and blood from my nose. My hearing gradually improved, and soon I could hear Dave and Brian yelling to each other for ammunition and calling out targets.

Brian now selflessly ferried ammunition from the ditch I had just been wounded in. He darted back and forth several times, tossing the ammunition into the back of the truck.

A volley of three RPG rounds came in and hit the northern school wall beside our truck, peppering the vehicle with razor-sharp metal and debris. Dave dipped down from the turret, shaking and squeezing his hand and cursing. A bit of shrapnel had gashed it open. More mad than hurt, he grabbed the butterfly-shaped wooden handles of the machine gun, cranked twice, and went back to work.

I crawled into the back of the truck and heaved two luggage-sized cans of ammo onto the turret for Dave. I could feel the breeze blow through my pants. My desert camouflage trousers had been torn from my rear at the waist all the way down to the inside of my thigh. There was no time to change. Dave's gun soon went dry again, and I helped him change out ammunition cans. My M240 machine gun hung limp in the bracket near my door. I pulled a box of ammo, loaded the belt into the feed tray, and slammed it shut. Setting the buttstock into my shoulder, I went back to work.

That day I fired thousands of rounds at fighters in the buildings and ditches that surrounded Sperwan Ghar. It was my way of getting the fear out of my system. Whatever enemy was out there had tried to kill me and failed. Now I would eat, sleep, live, and breathe to make them regret it.

I planned to sleep behind my truck with my body armor propped up in front of me that night. My armor had saved me twice from certain death. We would all rest again to the sound of the Spectre engines above us.

I stopped to talk with Shinsha on the roof of the school before getting some rack time. That miserable bastard of a sun had set as I stepped onto the broad flat surface, but I instinctively bent forward at the waist, ducking to stay low, even though it was dark. I was taking no chances. I flopped down on the bright red-and-black-patterned pillow next to Shinsha. He swung his massive head toward me and squinted through the cigarette smoke.

"Roostie," he said in his usual gruff tone, pointing toward a small Chinese-made hand-cranked radio by his feet, which was tuned to a Pakistani national radio station. Shinsha seemed unusually happy and laughed deeply several times during the broadcast. I sat and drank chai while listening, acting as if I understood every word. Finally, when it was over, Shinsha explained the broadcast to me in Farsi through an interpreter. "A Taliban spokesman in Quetta, Pakistan, admitted that more than three hundred fighters had been martyred in the past two days," he said with a satisfied smile.

The first truly inspiring piece of news from the battle had come from the Taliban themselves. There was no explaining away the enormous number of fighters arriving at the hospitals in Pakistan. There was no way they could hide their growing casualty numbers, something they'd been able to do in the past. We had them on their heels. Their commanders fought internally about how they would receive reinforcements. They knew their dreams of taking Kandahar by winter were slipping away. Now all we had to do was keep the pressure up, pursue them when they ran, and punish them.

Chapter 20

A WORLD OF HURT

You ask, what is our aim? I can answer in one word. It is victory. Victory at all costs. Victory in spite of all terrors. Victory, however long and hard the road may be, for without victory there is no survival.

—WINSTON CHURCHILL

The long stream of dust could be seen for miles. Civilians continued to flee.

Numerous requests for Rangers, Marines—or any assistance—had fallen on deaf ears for several critical days, but after the second counterattack in less than twenty-four hours, the ISAF headquarters in Bagram finally sent Comanche Company from the 10th Mountain Division and another Special Forces team. Major General Freakley, God bless him, was true to his word. They also sent two 105-mm howitzers, slung under Chinook helicopters. Less than twenty minutes after the helicopters dropped off the guns at Keybari Ghar, the crews were ready and on the radio asking Jared for a fire mission.

The infantry company from the 10th Mountain Division arrived next. It had driven straight down Highway One from Kabul, stopping only to refuel the trucks. We didn't care where they came from, we were just glad they were here. The convoy formed a huge defensive perimeter around the artillery. Special Forces Team 376 from the 3rd Battalion also arrived with the infantry, along with an additional ANA unit. I knew their team leader, Mike, from the qualification course. He hopped out of his truck and pointed to the menacing-looking six-barreled minigun atop one of his vehicles. "I brought the scunion," he said. A world of hurt.

Help had truly arrived.

The appearance of the 10th Mountain's Comanche Company marked the first time conventional forces were under operational control of a Special Forces unit in Afghanistan for a large-scale operation. Jared had planned a broad sweeping action to clear Objective Billiards, the entire area north of Sperwan Ghar. Comanche Company would infiltrate from the desert, punch straight into the villages, and sweep southwest, clearing everything in front of Sperwan Ghar. Jared wanted volunteers to go with the new ANA unit and lead the reinforcements into the labyrinth of villages and compounds with Comanche Company. Riley, Casey, and Smitty agreed to go.

As the soldiers moved through the village below, I got into my truck and drove to the top of the hill. Bill pulled up next to me just as Smitty's voice exploded over the radio.

"Talon 30, this is 31 Sierra. Troops in contact. Heavy contact. Over one hundred AAF [Anti-Afghanistan Forces]. Small arms fire, RPG and machine-gun fire. One hundred meters northeast of our position. Trying to get ANA to maneuver. Need immediate air support," he said breathlessly. I could hear the rattle of gunfire in the background and see the fight erupting before us.

The Taliban had ambushed them. From a distance, it looked like fire ants pouring out of a great mound as about fifty fighters emerged from the irrigation ditches as the Afghan soldiers and American infantry pursued decoys. Smitty finally got some helicopters on station and began making gun runs on enemy targets. A Taliban commander could be heard trying to rally his men, while others simply fell back to other buildings. His fighters were getting pushed into a constricted area. Signs of the enemy were everywhere, bodies of dead and wounded fighters scattered throughout the compounds and grape huts. Other rooms were packed with weapons, food, spare parts, and cheap Chinese motorcycles.

I had stepped away for a moment when I heard Dave curse. Someone was hit. As I got back to the radio, a second soldier was reported as wounded. Then: "We have four casualities, one American."

An ETT working with the Afghans had been killed trying to get over the thigh-high hedges lining the vineyard. One ANA soldier had also been killed and two wounded. The four were carried out and loaded into the back of a Ranger, which sped off in a cloud of dust to Comanche's main position. I watched as eight Rangers loaded with ANA soldiers took off for the highway, clearly not intending to stop until they got to Kabul. At least we now knew that the new ANA weren't going to turn on us. They were just going to run.

The 10th Mountain commander, Comanche 6, called for support. His men were getting fired on from an area between the hill and their location in a field near the river. We needed to get a better vantage point, so Brian threw Ole Girl in reverse and peeled out. Zack and Chris followed in their truck. Working our way down the hill, we finally saw movement near a group of grape huts not far from Sperwan Ghar. Setting up below the school, a group of nearly one hundred fighters attacked the hill as we arrived—the third counterattack on Sperwan Ghar. They were in a pressure cooker, compressed between Comanche Company and us. Their machine guns opened up on us.

Brian and Dave switched, since Dave had spent most of the morning baking in the turret. Brian worked the gun while Ron and I started working on the grids for an air strike and made sure the aircraft wouldn't drop on our own people. Ron jumped off the back of the truck as the firing picked up and set up at the corner of the schoolhouse. It was safer and he could still talk to me over the radio. Just then I caught the flash of an RPG smash concrete off the schoolhouse, where it broke into pieces instead of exploding. The warhead landed two feet from Ron. The enemy was so close that the rocket did not have time to arm itself.

Looking through my scope, I quickly swept the fields from left to right, looking for a head with an RPG tube. There. "There, there!" Brian yelled at the same time, raking the small animal barn with fire. Surrounded by trees, it was about the size of a toolshed and had a three-foot-tall wall running along it.

The fire from Brian's machine gun blew cinder-block-sized holes into the wall in a connect-the-dot pattern. An explosion flung part of a human torso into the air, followed by another explosion and a whitish-pink mist. The fighter wore a backpack full of RPG rockets; one must have caught a bullet. Brian continued to pummel the wall with fire until it collapsed and nothing else moved. Hodge's team, on the other side of the hill, caught six guys running for the building to the north.

"The enemy is coming up from the south. We can close this gap. You should probably get back to the other side of the schoolhouse," he radioed. Hodge had the commanding view and I took his advice.

We raced back to our previous positions. I heard Jared talking to Hodge and Bruce over the radio. Tomorrow, we would absolutely have to recon the hills of Zangabar Ghar, also known as the Dragon's Back.

Down in the grape fields, Riley and Casey moved swiftly as the remaining Afghan soldiers kept the Taliban fighters' heads down with accurate fire and stuck close by them. As they worked their way down one of the narrow irrigation ditches, Riley could hear the screams of a Taliban fighter over the radio. Lining up on the outside door of the compound where the Taliban fighters had gone, Riley and the Afghans burst through the door.

A Taliban fighter with an ammunition vest strapped across his chest, radio in hand, started to crawl toward his AK-47 several feet away. Binoculars lay beside the rifle. He had bullet wounds in both legs, and a trail of blood followed him as he clawed his way toward the rifle.

After securing his hands and feet, Riley searched his pockets. The satellite telephone, two cell phones, and a fist-sized wad of cash made it clear this guy was a commander.

"I bet that hurts like shit," Riley said, looking at the ANA. "He's all yours."

Six sets of hands reached for the Taliban leader who had just ambushed them. He was responsible for the death of their friends and atrocities against some of the local civilians.

Up on the hill, Bill came over to the truck. He'd been listening to the battle. "If this thing turns south and they get in trouble, I say we go straight down the hill and attack the enemy in the blind side," he said in his slow Texas drawl. "They'll never see it coming, we can kill a bunch of 'em and fall back to the hill. I ain't letting our boys get stuck down there." I nodded in agreement.

We prepared for our assault and staged at the schoolhouse. Bill coordinated with Riley, Smitty, and Casey for our attack in case the battle turned, but things got quiet over the next hour. Fighters took a few shots at us, but nothing like the previous days. We stayed either in the trucks or in the school to be safe. Evening was falling fast. Facing southwest, I stared at Zangabar Ghar. We knew Taliban fighters were coming from that area; Jared had tapped Bruce's team to go over there the next day and patrol the area.

Sitting in Ole Girl, I reached into the ammo can next to my leg and hit the play button. "I'm just a middle-aged, Middle Eastern camel-herdin' man, I got a little two-bedroom cave here in North Afghanistan . . ."

Brian, who was typically very reserved, and Dave jumped right in, and we sang like drunken sailors. Beside that hill, we could relate to Toby Keith's hit. Brian and Dave were better fighters than singers. As they butchered the song, I watched a small finch hop from limb to limb on the grapevines below. My attention was finally diverted when Victor jumped off the truck, his prayer rug under his arm.

"Stay on the truck, Victor," I said. "We have to be ready to move in case the dismounted guys down in the village need us."

"I am going right over here," he said in broken English. Taking only a few steps from the truck, he rolled his rug and laid it out neatly.

"Victor, I am telling you . . . you are gonna get shot, stay on the damn truck!"

"*Inshallah.* If it is Allah's will, but I will pray now!"

He had no more than hit his knees when an RPG raced by my door and exploded in the powdery dirt hill directly behind him. He fell to the ground, and I was sure he was wounded. I pushed my gun out of the door and started toward him. I had barely touched the ground when Victor leapt to his feet.

"Sheet-sheet-sheet. I will pray later!" he said, as he scrambled back into the truck.

Right then I really missed my two interpreters who had been killed in Panjwari with Shef's team.

"You dumb sum bitch. We are trying to keep you alive," I growled.

"I know, I know. I listen every time now, *Turan,* every time," Victor panted.

The single RPG was followed only by sporadic shots. We held our fire.

Bill called over the radio. "Did anyone see the launch? If there is no more fire then this is a feint. Hold your fire. Hold and see what happens."

I could see Brian in my peripheral vision nodding in agreement. It was a game of cat and mouse. *Where are you?* I thought. It didn't matter. We held the high ground. If they wanted it bad enough, they'd have to come and get it. We could hear the Taliban fighters chattering on the radio, a midlevel commander ordering his fighters to attack Sperwan Ghar. I glanced at Victor, who had his notepad out.

"Don't fuck this up. Write every word," Dave said.

The Taliban commander was berating the RPG gunner for not coordinating with another gunner, yelling that he'd missed our truck and wasted another round. They were only two hundred meters away and had wasted an opportunity. Turning his attention back to us, he gave a new order. *"Hamla, hamla, za, za,"* he barked into the radio. Attack, attack, go, go.

Victor shouted something that got lost in the chaos. Sparking rounds and puffs of dust stuck the vehicles as I called Jared on the radio. He was managing two fights and trying to communicate as more machine guns fired. "Set," screamed Brian as we bolted backward. I peered over the small three-foot-tall berm into the tangled mess of compounds, ditches, and fields and stared at the map. They could be any damn place. I crawled through the truck to talk to Ron.

"Here and here," I said, pointing at targets. "If it was me, I would only be operating from two places." Both were irrigation ditches running east to west, about 150 meters apart.

Ron nodded and called in the grid to the waiting aircraft above. A jet made a low pass, looking for the Taliban fighters.

"No joy, Captain," Ron said. "We need to mark the target somehow so he can tell the difference."

I got with Bill. "Can we fire into one of the buildings or set something on fire to use as a marker for the aircraft?"

Bill ordered the mortars to fire smoke rounds into a dry field. The rest of us strafed the field, hoping that the red-hot tracers would start a fire. It wasn't much of a fire, not like the bonfire I envisioned. I turned to Ron.

"How is that?"

"Nothing. The pilot can't see it," Ron said, shaking his head.

On to plan B. Maybe we could kick up enough dust for the pilot. The enemy rounds kept coming, and Zack fired the grenade launcher at a series of grape huts near the closest irrigation ditch.

"Zack, when I hit that grape hut with an AT4, you fire about twenty rounds into it to create as much smoke as possible."

He laughed.

"You can't hit that from here," he said.

"Case of beer?"

"Bottles or cans?"

I took the AT4 rocket from behind the seat in my truck and headed for a small washout between the vehicles. I signaled Bill when I was ready.

"Covering fire," he called into the radio.

I looked down the small black plastic sights and realized how far away it was. The massive grape hut looked small, and I began to doubt myself. I pulled as tightly as possible on the front strap, lifted the safety, and pressed the small red firing button. The rocket streaked out of the launcher as the concussion took my breath away.

The rocket hit the roof, starting a fire that grew quickly as it burned through the dry thatch. I dropped the tube and sprinted back to the truck. Brian and Dave were laughing. I had not only hit the building but started a fire that a blind pilot could see.

"Target marked."

Brian called Zack on the radio, who had nothing to say, but when I looked at him he was grinning like a thief. Hell, even Bill was shaking his head. In ten seconds, I had redeemed myself for missing the Taliban in the river during our infiltration to the desert.

"Zack, I like Guinness. Cans. Tallboys, if you please."

Ron reported that the pilot saw the fire, and he talked him onto an irrigation ditch just behind a long wall.

"Bombs away, cover," he said.

The F-18 swooped down and dropped. The blast rocked our trucks, and debris and dirt fell everywhere. As the dust cleared, I keyed the radio.

Ron looked upset in the back. "Damn it," he said. The bomb had fallen two hundred meters short, but it was still in the ditch.

"How did you miss with the biggest bullets on the battlefield?" Brian asked.

Our ribbing was cut short by the blood-curdling screams coming over Victor's radio.

"They have killed us! Nine brothers are sleeping! Everyone is hurt. Come quickly. We are dying!"

"Zack, the impact site is your target. One can of forty mike mike grenades, if you please. All guns converge on the tree line. Fire."

The bomb had fallen directly on top of the enemy position. Ron smirked. We had guessed the enemy position incorrectly, but Ron had put the pilot and the bomb in the right spot. "Guess I didn't miss, did I?"

Chapter 21

——

THE DRAGON'S BACK

Anything worth fighting for is worth
fighting dirty for.

—UNKNOWN

The midday sun beat down on Bruce's team as they walked cautiously, weapons at the ready, toward the Arghandab River. Jared had sent them down to the river that morning to check out the rock formation known as Zangabar Ghar. From the top of Sperwan Ghar, the jagged mountain poking out of the thick green fields looked like the scales on the back of a dragon. A few days before, a Taliban radio transmission had identified the Zangabar hills as a meeting point for fighters coming across the river.

The team tried to get to Zangabar Ghar in their trucks, but they couldn't get through the tangle of irrigation ditches. Bruce and two of his teammates took twenty Afghan soldiers to investigate. J.D., one of Bruce's medics, had an uneasy feeling moving through the open. Fighters had to be in the area; the team had uncovered a massive irrigation ditch that the Taliban used to move supplies and fighters to their fighting positions near Sperwan Ghar and the river. It was so big, they could have driven a five-ton truck through it, but most of it was covered by trees, rendering it invisible to pilots circling overhead.

Pushing all the way to the banks of the chocolate-milk-colored riverbed, Bruce and Ben talked about laying ambushes in the irrigation ditches. They scouted out several locations, but none offered a big enough field of view. Hiking back to a compound they had identified on the way in, they noticed that it sat in the middle of the several trails the Taliban used to get to Sperwan Ghar. It was the only place where they could see the whole area.

A typical Afghan square house, it had high, thick mud walls. Its main door was on the west side; there was also a side door on the south side. The compound looked abandoned. Stacking on the door, the ANA soldiers under Pete's and Ben's leadership burst through. Pete was an ETT assigned to Bruce's team. Chickens and goats scattered into the courtyard. The compound was in disarray, clothes and food spilled on the floor. Whoever lived there had left in a hurry. The only resistance was a growling, snapping dog. When it finally attacked, they shot it.

Fanning out, they opened each room, searching for Taliban fighters. Pete and Ben told the Afghan soldiers to be careful and not to break anything, and to be respectful. This was someone's house. With the compound secure, Ben arrayed the ANA soldiers on the roof, setting two machine-gun teams to cover the paths leading to Sperwan Ghar. Nearby, two teams of Afghans armed with RPGs stood ready. Ben set up five more soldiers with AK-47s on the roof, making sure their sectors of fire overlapped with the machine guns.

In the courtyard below, Bruce set up the radio and listened to reports of a firefight between Taliban fighters and 10th Mountain Division soldiers north of Sperwan Ghar. Jared came over the radio and ordered Bruce's trucks to go pick up an Air Force controller and another soldier. As the trucks sped off, Bruce knew he was now without any heavy weapons. He and his men were alone.

Ben, crouched on the roof next to a machine gunner, saw eight Taliban fighters moving down one of the irrigation trenches toward the fighting. He let the fighters close to one hundred meters and opened fire, cutting them down almost instantly. Alerted to their presence, other Taliban fighters began to converge on the compound from the north and southwest. A Taliban machine gun on a nearby grape hut started raking the rooftop, sending mud and wood splinters into the air. Volleys of RPGs smashed into the walls and showered the soldiers with shrapnel.

J.D. watched a tree line near the compound erupt. Then the RPGs started coming down. They hit the walls and sent shock waves through the compound. The level of fire and the growing swarm of fighters were completely unexpected, and J.D. knew they couldn't keep the Taliban at bay for long. He could see machine-gun tracers and RPGs coming from three sides.

Bruce called "troops in contact" over the radio. Ben yelled down that Taliban fighters had surrounded the compound.

"We need air ASAP," Ben yelled. "We are going to get overrun unless we get some help."

Standing on top of the school near Sperwan Ghar, I could hear Bruce's calls over the radio. He could see the enemy racing toward him across the river in groups of four to six vehicles, which were crowded with fighters carrying PKM machine guns and RPGs. I dropped my MRE and climbed to the top of the hill. When I got there, I could see the Hilux dust trails coming from the dry Arghandab River.

"Where are they going?" I asked one of the soldiers at the summit.

"Toward Bruce's team."

I marked the grid on the map and tried to call Jared. No response.

I ran down the slope of the hill and burst into the operations center. Jared and Hodge stood near the radio, listening to Bruce calling for assistance. Bill and Shinsha were standing nearby. Jared had the handset pressed to his ear and was staring at the speaker box. We could barely hear Bruce over the roar of the guns. Hodge, scowling, shook his head.

I heard Bruce call for the trucks that had inserted his team, but Jared had already ordered them to go pick up the critical new Air Force combat controller. "CAS is on the way," Jared radioed back calmly. "It will be there shortly. We'll send help." Back at Kandahar Airfield, a runner monitoring the transmissions found Bolduc, who then listened in from the operations center.

"I am in contact with a couple of enemy platoons. One element has closed to fifty meters. We are taking accurate small arms fire. I have two WIA [wounded in action]. I am going to need a medevac, but no LZ set," Bruce said tensely. "We are going to fucking die if you don't get in here. Do you understand? We are going to fucking die if they do not get us some air." He wasn't buying the lip-service, "help is coming" line.

Bolduc knew that Bruce had to stay calm. Close air support was on the way and if his soldiers panicked before it arrived, he'd lose a team. Soldiers packed the operations center. All were there to help, but Bolduc knew they were also watching for his reaction. Sometimes just hearing a commander's voice helps.

Bolduc took the mike. He wanted Bruce to know that the aircraft were on the way and that he was working to get more help. "This is Desert Eagle 6. You are doing a great job out there. You've got the enemy right where you want them. Keep the pressure on. It is coming. Hang in there."

It worked. Bolduc's calm, professional manner reassured Bruce. Coming from the Indian Ocean, the Navy F-18s needed fuel, but they were only ten minutes out.

Now fully surrounded, Ben ignored the Taliban gunners as they tried to draw a bead on him. Walking uncovered on the roof, he directed the Afghan soldiers to fire back at the ever-growing number of fighters. Within ten minutes, a third group of Taliban had arrived. Bullets smashed into the roof and wounded three more Afghan soldiers. Ben continued to rally his Afghans, once stepping out in the open to kill two Taliban fighters who got close enough to throw grenades over the wall. Rounds impacted all around him, but the move rallied the Afghans and prevented the Taliban from overrunning the compound.

Between radio calls, Bruce protected the southern side of the compound. Huddled in a doorway, he knew that the only way out was to the south. He stationed several Afghan fighters on the wall, but when the RPGs hit, the Afghans lost their will and left it to Allah. If he willed it, they wouldn't get overrun.

Another RPG slammed into the compound, piercing the mud wall and exploding inside.

The next call sent chills down my spine. Bruce was no longer on the radio. A new voice, J.D., the medic, came over the radio.

"The captain is down. Six of the ANA are wounded. Ben and I are the only ones left," he said.

I turned to Hodge. He'd been in the area before and knew where Bruce had gotten out of his truck.

"We've got to do something."

He had made his decision already and was moving toward the door. "I'm going to go down there and try and get them out," he said.

"You knock a wedge in. See if you can get some close support," I said as we left the operations center. "I'm going to bring everything up onto this hill and support you."

As Hodge and his team ran to their trucks, I called Bill over. "Collapse the perimeter!" I barked. "Bill, get me everyone that can fire a weapon on top of the hill NOW!"

The Taliban commanders smelled blood in the water. They knew the small unit was surrounded and cut off. We heard them calling for reinforcements from the north side of the river, elated at the thought of killing or capturing Americans.

I could see the plumes of dust as Hodge and his team sped toward the Dragon's Back. He knew the clock was ticking on Bruce and any hesitation would cost lives. If we took a minute too long, there would be nothing left for his team to bring back.

Shaking off the RPG blast, Ben called out twice before climbing down the wooden ladder. He found Bruce lying facedown on the ground. Bruce had a blank stare when Ben propped him up.

"Hey, Captain, you okay?" Ben asked.

Slowly, Bruce started to come back, and with Ben's help, he again took up a position in the doorway. Shouldering his rifle, he fired at the fighters in the grape huts and irrigation ditches on the south side of the compound.

J.D. continued to go back and forth between Bruce in the court-yard and Ben on the roof. That meant scrambling up a rickety ladder that led from the courtyard and exposing himself to Taliban fire, but he had no choice. He had to get up and down to treat the wounded. After climbing up and dodging rounds, he saw a Taliban round slice through an Afghan machine gunner's foot. J.D. watched as the soldier stoically looked at the wound, shrugged it off, and continued to fire back. Staying covered, J.D. tried to get the Afghan to crawl to him. If he got shot he'd be useless to the rest of the team. The soldier finally stopped shooting long enough to move to J.D. and have his foot bandaged. It wasn't a life-threatening wound, and in minutes the gunner was back firing at the Taliban fighters surrounding the com-pound.

I dropped four cans of ammunition where we could use them and turned to Bill.

"Do not let a single soul make it across the river."

The array Bill had created was fearsome. We had five .50-caliber machine guns, three grenade launchers, more than a dozen Ameri-can and Soviet medium machine guns, and four Gustav recoilless ri-fles. Ammo bearers set up an assembly line so that the guns could keep up a constant rate of fire. It was a killing machine set on de-stroying everything between the Dragon's Back and the river. We had to keep up a level of fire so hellish that the Taliban would retreat and never return. If they wanted blood today, it would be theirs, and it would flow like a river.

I watched a group of trucks drop off about two dozen fighters and drive back across the riverbed to get more. Marking the drop-off point on the map, we waited anxiously for the trucks to return.

I stared intently through my binoculars. Bill focused on the vehicles. When they came within range we'd cut loose. "Now," I said. "Open fire!" Bill screamed, and every weapon system belched fire and rounds. The machine guns and grenade launchers raked the irrigation ditches and roads hiding the newly arrived enemy. We cut an alley of death nearly half a mile wide through the northern half of Panjwayi. A constant roar thundered down the valley. Every gun went full auto for thirty seconds. After that, we went to firing six- to nine-round bursts. The only lull came when we changed the white-hot barrels.

Wailing cries pierced the airwaves as Taliban soldiers clutched radios and cried for help. I wondered if they asked for forgiveness before they died for disemboweling my interpreters a few months ago and torturing innocent civilians in Panjwayi. This was a dish best served cold.

The first two Taliban trucks caught fire immediately and exploded. Another spun hard right and flipped, sending its passengers flying. We allowed four farm tractors coming from the northwest to make it halfway across the riverbed before we decimated them and the other vehicles with them. Some caught fire and burned. Others turned around and headed for the safety of the far side of the river before being destroyed. The rest were abandoned and continued to roll forward into the riverbed. Their drivers ran furiously back and forth until they, too, were finally killed.

The AH-64 helicopters arrived soon after and flew directly over Sperwan Ghar.

"Talon 31, this is Viper 04, lookin' for a party. Request guns hot, inbound," the lead pilot said.

"Viper 04, you are cleared hot. Come on heading of two zero two degrees. My position is on the volcano with a large orange visual recognition panel. Listen carefully; there are no friendlies north of the Arghandab River, except west of the thirty grid line. Taliban are attempting to overrun a Special Forces team on the south side of the river. You have no restrictions. My initials are Romeo Bravo. Bring the heat NOW, we need it."

"Whoa, that's all enemy," the pilot said. "Let's even the odds." I looked up to the large H on the brown helicopter's belly and wondered if it was the same pilot who had saved us last year in the mountain pass where my team sergeant had gotten shot.

Dropping its nose down toward the oncoming vehicles on the other side of the river, the lead Apache shot six pairs of rockets that arced toward the ground, destroying the fleeing vehicles.

Within minutes, the Apaches were making a final gun run before turning sharply back toward Kandahar. They had unloaded everything they had.

"Talon 31, this is Viper 04. Coming out. Winchester." That meant he was out of ammunition, that he'd given us everything he had. I vowed right then and there to keep at least twenty dollars in my pocket in case I ever ran into a thirsty gunship pilot.

Like a conductor, Bill kept the whole orchestra of death going. He made sure the Afghans fired in their sector and got other guns to cover during ammunition and barrel changes. During the short lull, fighters fleeing the 10th Mountain soldiers stopped in a series of nearby huts. Seeing our position, they started firing. Rounds bounced around the rocks. Bill turned, snapped his rifle into his shoulder, and sent a short burst into one of the windows. I saw him and ran to his side.

"Right there. Right there, two o'clock, fifty meters!" he screamed without taking his eye from his scope.

Another round skipped between us as I stood alongside him and started firing too. There were now Taliban fighters near the base of Sperwan Ghar firing up at us.

"ALL GUNS, open fire!" Bill screamed, beating me to the punch.

The roar of the weaponry started again, and the rounds chewed into the walls of the nearby hut, killing the fighters. For the next hour, every soldier on the mountain, including myself, either fired, ferried ammunition, donned asbestos gloves and changed barrels, or carried guns up the six-story hill to replace worn out or broken weapons. There could be absolutely no relief in the intensity of fire we inflicted on the enemy.

The fighters were so close, J.D. could see their faces. He had no idea how many waited in that enormous irrigation ditch near the river or in the tree line. Ammunition was going fast, and soon Ben started telling his gunners to conserve what they had and be selective. No spraying and praying.

Hodge and the rest of the team's trucks arrived at the field south of Bruce's team and immediately got into a fight with Taliban soldiers heading for the compound. The situation could not have been more chaotic. SF teams held a compound, surrounded by Taliban. We now engaged the Taliban from the south, east, and north.

Suddenly, an F-18 thundered over the battlefield, prompting a brief lull in the fire. From the rooftop, Ben used the moment wisely and surveyed the terrain. To the south, he saw an escape route.

Hodge looked up just in time to see the first F-18 swoop down and roar over the compound. The jet was so low, Hodge swore he could see the pilot's visor and patches. This guy meant business.

"Where did an F-18 come from?" he called over to Mike.

"An aircraft carrier!"

Ben and J.D. brought the F-18s on low passes over the compound as the Afghan soldiers climbed off the roof, wounded first. Ben stayed until everybody got down. J.D. was the last off. As he climbed down, an RPG hit nearby, throwing him off the ladder to the hard floor of the compound and showering the others with debris and shrapnel. Staggering to his feet, J.D. peeked through a sliver in a door. A pair of

Taliban fighters were approaching the compound. With the world still spinning, he tried to focus. Looking down the scope of his rifle, he fired, hitting one of the fighters. Turning to fire at the other fighter, he found himself looking down the barrel of the Talib's AK-47. The moment froze in J.D.'s mind. The Talib had him, but hesitated. J.D. fired, hitting the enemy in the nose and sending him sprawling to the ground.

"Why didn't he shoot me? Was he out of ammo?" J.D. would never know.

With everybody outside the compound, they still didn't know the best route to Hodge and the trucks. Taliban fighters headed to the compound stumbled across the trucks and opened fire. J.D. volunteered to find a route. Running out of the door on the south end of the compound, he snaked his way two kilometers through the irrigation ditches despite a serious head wound. It was his second dash to get help, but one that he wouldn't remember.

As the minutes passed, Bruce worried that J.D. had run into a group of Taliban fighters. Ten tense minutes later, Hodge called back that J.D. had made it.

Hodge popped a smoke grenade, and Ben led the others to the trucks. F-18 fighters flew so low they could distinguish between the SF and ANA soldiers. The pilots gashed the Taliban fighters with gun runs in front of the element, clearing the way for Bruce and his men.

It was more than a reunion when they all came back to Sperwan Ghar.

A medevac helicopter came in and took J.D., who had a fractured skull, and six Afghan soldiers with gunshot and shrapnel wounds back to Kandahar.

When the helicopter landed, Bolduc and the battalion's command sergeant major, Hedges, stood on the tarmac waiting. Both had spent the balance of the day filing reports with their superiors explaining what had happened. But it was their policy to be the first people their wounded soldiers saw when they got back to the base. Running next to J.D.'s stretcher, they followed him all the way into the hospital.

Back at his room, Bolduc finally relaxed and reflected on what had happened. Looking at CSM Hedges, he admitted what he couldn't in the operations center.

"We were lucky. Very, very lucky."

Chapter 22

———

FIREBASE SPERWAN GHAR

We are determined that before the sun sets on this terrible struggle our flag will be recognized throughout the world as a symbol of freedom on the one hand, of overwhelming power on the other.

—GENERAL GEORGE C. MARSHALL

The plum-colored phone buzzed rather than rang in the operations center. The nine a.m. call was for either Bolduc or Command Sergeant Major Hedges, and the sergeant in charge of the operations center in Kandahar knew it.

He didn't want to answer it. The command staff in Bagram, Bolduc's bosses, had been calling for hours. This was the third call. On the fifth ring, he finally picked up.

"Sir, I think they are in a meeting or something, but let me go find them and they will call you back."

"Get Bolduc on the phone now," the officer in Bagram said. The stalling tactic had played out.

A few days before, CSM Hedges had told Bolduc that "higher," the commanders in Bagram, didn't want him going out to Sperwan Ghar. It wasn't an order, just a heavily emphasized suggestion. No one ever told Bolduc specifically not to go.

"We just want you to stay close to your FOB [forward operating base] a little more than in the past," is all they said.

It was dangerous to circulate to the different firebases, and Bolduc had a reputation for finding trouble. On a previous rotation, his helicopter had gone down, and once he even had directed his helicopter to pick up ambushed paratroopers and ferry them off the battlefield.

The battle at Sperwan Ghar had become too fierce to endanger an entire command team. So, the night before Bolduc left for Sperwan Ghar, he instructed the sergeant to stall Bagram until he could get to the hill. Bolduc was smart enough not to ask permission, because he knew they'd say no. It is easier to ask for forgiveness. Plus, he knew that if the battle spread, we would need his rank out there to get assets and assistance.

"Sir, they are at Sperwan Ghar," the sergeant finally told Bagram.

The amber sun was up before I woke on September 11, 2006. Startled, I realized that I had not been awakened for my guard shift. Had someone fallen asleep?

I rubbed the sleep from my eyes, snatched my weapon, and got up to see. It took me a second to will my swollen and stiff body off the ground. I still had a large tear in my pants, and my back, butt, knee, and shoulder throbbed relentlessly. I had had a horrible ringing in my ears since the blast. My men had not complained of their wounds, nor allowed themselves to be medevacked, and neither would I. I made a mental note to see Riley about some medication for the swelling.

Walking the short distance from my truck to the command center in the schoolhouse, I found Bolduc and CSM Hedges inside, monitoring the radio and pulling security. Jared walked into the hallway scratching his filthy red beard.

"How did you sleep?" Jared asked. "Commander and the CSM insisted that they pull guard duty the entire night."

We had badly needed some rest. The past two weeks had been total sensory overload. A good six hours of sleep was just what the men needed, including me. It was rare indeed to have two leaders who cared so greatly for their men. Humbled, I headed back to my truck. As I left, my eyes fell on the words written in chalk on the ash-gray walls of the hallway: "From this day, until the end of the world, we in it shall be remembered. We few, we happy few, we band of brothers. For he who sheds his blood today with me shall be called my brother. —Shakespare." I had misspelled Shakespeare.

I broke out the coffeepot and plugged it into the truck. The dusty socket sparked angrily but pushed enough power to the ten-dollar kettle. I dug deeply into my backpack for a bag of pure Kona coffee, Hawaiian gold that I saved for special occasions. If the commander and CSM were going to pull guard duty for my men all night, the least I could do was to make them a damn fine cup of coffee. I would not mind being a coffee gofer today.

Bill came up while the coffee brewed and wanted to know what had happened to the guard shift.

"Bolduc and Hedges are here and pulled them."

"No shit?" he said. Seeing the coffee, he fished out his canteen cup. "First things first, I'm getting a cup of that right there!"

I poured the water slowly over the small yellow filter full of coffee and filled four canteen cups with the deep-almond-colored liquid. As I walked with Bill back toward the school, I held the cups close to my face, inhaling the aroma. Bill didn't wait and took a big gulp.

When we got to the school, Jared, Bolduc, and Hedges were sitting on MRE cases and ammunition cans, talking about the last eleven days. Bill and I listened to the discussion, and its tally was impressive: we'd completed a clandestine desert crossing with an indigenous force, survived a massive ambush, assaulted a known enemy fortified position, seized the key and decisive terrain feature, repelled two counterattacks and two direct assaults on our defenses, killed or wounded nearly eight hundred enemy fighters, including eight Taliban commanders, "assisted" NATO's largest combat operation before becoming its main effort, and liberated a valley the Soviets never conquered.

"Whew," I mumbled when Bolduc was done. "Not bad for thirty Green Berets and fifty Afghan soldiers."

"It will be the greatest battle no one ever heard of," Bill chuckled.

Then Bolduc delivered the news. Sperwan Ghar was now officially a firebase. We'd fought hard to get the hill, and now we'd use it to hold the valley. The Canadian task force had finally managed to seize and hold their hard-fought objective, Rugby, and established a firebase of their own at Masum Ghar. But we didn't have time to dwell too much on our successes. We still had to cross the river and secure four more objectives. We knew the order was coming because the Canadians couldn't do it with their mechanized vehicles.

With the coffee gone, Bill and I went back to our trucks. It was eerily silent, but I didn't have that feeling of impending doom. Something had changed. Looking down into the fields and compounds, I didn't see any activity. Nothing. I woke Victor and told him to scan the radio. He listened for several minutes to mostly static. Then there was a short message in Pashto. Victor's eyes lit up. Grinning like an opossum, he held the radio in the air.

"They are leaving, they are leaving."

The Taliban commanders were collecting the remaining fighters and leaving for Helmand Province and Pakistan. Listening to the radio calls, I could hear their humiliation. An Apache helicopter flew across the river, searching the fields and tree lines for a fight. Bill called him on the radio.

"Razor aircraft, this is Talon 31, requesting a situation report, over."

"Talon, it looks like a ghost town. Everyone is gone. It looks like they've had enough."

Bill looked at me and shrugged his shoulders. "Too bad, we were just getting a rhythm going," he said.

I stood up straight for the first time in more than a week. I was now less worried about snipers or machine guns; I looked out over the valley. It was my first concentrated look at the massive devastation precipitated by the Taliban. This was all their doing. To say any less would be asinine and ignorant. I had to shake my head. The protected and self-righteous regularly toss knee-jerk, ill-informed accusations toward the militaries of the Western world every time civilians are killed in combat, yet they sit by quietly while the Taliban and many other terrorist organizations intentionally fight and hide behind or within innocent civilian populations. Not a damn word is said nor deed done about *that*.

A landscape of destroyed grape huts, impact craters from bombs, fires, and carnage unfurled before me. It looked like a monster had stomped through the valley, leaving the skeletons of compounds smoldering and the tops of trees jagged and twisted. It didn't look like victory to me. It was all the Taliban and Al Qaeda had to offer Afghanistan. We didn't start this battle. They had picked the fight with the wrong hombres, and in turn laid waste to others' homes.

We walked down the hill and told Jared, Hedges, and Bolduc that we'd planned a ceremony later that morning to commemorate September 11 and to remember why we'd fought for the hill in the first place. Before the ceremony, Bill got the team together to clean weapons, check the radios, and fix up the vehicles. Dave asked me to play DJ with my iPod because he had only techno music suitable for the next assault, workout session, or rave. "Maestro, something patriotic, if you please!"

I plugged in my speakers and scrolled through the play list. "Courtesy of the Red, White, and Blue" by Toby Keith kicked things off. Everyone gathered around the truck and began to bellow out the tune. For the next hour, we sang along with Toby, guzzled warm soft drinks, and ate cookies courtesy of the CSM and commander. It was a caffeine and sugar high. The guys from 3X, a few hills away, got the same resupply that had flown in with the commander—with one special addition. A case, not just a box, of tampons. Our community does have a unique sense of humor.

Bill hollered that it was time to go. The ceremony would begin in ten minutes. Hodge, Bruce, and their teams started to gather up around ten o'clock. Most of the men carried small flags that had been stuffed in their equipment pouches for the last two weeks. It was an essential military tradition. With everyone on top of the hill, we fashioned three flagpoles.

Our combined force went to the top of Sperwan Ghar and proudly planted the flags of Canada, Afghanistan, and the United States of America, together. It was the first day since the initial assault that not a shot was fired by either friend or foe. "COMPANY, attention!" the command sergeant major yelled.

The three flags were raised in unison. We then all bowed our heads in silence. It was a moment to reflect—on the tragedy five years ago, the sacrifices made and those yet to be made for the hard struggle ahead. Bolduc then fished out a letter written by General Fraser. The coalition commander for southern Afghanistan wanted to personally thank us. We gathered around Bolduc as he read parts of it to us:

> I want to express my personal thanks to the soldiers and offi-cers of United States Army Special Forces Task Force 31 for their recent efforts as part of Operation MEDUSA, perhaps the single most important and successful combat operation to be conducted in Afghanistan since 2002 . . . As has been made very clear to me by my superiors, it is no exaggeration to say that the future of NATO, and of Afghanistan, hung in the bal-ance. In this time of need, when failure was not an option, the soldiers of TF 31 stood and delivered, and by their brave ac-tions made a contribution to victory out of all proportion to their relatively small numbers.
>
> The personal courage demonstrated time and again by the soldiers of TF 31 was remarkable, and I stand in awe of their

mission focus, offensive spirit, and dedication . . . To the soldiers of TF 31: I am proud of your accomplishments and humbled by your warrior spirit. You are true warriors and epitomize the traits expected from the Special Forces community.

After the ceremony, I flew two American flags. The first one was for Greg. I had gotten word several days earlier that Sean had lived, but there was still no word about Greg. He had been transported from Kandahar to Germany. If he died from his wounds, I wanted to present the flag to his wife after the funeral. There I would make the same promise I had to Charlie's wife. Six months later, I was privileged to be able to give the flag to Greg himself. He had survived by the grace of God.

The second flag I flew for someone else. After hoisting it up, Bill helped me neatly tuck it back into the box. I wanted to present it to Bolduc, to thank him for his incredible leadership.

Walking down the dust pile of a hill after the ceremony, I asked to speak with the boss. I presented the flag to Bolduc. It was the only way I could show my appreciation. He should own a piece of this history.

Bolduc grabbed my arm and looked me dead in the eye.

"Your men did a good job here. Remember that."

We spent the rest of the day planning for the next operations across the river and the reconstruction of the area. We had to repair the damage, build dirt roads, and start establishing rapport with the people. The Soviets hadn't been able to conquer the valley, but we now had a chance to not only control the Taliban's backyard, but to win over their home-field support. We just had to capitalize on our victory by returning the ravaged district to its heyday as Afghanistan's breadbasket.

Days had passed since I had called home, and I knew my wife hadn't been well. At dusk, I went outside and called her on my satellite phone. I knew that the battle was big news, and any Green Beret's wife who has been around more than a day knows how to put two and two together. I knew that watching the battle on the news would have made her anxious; I knew I was fine, but she did not. The sheer weight of the unknown is crippling, as I was about to learn firsthand. Pressing the hot black plastic against my ear, I listened for the clicking sound of connection. I could hear it finally make contact thousands of miles away. But instead of my wife on the other line, my mother answered. Startled, I asked if anything was wrong.

"She was taken to the emergency room for spinal surgery," my mother told me. I couldn't catch my breath.

My wife had never mentioned anything that serious when I talked to her before the first assault. A strong soldier's wife, she did not want me to worry about her. Army wives are a special breed.

My mother was waiting for news from the hospital. "Call back when she gets out of surgery," I said, numb.

I still had the small black Iridium phone in my hand when Bolduc came out of the building. By now the moon was full and gleaming white like a celestial flashlight. He walked over and handed me a paper. I read the first line and almost dropped the message.

FROM: The International Red Cross . . . Your wife . . . Surgery . . .
    Requests your immediate presence . . .

I was faced with toughest decision of my life: go to my wife and help my family or stay with my men, who were closer than family. It had been only a short time since I'd talked to my mother, but I called back anyway.

"Your wife is fine and in recovery. She is going to need a lot of help, though," my mother said.

I turned to Bolduc, still stunned. He knew that I needed some advice, and I just listened as the words streamed out. I knew my wife needed me, but I also knew that we faced some difficult days rooting out the remaining Taliban fighters across the river. We had a firebase to build, and I didn't want to leave my men in harm's way without me. Seven of my twelve men had been wounded, including me. When you are so close to your men, command is much more personal and much more difficult. I needed to be with them.

Finally, I asked the question.

"Sir, what do I do? I can't leave my men in combat," I said.

Bolduc knew that if I stayed, I'd be distracted. If I went home and took care of my family, when I returned I'd be committed, knowing that I didn't have to worry.

First he gave me the setup. "We have this dichotomy as soldiers where we must balance between our families and our mission. Families always seem to come second," he told me. "The team is trained well. They will do fine without you during this period."

Then he let me off the hook.

"I will make it easy for you. You will get your big ass on that helicopter and go home and take care of your family. Right now, your priority is at home. I am not asking you," he bluntly stated. I would have hugged him, but he would have punched me in the mouth. I knew he was right, but I didn't feel any better because now I had to say good-bye to my men. I knew we'd get the mission to clear the objectives the Canadians couldn't get to in their vehicles. There was a good chance I'd be shaking one or some of these men's hands for the last time.

I found Smitty and Bill first. "Guys, I have a problem. I have to talk to you. My wife has had emergency surgery. I don't know exactly what's wrong," I said. "I've never been there for anything. I missed the birth of my child. I've missed the death of relatives. My wife has carried the rucksack for our entire marriage. I have to go."

After an awkward silence, Smitty spoke. "There will be lots of fighting here when you get back. Go take care of your family."

That is what I needed to hear from my men. I stopped at all the trucks before going to my truck and picking up my kit. All the handshakes were strong. The smiles were big. Not a lot of words, just "I'll see you soon." Throwing the last of my gear into my bag, I left behind grenades, batteries, magazines of ammunition, snuff, and socks for Brian and Dave. They'd need them.

By now, I could hear the rotor blades of the Chinook echoing through the valley. An Apache circled around Sperwan as the helicopter landed. I could see the static electricity from the Chinook's two rotors cut through the dust, creating a speckled halo over the bird as it touched down at the base of the hill. The tailgate dropped. Bill grabbed my backpack. Bolduc came over with Jared and both gave me a hug. They stayed at the truck as Bill walked out with me.

I stepped up on the ramp, grabbed my bag from Bill, and clicked my snap link into the aircraft. I felt like I was dragging myself onto the helicopter. I didn't want to go, but I knew I had to. I knew my wife needed me. The noise from the helicopter made it hard to talk. Bill stepped up on the ramp and shook my hand.

"Remember rule number one, Ranger," I said.

"I'll walk my post from plank to plank and take no shit from any rank," he said, grinning broadly.

"Watch after the boys until I get back, Bill."

He gave me a thumbs-up and walked off the ramp.

I turned to the crew chief and gave him a thumbs-up. Bill stepped back. The engines whined as they gained power, and I watched Bill, the hill, and the ground fall away beneath me. I stood on the chilly metal ramp and looked down at the Panjwayi Valley and Sperwan Ghar. I wondered in absolute amazement how I or my men had not been killed. I tried to burn every second into my memory. We crossed the ridgeline where our blocking positions had been a week earlier. The Chinook's nose dipped down as we turned toward Kandahar.

The helicopter turned to follow Highway 1, and soon the entire city of Kandahar could be seen out the back of the helicopter's rampway. The lights and smells of the city—burning fires, exhaust, and dust— rose to meet me. I could see a few cars and trucks moving around. The bazaar, which normally would be full of hundreds of shoppers, was lifeless. Everybody was home asleep. Safe.

Epilogue

———

Blessed be the Lord, my rock,
who trains my hands for war and my fingers for battle.

—PSALM 144, VERSE 1

I boarded the plane in clean clothes. I felt guilty even taking a bath because my guys were still out there. I'd sat in the TOC until it was time to board the plane. I listened as my guys got word to move north across the Arghandab River to clear the villages where the Taliban had maintained their stronghold for weeks. There was little contact, and it was mostly a clearing operation.

The plane was empty except for about ten passengers. The medics had braced my knee and given me shots in my shoulder to ease the pain for the long flight home. My thoughts drifted between my family and my men. I pulled out my notebook and began to utilize the many hours I had on the flight to try to compose statements for the valorous awards recommendations. I tried to put together everything I remembered. I stared intently at the pages I had written on the hill and tried to summarize all that had happened.

For such a strategic and significant battle, only a few valorous medals were awarded. The most important of these, to the men who fought there, was to Jude. His willingness to selflessly charge into what should have been certain death will forever be burned into the memories and lives of those who witnessed his actions. In reference to Staff Sergeant Jude Voss, I'd scribbled a page for an award recommendation that night on Sperwan Ghar:

> This single HEROIC act, by my account, as a witness and as
> the Ground Assault Commander for the operation to seize
> Sperwan Ghar, was the BRAVEST and most VALOROUS
> thing I have ever witnessed in 3 combat rotations in Afghanistan, 14 years in the Army and my 36 years of life. SSG Jude
> Voss's quick, decisive and selfless actions that day directly
> saved two soldiers lives' and carried the initiative of battle. If
> SSG Voss had not been there doing what he was doing, it is an
> absolute certainty that SFC Greg Stube and SFC Sean Mishura
> would have been burned to death, killed by enemy actions or
> secondary explosions. SSG Voss went to the rescue of endangered American soldiers, not knowing the disposition of their
> lives, while showing a complete disregard for his own safety
> and under intense enemy fire. He then remained in a place of
> utmost danger and in extreme close proximity to a vehicle
> (about five to eight meters) while remaining under enemy
> fire, a vehicle fully engulfed in flames under continuous explosions from a triple load of ordnance and explosives now burning on the vehicle. He not only moved Greg from the vehicle
> to a ditch under enemy fire, leaving only himself exposed, but
> applied absolutely critical life-saving first aid to Greg until Riley, my senior medic, arrived and provided advanced trauma
> management. Upon my arrival, had I not seen SSG Voss there,
> doing what he was doing, I would never have known that Sean
> was unaccounted for and gone looking for him. Without Jude,
> Greg would have burned to death and Sean would have succumbed to inhalation and burns . . . There is no higher honor
> in the place of time and military history than the way Jude
> conducted himself that day as an American soldier. It was a

day I shall never forget. I have walked with heroes. I hope someone finds this note.

"You're just doing your job when you're out there," Jared had said. "Any one of the other guys would have done it, but Jude did it."

The entire Desert Eagle chain of command recommended Jude for the Medal of Honor, our nation's highest valor award. The recommendation was downgraded in Afghanistan. Whatever politics came into play, Jude's actions will never be downgraded in the eyes of those who knew what he had done.

Ultimately, our struggle for Panjwayi would continue. Coalition and NATO units taking over after our rotation could not reinforce our successes. Failing to control the valley by establishing a permanent security presence created an environment that allowed the Taliban to easily repopulate Panjwayi in late fall 2006. Our forces followed Operation Medusa with an even larger operation, called Operation Baaz Tsuka, or "Falcon Summit." Operation Baaz Tsuka focused on removing the newly returned Taliban influence and reestablishing security. In a familiar story line, the ISAF forces could not maintain the initiative due to operational, strategic, and political issues. The Desert Eagles of Charlie Company, 1st Battalion, 3rd Special Forces Group again stepped in to clean out the enemy and secure objectives deemed "too dangerous," then stayed to do damage control.

Two months after we took Sperwan Ghar, tragedy struck. Bill, my friend and the best soldier I ever knew, died three hundred meters from the hill when an IED exploded under his truck. Bill did not die the way he wanted, but he died the way God intended. That is the only way I can understand it. I know all soldiers want to live long and full lives, but we have our purpose as warriors. When that purpose is fulfilled, we are called home to our creator. I know that those who have seen battle understand this without question.

If in fact it is your time to be called before God, you typically won't know it. Sometimes you will, and these are the hardest of times: When the blood pours from your nose and down your throat, clogging it, causing you to spit and gag. You heave for breath in the smoke and dust. Your equipment seems to suffocate you. You wipe the salty sweat and grime from your eyes, only to realize it is blood, either yours or that of the enemy. You would stand but you can't move your legs. You grasp the open, gaping wounds in your body, trying not to pass out from the pain. You feel the anger thinking of the loved ones you will never see again, and losing your life infuriates your soul. You rage to get to your feet and grab for a weapon, any weapon. Regardless of your race, culture, or religion, you want to die standing, fighting like a warrior, an American, so others won't have to. For those looking for a definition, this is the price of freedom.

Our objectives on Sperwan Ghar and in Afghanistan were clear. We knew and understood that as an army and as a nation, we cannot and will not accept failure. Ours was not a mission that ended in near escape, but in victory and defiance on a small hill in the heart of the enemy's birthplace. The battle made few headlines. The fact remains that the actions of the 3rd Special Forces Group soldiers, the ISAF, and their Afghan Army allies disrupted the largest-ever Taliban offensive aimed at taking over Kandahar city. History cannot change the fact that five years to the date after our nation was attacked, a small group of men stood in the midst of the enemy's birthplace and swore, "We shall never forget."

Acknowledgments

———

I would be remiss if I did not give credit to all those who were involved in this endeavor. Whether you were the boots on the ground, family, or a supporter of this project, I humbly say, "Thank you."

To my family: the mere thought of you, in one way or another, kept me alive more times than you will ever know.

To the men of Detachment 331: Because of you, I now know what the word "honor" really means. You are all ordinary men who have proven yourself extraordinary. This project is for you. There never seemed to be an end to the ridiculously dangerous tasks force-fed to us, and with little or no help, through professionalism and tenacity, you refused to accept failure. You pursued with the cunning of an obsessed hunter every target, every objective, every bad guy. Your eyes have beheld the savagery of our nation's enemies, and you never faltered, never. Voluntarily you stepped between them and the citizens of our great country. My proudest days as a man, as a soldier, and as an American were spent walking that ground with you, and I will spend the rest of my life wishing I was still fighting by your side. *March or Die.*

To my commanders, who stood their ground, gave sound advice under the worst of conditions when it was most needed, and kept their word in the face of insurmountable odds: Never did I feel that whatever I asked for, whatever I needed, you would not break your back or sacrifice your career to provide. You gave top cover for those doing what was needed to get the job done and did not bow to political pressure or let us get railroaded when things went bad. Hopefully our organization will recognize your true value on the battlefield and in the future of Special Forces.

To the other detachments who fought by our side: God willing, may we never face such a thing again. All who were there and participated know the magnitude of this event. We also know that within us, this will never be forgotten. We have written a chapter into the history of United States Army Special Forces and Afghanistan that can never be removed, ever. Even today the enemy, those who managed to escape, remembers the "long beards" of Sperwan Ghar.

To Willie, Paul, Wayne, Pat, Red, and all the support soldiers who endured day upon day of sleepless, back-breaking work, in 120-degree temperatures, building pallets and pushing supplies: I knew you would get us everything we needed. You made something out of nothing. When we or our equipment were broken, burned, bleeding, damaged, or destroyed you fixed, repaired, patched, and replaced what was needed so we could keep fighting. This was the first time in fifteen years as a professional soldier that I was properly supported. You have set a standard few if any can achieve again.

For men like Bill, Zack, Smitty, Jude, Dave, Greg, and Sean, you sacrificed your bodies, health, and lives so that others may live and continue to protect the greatest country on earth. You all, either in memory or in example, set the standard by which we all should live. Your honor, integrity, and selfless service shall never go unrecognized as long as we still have breath in our lungs.

I would like to extend my thanks to Kevin Maurer, who was instrumental in capturing this monumental event, putting it on paper, and producing something of value to future generations of warriors. Kevin, you are a deceptively keen man who has earned the respect of a community that distrusts the media, and for good reason. Your guidance, hard work, and dedication to this project will not be forgotten. You are a credit to your profession.

To Colonel Nye, Ms. Carol Darby, and Clearwater from the United States Army Special Operations Command (USASOC) and the United States Special Operations Command (USSOCOM), I thank you for your encouragement, guidance, and support. Through you and your persistent mentorship, we were able to stay on track with re-creating a small piece of history and telling a story that needed to be told. Without you and your confidence in this project, it would never have flown.

Finally, to the families of the fallen, you are as important as the soldiers themselves. Please never forget that. You give us the strength to continue fighting, even when our grief calls us to pause. Without hesitation, military families allow soldiers to go forth into battle with the understanding that they have your full support, and this allows them to act as the warriors they are. You guard our freedom with the most valuable assets you have, your loved ones, husbands, and fathers of your children. This freedom is paid for by the blood of citizen soldiers, volunteers, those who have proven themselves better than we. You above all know that freedom is not free.

Kevin would like to thank our agent, Scott Miller, and his staff for seeing this book in a series of newspaper articles. Your faith in us made this project possible. Thanks to John Flicker and Tracy Devine at Random House for their patience and insight in helping us capture this important battle in these pages. Thank you to the U.S. Army Special Operations Command for all their help running down my many requests. Thanks to folks who were there, and you know who you are, for talking to me and answering my questions, even when I know sometimes you didn't want to. Thanks to Lieutenant Colonel Don Bolduc not only for making sure I didn't make mistakes, but for teaching me the art of counterinsurgency. It is because of officers like you that we can win this war. Thank you also to the crew of C-17 00184 who flew me from Pope Air Force Base to Bagram, Afghanistan. We couldn't have finished this book without the ride. Thanks to Andrew Craft for taking time to spend his vacation in Afghanistan and Kristen Henderson and Kelly Kennedy for reading chapters and helping me make each one better, one word at a time. Thanks to Bill at AWS for providing me with tactical gear for my embed. And finally, thank you to my family, especially my wife, Jess, for supporting me during the long nights in the office and weeks in Afghanistan.

About the Authors

———

MAJOR RUSTY BRADLEY was wounded during the Battle of Sperwan Ghar in command of a Special Forces A-team, on his third combat tour as a Special Forces team leader. A native of North Carolina, he graduated from Mars Hill College and enlisted in the Army in 1993, serving as an infantryman for six years before earning his commission from Officer Candidate School in 1999.

KEVIN MAURER has been embedded as a reporter with the U.S. Special Forces and 82nd Airborne Division in Afghanistan and Iraq more than a dozen times in the last five years.

About the Type

———

This book was set in Monotype Dante, a typeface designed by Giovanni Mardersteig (1892–1977). Conceived as a private type for the Officina Bodoni in Verona, Italy, Dante was originally cut only for hand composition by Charles Malin, the famous Parisian punch cutter, between 1946 and 1952. Its first use was in an edition of Boccaccio's *Trattatello in laude di Dante* that appeared in 1954. The Monotype Corporation's version of Dante followed in 1957. Though modeled on the Aldine type used for Pietro Cardinal Bembo's treatise *De Aetna* in 1495, Dante is a thoroughly modern interpretation of that venerable face.